PATSY J. HALLMAN
Professor and Associate Dean
College of Education
Stephen F. Austin State University
Nacogdoches, Texas

◆

J. LYNN JOHNSON
Associate Professor of Management
College of Business Administration
University of North Texas
Denton, Texas

Delmar Publishers Inc.

NOTICE TO THE READER

Cosmetology photography by Michael A Gallitelli, on location at the Austin Beauty School, with Dino Petrocelli and by Steven Landis, with direction from Vincent and Alfred Nardi of Nardi Salon.

Cover design: Silvers Design

Delmar staff:
Senior Acquisitions Editor: Mary McGarry   Production Supervisor: Karen Leet
Developmental Editor: Sheila Furjanic   Design Supervisor: Judi Orozco
Project Editor: Judith Boyd Nelson   Art Coordinator: John Lent

For information, address Delmar Publishers Inc.
3 Columbia Circle
Albany, NY 12212

Printed in the United States of America
Published simultaneously in Canada
by Nelson Canada,
a division of The Thomson Corporation

1 2 3 4 5 6 7 8 9 10 XXX 99 98 97 96 95 94 93

Library of Congress Cataloging-in-Publication Data

Hallman, Patsy Spurrier.
    Building a professional life / Patsy J. Hallman, J. Lynn Johnson.
        p.   cm.
    Includes index.
    ISBN 0–8273–5240–9
    1. Career development—United States.   2. College students—
Employment—United States.   I. Johnson, J. Lynn.   II. Title.
    HF5382.5.U5H337   1993   92–28104
    650.14—dc20   CIP

CONTENTS

PREFACE IV

ABOUT THE AUTHORS VI

UNIT I WHO YOU ARE: JOB AND CAREER PLANNING 1

CHAPTER 1 Investigating and Choosing a Career 3

CHAPTER 2 Communicating Who You Are 27

CHAPTER 3 Professional Dress 55

CHAPTER 4 Getting a Job 94

UNIT II WHO YOU WANT TO BE: BEGINNING A JOB 123

CHAPTER 5 Understanding the Business You Join 125

CHAPTER 6 Everyday at Work 141

CHAPTER 7 Communication: Personal and Professional 165

CHAPTER 8 Away From the Office: Representing the Company 189

CHAPTER 9 Corporate Etiquette 216

UNIT III MOVING IN, MOVING UP: PROMOTION AND GROWTH 239

CHAPTER 10 Productivity and Promotability 241

CHAPTER 11 Ethics in Professional Life 256

CHAPTER 12 Personal Health 275

CHAPTER 13 Personal Finance 309

CHAPTER 14 Professional Growth 333

INDEX 353

PREFACE

Building a Professional Life is a text written for college and university age students who are preparing to enter the world of work. Readers will find information to help them find a job, to enter the work force successfully, and to progress upward on the career ladder.

The text is enjoyable reading for people in formal classes as well as for people who are working individually toward career advancement goals. *Building a Professional Life* contains information about how to handle actual tasks facing the new professional. The book is divided into three major units. The first unit discusses strategies for being successful in the job search through self-knowledge and self-evaluation. The second unit deals with information about successful practices in the workplace, while the third unit deals with events and behaviors related to career responsibilities. Topics range from practical skills, such as when to resign from a position, to abstract skills such as ethics in the business world.

Major topics in the text are self-knowledge, getting a job, practical communication, relationships in the workplace, self-management for professionals, growing professionally, and how to represent business and industry effectively. A section in each chapter highlights a critical skill related to the chapter topic. This feature is called "FOCUS ON." It provides straight talk about the real world that today's young professionals enter. End of chapter materials include summary questions, critical thought questions, and activities to promote skill building.

The U.S. Department of Labor recently identified seven basic skills needed by all workers. They are skills for 1) continuing education, 2) basic academics, 3) communication, 4) leadership, 5) personal management, 6) interpersonal relationships, and 7) problem solving. Students who read *Building a Professional Life* and complete the activities suggested at the end of each chapter will have opportunities to develop each of these skills.

We chose to write this book because in our work with college and university students, we saw a need for students to have such information. In addition, for many years we have had frequent requests to conduct workshops and seminars on the topic. We have provided the seminars for personnel in health care, banking, insurance, management, and other professional arenas. These frequent requests have convinced us that young professionals do want to know what principles and practices will smooth their climb up the career ladder.

We wish to express our appreciation to our students in business classes at the University of North Texas and in leadership classes at Stephen F. Austin State University who inspired the development of this text. We also appreciate the support we received from our university administrators as we worked on this project. We thank the members of our families, the Johnsons and the Hallmans, for their support and patience. We believe that this book could not have been completed without the work of several fine editors, namely, Carol O'Keefe and Mary McGarry; their faith in us and in our work and their highly ethical and capable support are a tribute to the publishing industry. We also wish to express appreciation to Jackie Coggin for her able assistance in researching and developing many of the Focus On features and Susan Merrill for her assistance in preparing the text and art manuscripts. And, finally, our thanks to all of you who are reading this work. Best wishes to you as you build a successful and satisfying professional life!

Patsy Johnson Hallman
J. Lynn Johnson

Chapter Opening Photo Credits

Chapters 1, 6, 11 (left to right): Courtesy of Leslie Fay Companies, Inc.; Courtesy of J.C. Penney Company, Inc., 1992; Courtesy of J.C. Penney Company, Inc. 1992; Courtesy of Clairol.

Chapters 2, 7, 12 (left to right): Copyright © Spiegel, Inc.; Courtesy of J.C. Penney Company Inc., 1992; Copyright © Spiegel, Inc.; Copyright © Spiegel, Inc.

Chapters 3, 8, 13 (left to right): Copyright © Spiegel, Inc.; Courtesy of J.C. Penney Company Inc., 1992; Photographer Steven Landis on location at Nardi Salon, Stylists Vincent and Alfred Nardi; Courtesy of North American Hairdresser Awards, Hair by Sabrina Hill.

Chapters 4, 9, 14 (left to right): Photo by Jack Cutler, hair by Sara Aiello, grooming by Cheryl Esposito; Courtesy of J.C. Penney Company, Inc., 1922; Copyright © Spiegel, Inc.; Courtesy of Leslie Fay Companies, Inc.

Chapters 5, 10 (left to right): Courtesy of Matrix Essentials; Photo by Havriliak, hair by Joico International U.S.A. Team; Copyright © Spiegel Inc.; Courtesy of J.C. Penney Company, Inc., 1992.

ABOUT THE AUTHORS

Patsy Johnson Hallman currently serves as professor and associate dean at the College of Education, Stephen F. Austin State University, Nacogdoches, Texas. She has more than twenty years of university teaching experience, which includes teaching courses dealing with professional development. She has authored and coauthored *Home Economics Instruction, Family Health,* and numerous articles published in scholarly journals. Dr. Hallman frequently speaks to professional and civic groups on topics related to professional life. She holds degrees in home economics and in education from East Texas State University, Stephen F. Austin State University, and Texas Women's University. She is married to Dr. Leon Hallman and they have eight young professionals in their family. They live in Nacogdoches, Texas.

J. Lynn Johnson is an associate professor of business administration at the University of North Texas in Denton, Texas. He is coauthor of *Management: Theory and Practice,* and has published over 20 other journal articles and training manuals. He has been active in designing the curriculum for undergraduate and graduate programs focusing on personnel and industrial relations, hotel and restaurant management, and small business administration.

Beyond his academic work, Dr. Johnson is an active consultant with major corporations throughout the Southwest. His primary consulting interests are in the areas of business communication, career development, outplacement services and supervisory training.

Dr. Johnson received his Ph.D. from the University of Arkansas after earning a Masters degree from the University of North Texas and an undergraduate degree from East Texas State University. He continues to teach, write, and offer training programs for today's business world.

UNIT 1

WHO YOU ARE: JOB AND CAREER PLANNING

CHAPTER 1
INVESTIGATING AND CHOOSING A CAREER

CHAPTER GOAL

To help you establish career goals and plan strategies to reach them.

CHAPTER OBJECTIVES

After studying this chapter you should be able to:

1. Conduct a self-assessment of your abilities, interests, and aptitudes.
2. Implement strategies for gathering information about specific careers.
3. Set career goals.
4. Identify skills needed to reach your career goals.
5. Outline ways to prepare for a chosen career.

The career choices you make are among the most important of all your life choices as you search for personal happiness and satisfaction. Where you work, what you do on the job, whom you work with, and how much money you make will all be determined by your career choices. In fact, although your life-style preferences affect your career choice, the career you choose affects every aspect of your life-style.

Making a career choice is not easy. You may feel anxious, wondering if you have enough information to make a good choice. Perhaps you are afraid that you will make the wrong one. These feelings and fears are normal. Talk to your friends and you will probably learn that they have some similar feelings and doubts.

Actually your career choice is just one of many choices that you make all through life. The good thing is that you can usually change them. If you make a choice that proves to be dissatisfying, you generally have an opportunity to make another one.

Isn't it exciting to know that you have the freedom and the opportunity to make your own career choice? You can make the choice that is right for you if you accurately assess yourself and if you gather information about various career options (see Figure 1-1).

Experts have identified four stages in the career choice process. The first step is simply daydreaming about or imagining yourself in a particular career. Like the child who watches a TV newscast and dreams of being a network anchor, adults also fantasize about performing work that has special appeal for them.

The second step involves investigating a specific career. Reading about a career, interviewing experienced people, and visiting work sites are all part of the second step. The third step is entering some temporary relationship with the career. This step may take the form of part-time employment, or it may be taking courses related to the career field. The final stage is actually beginning to work in the career field. When a person begins work, then he or she has made a significant career decision.

STAGES IN THE CAREER CHOICE PROCESS

Stage 1
Think About a Career

Think about a career, perhaps daydreaming about your life and work in a particular field.

Stage 2
Learn About a Career

Learning about a particular field; gathering information.

Stage 3
Prepare for a Career

Beginning some relationship with a field of work, either taking classes to prepare to work in the field, beginning a temporary job, or taking a part-time job in the field

Stage 4
Commit to a Career

Committing yourself to a specific career choice by beginning a full-time job in your chosen field

Figure 1-1 You might choose a career as (a) a child-care worker, (b) medical secretary, (c) cosmetologist, or model. (Child-care worker courtesy of Wee Care, Department of Labor, Albany, NY; medical secretary photo by Jeff Greenberg, Inc.; cosmetologist/model photo by Stevin Landis.)

You have probably gone well beyond Stage One—maybe you are even ready for Stage Four. Wherever you are now in your career decision-making process, this chapter can help you evaluate yourself and your choices and move you closer to that important career choice.

UNDERSTAND YOURSELF

Self-assessment means knowing your likes and dislikes, your strengths and weaknesses, your interests and abilities, and the kind of work environment you enjoy. You can learn more about yourself in a variety of ways.

TALK WITH PEOPLE

Many people are available to help you learn more about yourself. If your school or college has a counseling and guidance service, begin there. Counselors are trained to help you understand yourself. They will talk with you in ways that will help you explore your feelings and interests. They can help you identify your strengths and weaknesses. You may get all the help you need from only one session with a counselor, or you may wish to have a series of sessions for in-depth career counseling.

Others who are not trained counselors, such as friends, family, teachers, and people you work with, may also be helpful. An older person whom you respect may offer valuable information based on years of experience. The very process of talking will sometimes help you decide what is right for you.

EXPLORE WHO YOU ARE

Ask yourself these questions as you seek to learn more about yourself.

- What kind of work do I like?
- Do I like to work with things, data, or people?
- Do I work best alone or with others?
- What kind of people do I like?
- What kind of people do I avoid?
- What am I good at?
- What kind of work am I doing when I feel happiest?
- What skills do I have?
- What skills do I wish I had?
- How much training and education am I willing to get?
- Can I make sacrifices in time, money, and effort to prepare myself for the career I want?

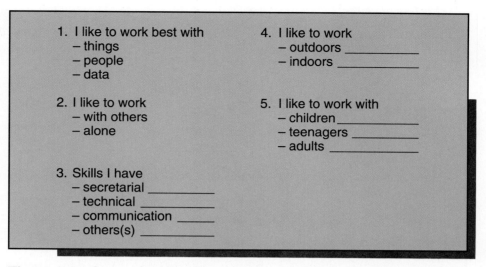

1. I like to work best with
   – things
   – people
   – data

2. I like to work
   – with others
   – alone

3. Skills I have
   – secretarial _____
   – technical _____
   – communication _____
   – others(s) _____

4. I like to work
   – outdoors _____
   – indoors _____

5. I like to work with
   – children _____
   – teenagers _____
   – adults _____

Figure 1-2   Create checklists like this one to help you identify your work preferences.

Review the personal checklist in Figure 1-2. Then prepare such a checklist for yourself.

EVALUATE LIFE EXPERIENCES

Think about the various experiences you have had in your life in such areas as work and leisure. For example, you will want to include participation in church or community projects, caring for a sick family member for an extended period, babysitting, working as a lifeguard or camp counselor. Which of your experiences were satisfying and which were not? Why were you happy or unhappy with the experience?

The form shown in Figure 1-3 provides an exercise that will help you evaluate your work and life experiences. The first two items on the form have been filled in as examples. Review the form and then prepare one for yourself.

TAKE TESTS

Most schools and colleges provide testing services to help students make career decisions. Ask a teacher or a school official whether your school offers such a testing service. Testing services may also be available in your community through the U.S. Employment Commission, through the Department of Human Resources, or through private counseling services.

Jobs or experiences I have had	What I liked about the job	What I disliked about the job
Examples:		
Babysitting	a. *Working with Children* b. _____ c. _____	a. *Salary* b. *Restrictions* c. *Hours*
Clerk at Convenience Store	a. *Handling Money* b. *Responsibilities* c. *Selling*	a. *Long Hours* b. _____ c. _____
1. _____	a. _____ b. _____ c. _____	a. _____ b. _____ c. _____
2. _____	a. _____ b. _____ c. _____	a. _____ b. _____ c. _____
3. _____	a. _____ b. _____ c. _____	a. _____ b. _____ c. _____
4. _____	a. _____ b. _____ c. _____	a. _____ b. _____ c. _____
5. _____	a. _____ b. _____ c. _____	a. _____ b. _____ c. _____
6. _____	a. _____ b. _____ c. _____	a. _____ b. _____ c. _____
Ranking:		
1. _____	2. _____	3. _____

Figure 1-3 Create a checklist like this one to help you identify your jobs and experiences.

There are no right and wrong answers in these tests, nor can you fail them. They simply help to identify your interests and show where your greatest potential lies. They provide strong information in your quest for self-awareness and a rewarding career.

Tests typically deal with individual interests, personality traits, and work aptitude. Interest inventories are the most widely used tests in career counseling.

Interest inventories may vary from simple take-home questionnaires for self-analysis to more sophisticated computer interaction programs. The interest test may be completed by the student in the guidance office in about an hour's time. It is followed by a conference with a counselor who interprets the results. The interest test identifies the individual's interests and then compares them with interests of people who are satisfactorily working in specific career fields. Frequently used interest inventories include the "Strong-Campbell Interest Inventory" and the "System of Interactive Guidance Information."

Aptitude tests measure a person's ability to perform specific tasks. They are often given when a person wants to enter technical fields of work. An aptitude test may help you decide, for example, if you can succeed at electronics, drafting, or secretarial work, or any of many careers that require technical skills. A frequently used aptitude test is the "General Aptitude Test Battery."

You may also take *personality inventories* to help you identify specific personality traits. These tests are not administered as often as interest inventories, but you may wish to ask your counselor for one if you are having difficulty deciding what is right for you. For example, you may be interested in a career in sales. The personality test may reveal that you do not handle rejection well, which may prevent you from finding happiness in a sales career. The personality rating sheet in Figure 1-4 will help you examine yourself. Review the rating sheet and then prepare one for yourself. A commonly used personality inventory is the "Minnesota Multiphasic Personality Inventory."

INVESTIGATE VARIOUS CAREERS

Career investigation is another service provided by many schools and colleges. You may have already investigated several careers that interest you. If you want more information about any of these careers, or if you want to investigate new ones, begin with the counseling service at your school, which can provide you with information on a wide range of jobs. Counselors can interpret information about specific jobs, give you long-term career information, and provide computer programs to guide you in career investigations.

CHARACTERISTIC	Always	Usually	Seldom	Never
1. Outgoing				
2. Friendly				
3. Decisive				
4. Tactful				
5. Honest				
6. Positive				
7. Courteous				
8. Dependable				
9. Moral				
10. Open-minded				
11. Self-controlled				
12. Well-groomed				
13. Interested in others				
14. Unselfish				
15. Communicative				

Figure 1-4 Create a checklist like this one to help you identify your personality characteristics.

GATHER OCCUPATIONAL INFORMATION

Information about specific careers is available from many other sources. Career literature can be obtained for public libraries, various federal agencies, and professional organizations.

Two major publications supply comprehensive information about careers in the United States. They are the *Dictionary of Occupational Titles* and the *Occupational Outlook Handbook*. These references can be found in your local libraries. Although they contain much more information than you will want, they can help you with a wide range of career ideas. If you are not sure of a job title or don't know what workers like "microcomputer specialist" or "administrative assistant" do, these books can help you. You will find occupations listed in clusters. Here are examples:

◆ Office occupations (such as receptionists and clerks)

◆ Service occupations (such as plumbers and electricians)

◆ Sales occupations (such as product representatives)

- ◆ Construction occupations (such as brick layers)
- ◆ Occupations in education (such as preschool teacher's aides)
- ◆ Occupations in transportation activities (such as drivers)
- ◆ Scientific and technical occupations (such as health technicians and computer programmers)

INTERVIEW PROFESSIONALS AND VISIT WORK PLACES

Talk to people who have jobs that seem interesting to you. These may be friends or someone recommended by a friend; however, don't limit your research to someone you know. If you observe people performing jobs that seem interesting to you, ask if you could talk to them sometime about their job. As long as you are friendly and flexible about when and where this takes place, they will probably honor your request—and feel flattered that you asked.

Also, you may read a feature article in a local newspaper or magazine about someone in a particular occupation. You could write or call the person if a means of contact, such as company or organization, is listed in the article. Ask questions such as these:

- ◆ What training and education did you receive to qualify you for your work?
- ◆ What is a typical workday like?
- ◆ What do you consider the major benefits of your job?
- ◆ Would you recommend this field of work?
- ◆ Do you like your job? What don't you like?

When you visit a store, doctor's office, or business office, observe these things about the workplace and the activities of the workers:

- ◆ Geographic location
- ◆ Working conditions
- ◆ Physical surroundings
- ◆ Contact with clients
- ◆ Type of clients
- ◆ Relationships with coworkers
- ◆ Length of workday
- ◆ Flexibility in work tasks

Perhaps you can even arrange to spend a day at the office or store to get a more accurate picture of the career you are considering. Imagine yourself working there, and record your impressions and feelings in a notebook. Would you find this job a satisfying one?

Figure 1-5 Some people enjoy working with senior citizens. Does this type of work appeal to you? (From Hegner and Caldwell, *Nursing Assistant*, Delmar Publishers Inc.)

READ ABOUT PEOPLE IN SPECIFIC WORK ROLES

You may be surprised at what you can learn about various jobs by reading newspaper and magazine articles. For example, read what workers on strike tell news reporters. Read interviews with workers explaining new opportunities in their field. Newsstand magazines, such as *Working Woman, People, Ebony, Self,* and *Life,* have glamour stories, but they also have information about real people working at real jobs.

Don't overlook the want ads in newspapers and magazines (see Figure 1-6). You can tell where the greatest need for employees exists and what skills are needed for these jobs. You can also collect some information on salaries and work schedules from these small ads. When you have information

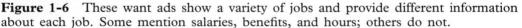

Figure 1-6 These want ads show a variety of jobs and provide different information about each job. Some mention salaries, benefits, and hours; others do not.

about job opportunities and about your own abilities, you can proceed confidently to the next step in career planning.

CHOOSE A CAREER GOAL

You should be ready by now to make a tentative career choice. Setting your career goal is a challenging experience! Determining the stepping-stones to your goals makes the goal seem more real and possible.

Goals may be defined as outcomes toward which a person works. They are broad statements of purpose. Goals grow out of our dreams and our desires for a satisfying life. They are usually based on our values, our needs, and our wishes. Goals give purpose to our actions.

Goals may be specific or general. They may be long-term or short-term. Some goals are known as *means-end goals,* meaning that they are short-term goals that are necessary to reach long-term ones. To earn a passing grade in a cosmetology course is a means-end goal for a person who wishes to become a hair stylist. Likewise, saving enough money for tuition to a technical school is a means-end goal for a person who wishes to become an auto mechanic.

It is important to realize that goals change because people or their circumstances are always changing. Also, as we reach some goals, we discard others or add new ones. The most important thing to know about goals is that establishing them will give you a more satisfying life. Your life will have a clearly defined purpose. For example, you may be unhappy with a part-time job, but you can get through each day by understanding that this job provides you with income and a good work record, which will help you achieve your goals of becoming a hotel chef.

LONG-TERM CAREER GOALS

Long-term career goals direct your work-related activity. They guide you in planning your education and your job search. Here are examples of long-term career goals:

- To have a career as an office professional
- To become a buyer in a department store
- To be a medical assistant
- To become an independent truck driver
- To open a day care center in my home
- To work as an airplane mechanic
- To become a hotel manager
- To own my own catering business

SHORT-TERM CAREER GOALS

Short-term career goals are the stepping stones to reaching your long-term career goal. Short-term goals typically relate to education and special training, to saving money for investments in your career, or to obtaining experience needed for your ultimate career. You may, however, have all sorts of other short-term career goals. For example, you may have a goal of making yourself more physically attractive or more physically strong to get the job you want. You may have a short-term goal of becoming acquainted with a person who can help you get started in a certain field. Even writing your resume is short-term goal that will be necessary to reach your final career goal. See the examples of short-term goals and their relationship to long-term goals in the following table.

HOW PEOPLE REACH GOALS

There are proven techniques for succeeding in reaching goals. Although there are times in life when a goal must be discarded because it cannot

Figure 1-7 An entry-level job in a day care center can help someone achieve a long-term goal of teaching children. Courtesy of Wee Care, Department of Labor, Albany, NY.

TABLE 1-1: SAMPLE GOALS

LONG-TERM GOALS	RELATED SHORT-TERM GOALS
To become an administrative secretary	To complete secretarial school To develop a resume and obtain interviews To work part-time or as a volunteer in a small office.
To become financially independent of my parents	To get a job To have my own apartment To pay my own bills
To have a career in child care services	To get an entry-level job in child care To get more training in early childhood development

be reached, most goals can be reached if certain techniques are used. Here are some guidelines for reaching goals.

◆ *Write out your goals.* Keep them where you can read them daily. You may tape them to the mirror where you get dressed or carry them in your wallet. Be sure to put the list where you will read it regularly.

◆ *Make a written plan for reaching your goals.* Determine what actions will be necessary for reaching goals. Then sequence them; that is, list them in the order in which they must be accomplished.

◆ *Be flexible as you plan.* Be prepared to change your plans. For example, if you plan to take a course at one school, but the course is dropped, do not give up on taking the course. Explore other schools or other courses.

◆ *Be realistic.* Create a workable plan. For example, few people who have taken courses in word processing, keyboarding, and supervision begin their career as office managers. Be willing to start at an entry-level job.

◆ *Be self-disciplined in carrying out your plan.* Research shows that self-discipline is one of the most important qualities a person may have to reach his or her goals. Sticking with a part-time job to achieve your goal requires self-discipline. Being a dependable volunteer in an office also requires self-discipline. Studying as much as necessary may be another exercise in self-discipline.

◆ *Prioritize your activities.* Decide what actions are most important and do these first. For example, you will need training or education before experience.

◆ *Keep a progress record.* Check progress toward your goals periodically. If you are not making the progress you think you should be making, you may want to rethink yours goals or plan new strategies for reaching your long-term goals.

◆ *Enlist the help of others.* Let family, friends, and teachers know what your goals are. Many of these people may be able to help you. By talking about your goals, you may learn about additional resources for reaching your goals.

◆ *Reward yourself.* Plan ways to reward yourself when you have reached short-term goals. For example, treat yourself and a friend to a special dinner when you have reached a savings goal, or allow yourself a weekend without studying when you have made a special grade you have worked toward. We all work more efficiently when we can look forward to a reward. Rewarding yourself is an effective strategy for reaching goals.

WHY PEOPLE FAIL TO REACH GOALS

Sometimes people fail to reach their goals. Although there are many reasons for this, here are the five most common ones.

Poor Decision Making. To avoid making bad decisions, use the scientific decision-making process. You probably learned this process long ago, but here is a quick review. The steps in the process are:

1. Define the problem.
2. Identify as many alternative solutions as possible.
3. Consider the consequences of each alternative.
4. Select the best alternative.

Evaluate the decision that seems the best to you by asking these questions:

◆ *What will be the outcome of my decision?* For example, ask yourself what education and special training will be required for the career you have chosen. What financial resources will be required? Where will you obtain the training? What life-style will you have with this career?

◆ *What do others think?* You will want to make your own decision, but getting the opinions of others can broaden your thinking and help you gain different perspectives. They may suggest alternatives and consequences that had not occurred to you.

◆ *How will my decision affect others?* For example, will you need to move your family? Will you need to use money set aside for other family uses? Will you be able to provide more opportunities for your family with this career than with another?

Insufficient Resources. There are three ways people may increase their resources. First they may "get more resources." Second, they may "use more effectively" the resources they have. Third, they may "lower their standards."

Examples of these three methods may be seen in the experiences of Abel, Benjamin, and Clair. Abel did not have enough money to pay his living costs and tuition fees, so he delayed enrolling in school for one semester while he worked to earn money. (He obtained more resources.) Although Benjamin had enough money for school tuition, he did not have enough for living expenses, so he took a job working in the school cafeteria to pay his room and board. (He obtained more resources.) He also restricted his entertainment allowance to school sporting activities (he used more effectively the resources he had). Claire, too, found that she did not have enough money for school costs, so she moved from her own apartment to her parents' home and gave up her car (she lowered her living standards temporarily to achieve an important goal).

Figure 1-8 A part-time job can provide the additional resources needed to help achieve goals, such as finishing school or getting additional training. (Photo by David W. Tuttle.)

Lack of Clear or Specific Goals. Goal statements need to be specific enough to guide actions. A career goal such as "to work in the oil business" is not specific enough. On the other hand, "to work as an accountant in the oil and gas industry" is specific enough to guide a person in career preparation.

Lack of Commitment to Goals. Having a commitment energizes a person. A person's commitment can be increased by putting personal resources into an endeavor. Writing down goals and talking about them also increases commitment. And finally, regularly acting on plans to reach goals increases commitment. These practices are very important, because when commitment is missing, people seldom reach their goals.

SIGNS OF COMMITMENT

1. **DEVOTES** time to the activity or idea.
2. **TALKS** about the activity or idea.
3. **INVESTS** personal resources in the activity or idea.
4. **GIVES UP** less important interests in favor of the activity or idea.
5. **STUDIES** to gain further information about the activity or idea.

Lack of Necessary Knowledge and Skills. Lacking knowledge or skill can be avoided by getting the education and training required for a specific job.

PREPARE TO REACH YOUR CAREER GOALS

Preparing yourself to reach career goals means developing certain personal skills. Important skills related to careers are:

1. Knowledge or education-based skills
2. Self-esteem skills
3. Interpersonal, or people, skills
4. Communication skills

KNOWLEDGE AND EDUCATION

You have already chosen the most important route to a professional career; you have chosen to seek an education. You are involved in educational experiences designed to help you acquire knowledge and technical skills necessary for a successful career. In this text you will find information for developing other important career skills.

SELF-ESTEEM

Self-esteem or self-confidence is one area of your life that may need work if you are to be successful in your career. "Successful" merely means "achieving your goals," whatever they may be. As you know, success often is measured in terms of money and prestige. Although income at certain levels may be included in your goals, success includes other things.

Your self-esteem is reflected in how you dress, how you present yourself in person and on paper, how you interact with friends and coworkers, and how you perform in class and on the job. Your self-

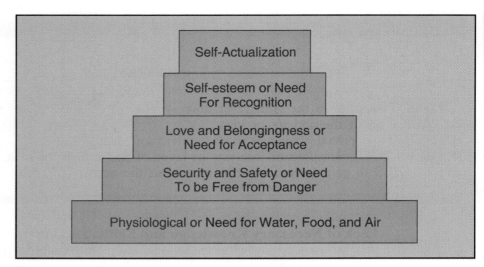

Figure 1-9 Everyone has the same basic needs.

Source: Maslow, A. (1954). Motivation and Personality. New York: Harper and Row, 1954.

image motivates you to do your best if your self-image is positive or to perform poorly, if your self-image is low. What affects our feelings about ourselves?

Although it is true that every individual is unique—different from anyone else in the world—it is also true that everyone has the same basic needs. Individuals have them in different degrees, but they are a part of all human existence (see Figure 1-9). The needs are:

1. Physical needs: food, clothing, shelter
2. Safety needs: protection from harm
3. Love needs: feelings of love and belonging
4. Esteem needs: respect and admiration
5. Self-actualization needs: fulfilling potential

Only when people's physical and safety needs are met can their self-esteem increase. Because they no longer have to worry about food or safety, they can feel good about who they are and what they have to give. They can also receive love and seek a sense of belonging. Then, when they feel loved and accepted, they have the confidence to reach out for some recognition for doing well at work and elsewhere. This level is not essential to life, like food or shelter, but it is so important to our well-being that it is classified as a "need." Last but not least is the level of self-actualization, the point at which you reach your potential.

Throughout this book you will learn ways to build your self-esteem.

As you implement the steps in Chapter 1 for preparing for and beginning a career, you will feel better about your ability to mobilize your resources and apply them to your goals. The ideas are here, but you are the one who **makes them happen** in your life. Pat yourself on the back for each success along the way. Try to learn something from disappointments; achieving small successes and viewing disappointments in a positive light can help motivate you.

What motivates people? Much research has been done on motivation. The results indicate that different people are motivated by different things. Some authorities say that today's workers, for example, are most often motivated by money and by having an opportunity to enjoy life and have fun. At other periods in time researchers found that young professionals in the 1950s were motivated by rewards and status.

In general, people are motivated by having their basic physical, safety, love, and esteem needs met. These are usually met through having an adequate income, a satisfying social life, and a satisfying job. Future chapters on grooming, dress, communication, and fitting into the work culture will help you achieve what you need at all levels.

INTERPERSONAL RELATIONSHIPS

Interpersonal skills are identified as critical to the success of most workers. Learning to work productively with others is as important as learning technical skills. People skills include the ability to be sensitive to others and relating to them in ways that bring positive responses.

Being Sensitive to Others. Listening is perhaps the most important way to show sensitivity to others. Listening skills are discussed further in Chapter 7 of this book. Other ways to show sensitivity to others are:

◆ *Viewing each coworker as a whole person.* Avoid responding to a worker in only the work role. Every individual has multiple roles, and people never completely separate their various roles. For example, the person who cleans your office may also be a mother who worries about her children; your boss is not only a manager, but may also be a caretaker for an aging parent. Be aware of the ways in which a person's private life impacts the work life.

◆ *Responding to people as individuals.* No two people will necessarily fill a role that you arbitrarily assign to them. For example, just because your supervisor is your mother's age does not mean that she will respond to you in the way your mother does.

◆ *Making people feel important.* For example, if you want Joe to help you arrange the tables in a banquet hall for a party, explain to him that he is the person who knows most about how to organize seating for

FOCUS ON:
AN EVOLVING CAREER

Jill Valdez's experience is a good illustration of how a career evolves. As a teenager in Milwaukee, Wisconsin, Jill had two strong areas of interest—nursing and office work. "I always liked the idea of working in a medical job where I could help people," explains Jill. "But I liked the idea of working in a busy office, too." Jill took both office education and nursing courses at Milwaukee Area Technical Center, and in her senior year she completed the school's practical nursing program. A few days after graduation, Jill was able to find nursing job at a St. Joseph's Hospital.

"I worked at the hospital for 4 years," says Jill. "I stayed at St. Joe's after I married Jose, and kept working right up until the week before my daughter Wendy was born. The experience was great, especially in the pediatric ward. But the night hours were hard to take."

When she needed to return to work several months after Wendy was born, Jill decided to look for a job that would allow her to work part-time during the day. "I decided to work as an office temp so I could earn some money while I checked out possible office jobs." Jill worked out her schedule with Jose so she could go to school two nights a week while he watched the baby. "I needed to brush up on my office skills," explains Jill. "I'm glad I signed up because a lot had changed since I was in high school."

After 6 months of temporary work, Jill was sent to a small publishing company where she worked in the editorial, sales, and telemarketing departments. "Publishing is great," says Jill. "There's something new happening every minute." The company was so impressed by her attitude and skills that it offered her a full-time job as an office assistant in the telemarketing department. She has been there for 3 years.

"I really like my job," says Jill, "but I think someday I'd like to combine my office skills and my nursing background. Maybe I'll find a job at a medical publishing company."

As you can see, Jill is always assessing her needs to determine if her work is meeting them. She is always eager to learn something new because this may help her achieve her long-term goals.

large groups. Three of the five basic human needs deal with the need to feel important: the need for love, respect, and self-actualization. When you make a person feel important, you contribute to pleasant and productive working conditions (see Figure 1-10). (Remember that it is impossible to make yourself look more important by making someone else look less important!)

Figure 1-10 We all feel better about ourselves when we are recognized for doing a good job. (Photo by Paul E. Meyers.)

Relating Positively to Others. As a new professional you will be more interested in ways to influence people positively. You may influence people in the workplace in positive ways with these actions:

◆ *Show interest in others.* Ask about their interests, their hobbies, and their families. Avoid talking too much about yourself and your interests.

◆ *Be friendly.* A smile is a powerful tool in developing good relationships.

◆ *Use people's names.* Every person enjoys hearing his or her name. Use titles when they are appropriate.

◆ *Be empathetic.* Listen to others and show concern for problems they may be experiencing. Respect their opinions. (You do not have to agree with a person to respect his or her opinion.)

◆ *Be tactfully assertive.* When asked for an opinion, give one; when asked for a decision, make one. Be tactful if you feel a need to be assertive on a sensitive topic. Criticize in a cautious and tactful manner. Never speak behind the backs of others.

◆ *Avoid arguing.* You may need to walk away from some unnecessary controversy, and you may need to develop skill in saying things like, "I don't see this issue in the same way as you."

- *Handle embarrassing situations tactfully.* Help others save face. Comments like "I can understand how that might have happened," is much better than, "that was the wrong way to handle the situation!"
- *Be positive.* Not only will you be sought after as a friend and worker if you become known as a positive person, you will be more productive.
- *Admit your errors.* If you have made a mistake, readily admit it. Not only will others respect your strength and honesty, but you will gain personal power from not having a hidden error.
- *Do your work well and in a timely fashion.* There is no better way to influence others in the workplace than by being a productive worker yourself.

COMMUNICATION SKILLS

Communication skills are so important to your professional well-being and success that a separate chapter (Chapter 7) in this text is given to the topic. Read that chapter for help in developing your communication skills. For now, it is important to remember that these skills are the most important ones you can develop in your search for personal and professional satisfaction. For example, you can "network" with friends and acquaintances. This means that you maintain contact with people who are working, with the expectation that they will let you know of jobs that become available. Once you are working, you can do the same for them.

ACTIVITIES RELATED TO YOUR GOALS

You can use your free time to reach your goals by engaging in activities related to your goals, such as taking personal enrichment courses and getting related work experience. Activities not directly related to school or work can also be helpful.

Personal Enrichment Courses. Personal enrichment courses are not required for your major field of study, but they support your career goals and enrich your learning experience. For example, a marketing student who plans to be a food retailer might take a course in food preparation as an elective. A person majoring in secretarial studies may take a course in accounting. People often take general personal enrichment courses, such as drama, art, and nutrition.

Work Experience. Every work experience you have is important. Even if you have a job that you will not want to hold for a long period of time, any job can be a learning experience. Regardless of what the job is, you can develop general work skills. The abilities to relate to clients and coworkers, to be prompt, to dress appropriately, to manage resources, and to present a positive attitude are important in any job. Therefore, any work experience can help you prepare for your chosen career.

General Activities. Participation in school and community activities is an excellent way to develop as a person and as a professional. Some reasons for participating in school and community organizations are:

◆ To develop leadership skills (and self-confidence)

◆ To develop a social circle

◆ To be with people who have the same interests as yours

◆ To gain experience in activities outside your major field

◆ To increase networking opportunities

◆ To broaden abilities and skills

◆ To contribute to the community well-being

◆ To build a record of accomplishment for your resume

Organizations that may be available at your school include professional organizations associated with major courses of study, student government, sororities and fraternities, religious groups, and honor societies. In addition, community organizations such as the Jaycees and others provide organizational activities for people of varied ages and interests.

REVIEW QUESTIONS

1. Describe the four steps followed in choosing a career.
2. Outline three ways to assess yourself.
3. Describe sources of career information.
4. Explain the difference between interest tests and aptitude tests.
5. Where would you find a copy of the *Dictionary of Occupational Titles*?
6. Define a "means-end" goal.
7. List five guidelines for reaching goals.
8. Name the five levels of human needs.
9. Explain why self-esteem is so important to achieving goals.
10. List five ways to motivate or influence others.
11. What is the best way to show sensitivity to others?

1. Interview three professional people and ask them how they decided to enter their career field. Prepare an oral report of your findings.

2. Visit your school counseling office and ask about career counseling services. Write a one-page report on your findings.

3. Write five career goals that you might pursue and prioritize them according to the interest you have in each of them now. When you have determined the one that has top priority, outline strategies for reaching that goal.

4. Identify one personal quality that you wish to develop to a greater degree than you now have. Consider how you may work to increase that quality in your life. Write your plan of action.

5. Write a paragraph explaining the value of participation in student or civic organizations to your professional development.

6. Interview a business person about the importance of goal setting in his or her life. Prepare a written summary.

CHAPTER 2

COMMUNICATING WHO YOU ARE

CHAPTER GOAL

To help you present yourself in ways that communicate to others that you are a successful professional person.

CHAPTER OBJECTIVES

After studying this chapter you should be able to:

1. Describe personal, internal qualities needed for professional success.
2. Explain the importance of a pleasing personal appearance in the professional world.
3. Use positive body language.
4. Use positive effective hygiene.
5. Use color to enhance personal appearance.
6. Exhibit good grooming habits.

WHO ARE YOU? WHO ARE *YOU*?

This compelling question can be answered in two ways. The first is based on the internal personal qualities you possess. The second is based on external factors, such as grooming and dress. This chapter describes the personal qualities needed for professional success and suggests ways that you can send positive messages to others about yourself through your self presentation.

Industrial leaders from across the nation have worked with the U.S. Department of Labor to identify the skills all workers will need by the turn of the century. These Workplace 2000 skills will be needed by all workers regardless of their professional level. For example, the skills will be needed by custodians just as they will be needed by managers. Analyze the lists that follow to determine what skills you need to develop further. Notice that the first list shows foundation skills. The second list showing competencies is an explanation of the foundation skills. The three key foundation points are further developed in the second part of Figure 2-1.

WORKPLACE KNOW-HOW *

The know-how identified by SCANS is made up of five competencies and a three-part foundation of skills and personal qualities that are needed for solid job performance. These include:

THE FOUNDATION—competence requires:

1. Basic Skills—reading, writing, arithmetic and mathematics, speaking, and listening;
2. Thinking Skills—thinking creatively, making decisions, solving problems, seeing things in the mind's eye, knowing how to learn, and reasoning;
3. Personal Qualities—individual responsibility, self-esteem, sociability, self-management, and integrity.

COMPETENCIES—effective workers can productively use:

1. Resources—allocating time, money, materials, space, and staff;
2. Interpersonal Skills—working on teams, teaching others, serving customers, leading, negotiating, and working well with people from culturally diverse backgrounds;
3. Information—acquiring and evaluating data, organizing and maintaining files, interpreting and communicating, and using computers to process information;
4. Systems—understanding social, organizational, and technological systems, monitoring and correcting performance, and designing or improving systems;
5. Technology—selecting equipment and tools, applying technology to specific tasks, and maintaining and troubleshooting technologies.

* The U.S. Department of Labor, SCANS Report, 1991.

Figure 2-1 Workplace essentials.

A THREE-PART FOUNDATION *

Basic Skills: Reads, writes, performs arithmetic and mathematical operations, listens and speaks

A. *Reading*—locates, understands, and interprets written information in prose and in documents such as manuals, graphs, and schedules
B. *Writing*—communicates thoughts, ideas, information, and messages in writing; and creates documents such as letters, directions, manuals, reports, graphs, and flow charts
C. *Arithmetic/Mathematics*—performs basic computations and approaches practical problems by choosing appropriately from a variety of mathematical techniques
D. *Listening*—receives, attends to, interprets, and responds to verbal messages and other cues
E. *Speaking*—organizes ideas and communicates orally

Thinking Skills: Thinks creatively, makes decisions, solves problems, visualizes, knows how to learn, and reasons

A. *Creative Thinking*—generates new ideas
B. *Decision Making*—specifies goals and constraints, generates alternatives, considers risks, and evaluates and chooses best alternative
C. *Problem Solving*—recognizes problems and devises and implements plan of action
D. *Seeing Things in the Mind's Eye*—organizes, and processes symbols, pictures, graphs, objects, and other information
E. *Knowing How-to-Learn*—uses efficient learning techniques to acquire and apply new knowledge and skills
F. *Reasoning*—discovers a rule or principle underlying the relationship between two or more objects and applies it when solving a problem

Personal Qualities: Displays responsibility, self-esteem, sociability, self-management, and integrity and honesty

A. *Responsibility*—exerts a high level of effort and perseveres towards goal attainment
B. *Self-Esteem*—believes in own self-worth and maintains a positive view of self
C. *Sociability*—demonstrates understanding, friendliness, adaptability, empathy, and politeness in group settings
D. *Self-Management*—assesses self accurately, sets personal goals, monitors progress, and exhibits self-control
E. *Integrity/Honesty*—chooses ethical courses of action

Figure 2-1   Continued

PERSONAL QUALITIES NEEDED FOR SUCCESS: INTERNAL FACTORS

Many studies have been conducted among employers to identify the personal qualities a worker needs to be successful. Certain qualities are listed again and again as essential. Here are the ones mentioned most frequently:

◆ *Willingness to learn.* Regardless of the amount of knowledge and skill that a worker brings to a job, there is always more that can be learned. Also, specialized information and skills are related to every position that may be unfamiliar to new employees. Therefore, a willingness to learn is essential for a worker to be productive.

◆ *Accepting of supervision.* Being able to accept suggestions for change and improvement, criticism, and correction are part of all productive work. The worker who cannot accept and learn from supervision will not be a valuable, promotable employee. Not only must an employee be able to accept criticism and make every effort to improve, but he or she must also be able and willing to follow instructions.

◆ *Energy.* The person who exhibits physical and mental alertness along with a willingness to work hard (physically and mentally) is valued by employers.

◆ *Enthusiasm.* When people like their jobs, it shows. Even on days when the work is not exciting or when the worker does not feel at his or her best, the worker finds something to enjoy. Perhaps it is the challenge of the work or the personality of coworkers, the drive to work, or the beauty of the day. Regardless, a spirit of enthusiasm is apparent in successful workers. Among the signs of enthusiasm are pleasantness, positive responses, and smiles.

◆ *Positive attitude.* Closely related to being enthusiastic is being positive. People with a positive attitude are not only pleasant to be with, but they are more productive than negative workers. They are also openminded and seek solutions to problems that might signal failure for a negative person.

◆ *Honesty.* The employee who tells the truth can be trusted and employers need to trust employees with information, time, money, and other company resources. Honest words and actions are respected in business.

◆ *Dependability.* Closely related to honesty is dependability. A dependable worker is not absent too often, does not make trivial excuses, finishes work on time, and follows through on commitments.

◆ *Organization.* Organized people manage their time, their possessions, and their tasks so that work is completed in a timely manner.

Figure 2-2 Enthusiasm and a positive attitude are important qualities for success in any job. (Courtesy of Brodock Press Inc.)

Figure 2-3 Stress levels are higher for disorganized people. (Courtesy of Knight-Ridder Inc.)

Frustration levels are lower for the organized person than for the person who has no sense of order or who gives little attention to schedules.

◆ *Loyalty.* Loyalty is valued by a company in the same way that it is valued in a friend or family member. It is the quality that enables an employee to think and speak positively about supervisors, coworkers, and the company. The loyal worker keeps company information confidential and is supportive of company policy and leadership. When a worker can no longer be loyal to a company, it is time to leave.

◆ *Cooperativeness.* The worker who is willing to share ideas, equipment, and information is valued as a person and as an employee. Today American businesspeople are investigating new ways for workers to work together to increase productivity. Some government agencies and companies ask for volunteers to participate in quality circles. These groups meet periodically to discuss issues or problems and suggest changes that will make work life better. Some companies give bonuses to workers for submitting ideas that save the company money. Sometimes employees are rotated within a department or from one department to another so they can learn more about the duties of others. This way, employees' skills are increased and they can learn from one another's experience.

◆ *Concern for others.* Indications of concern for others are courtesy, friendliness, empathy, and a helping attitude. Have you noticed that when you show concern for others, there is usually a positive result for you? This may come as increased cooperation on the job or increased support for your ideas and projects. It is also likely that others will show the same concern for you as you show for them.

◆ *Self-control.* Mature people control their emotions, their speech, and their outward responses, especially when the immediate reaction would be a negative one. This behavior gives them time to think about the situation and react appropriately to people and situations. Self-control saves people from potential embarrassment. It also helps to establish a worker's reputation as someone who is thoughtful and fair rather than unreasonable and immature.

Rate yourself on these personality traits with the chart in Figure 2-4.

PERSONAL APPEARANCE: EXTERNAL FACTORS

Your personal appearance is the outward expression of your inner self. The person you think you are is expressed in your posture, grooming, and dress. Your appearance makes a statement about who you are and how you feel. When you wear sweats and running shoes, you are saying "I am an informal, relaxed person today." On the other hand, when you

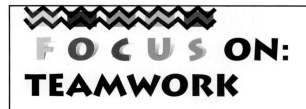

FOCUS ON:
TEAMWORK

LeisureCraft, of Redondo Beach, California, is a small manufacturer of sailboats and catamarans. Over the past 10 years, the company has managed to make quite a name for itself. Its corporate office is small, but LeisureCraft manages very well with a staff of only 11 people. How? Mario D'Oro knows the secret.

"I joined the company right out of high school," Mario says, "but it didn't take long to realize I'd stumbled onto something very special."

Mario is the assistant to the production manager. He is usually the first person in the office each morning, but whoever arrives first turns on the computer system and the copier, makes coffee, and so forth.

"It could be Connie Alonzo, the assistant in the sales department, or David Bascomb, the president of LeisureCraft. It makes no difference. Everyone pitches in.

"We're all in the same boat, if you know what I mean." Mario explains. "If I'm at the factory, or if one of the other assistants is out, everyone helps out by answering phones and taking messages."

Boating specs and periodicals are routinely routed by the president to various staff members, but anyone who sees an article of interest marks it for other staffers. If Mario is swamped with phytocopying or correspondence, others cheerfully pitch in to meet office deadlines.

"Connie has trained us all on the sales software package—even Dave Bascomb, our president!"

"We all wear a lot of hats around here. We couldn't make it work if we didn't. There are only four of us assistants, three sales reps, two order clerks, a production manager, and the president. The controller comes in only once a week."

Mario loves the friendly, cooperative spirit that motivates LeisureCraft employees.

"We're a real team," Mario says proudly. "We do whatever we have to do to get the job done. LeisureCraft couldn't manage without teamwork. It's what keeps us afloat!"

wear a nurse's uniform, you are saying "I am able to help you with your health needs." When you give special attention to grooming, you are saying, "This is an important day; I will look my best for people who are important to me." On days when you give no attention to grooming, you may be saying, "I don't care about myself or what others think of me today."

The first impression you make on others is formed in only 30 seconds. What can you see in that short time? A person's grooming, dress, posture, and eye contact (or lack of it). Once made, first impressions are slow to change; therefore, creating positive ones may be important to your job success.

PERSONALITY CHECKLIST			
Quality	**Always**	**Usually**	**Seldom**
1. Willing to learn			
2. Accepting of supervision			
3. Energetic			
4. Enthusiastic			
5. Positive in my attitude			
6. Dependable			
7. Organized			
8. Cooperative			
9. Concerned for others			
10. Self-controlled			

Figure 2-4   Rate yourself on each personality quality needed for success.

Your personal appearance is especially important when you want to be viewed as a professional. To create an attractive personal appearance, give consideration to your body language, daily hygiene, personal grooming, and your manner of dress. With careful consideration of these elements you can be confident that you will present a positive, professional image.

BODY LANGUAGE

As a professional, you can communicate confidence by the way you use your body. Your manner of walking, sitting, or shaking hands tells others whether or not you are self-confident.

Posture. Good posture—the way you move, stand, and sit makes you look good. The effect created by a carefully chosen, appropriate wardrobe and excellent grooming can be ruined by poor posture. People who stand in a slump and slouch in a chair may have low self-esteem that has developed over a long period of time. Such posture may also reflect a negative feeling about a current situation. At any rate, poor posture raises questions in an observer. However, standing tall is nearly always a sign that people feel good about themselves. If you are uncomfortable and have feelings of self-doubt, encourage yourself about the good qualities you possess and see how much easier it is to have good posture. The following suggestions can help you achieve the posture that communicates self-confidence (see Figure 2-5).

Figure 2-5 Good posture and a positive attitude communicate self-confidence and make you a more valuable employee. (Courtesy of Leslie Fay Companies, Inc.)

- *Sit* with your back straight against the back of the chair. Keep your feet flat on the floor. Balance your weight on both hips.
- *Walk* while holding in your abdomen; push your shoulders up by lifting your chest; let your arms hang relaxed at your sides. Balance your weight on the balls of your feet.
- *Eat* attractively. Some people slump in their chairs as they eat, lowering their heads close to the table. Watch people do this and you will see how it detracts from their appearance. Guard against adopting such a posture as you eat, even if you are tired at mealtime.
- *Exercise* to strengthen back and shoulder muscles. Many books, magazines, and videotapes offer exercise plans for improving posture. This is another area where self-discipline is needed, as well as the self-esteem to care about how posture affects your professional image.

Handshakes. The way you shake hands can communicate your feelings of self-confidence to others. Both men and women need to develop a firm, but not crushing, handshake. When business people meet, they often shake hands. Men have always shaken hands, and little boys learn about this practice from childhood. However, many women are sometimes unsure about initiating a handshake. If you have that problem, work on developing the habit of shaking hands in all appropriate business situations.

Figure 2-6 It is important to make eye contact when you shake hands. (Photo by Paul E. Meyers.)

To shake hands correctly, extend your hand immediately when meeting a colleague or a client. Shake "thumb joint to thumb joint." It is inappropriate to shake only fingers. Give one good firm shake, then drop the hand. Avoid patting the top of the hand and avoid pumping the hand several times. Of course, you will want to look directly at the person with whom you are shaking hands. If you are wearing heavy outdoor gloves, remove them before offering your hand. Stand up for all handshakes and remember that to refuse an offered hand is a grave insult; never refuse to shake when someone offers a hand.

Eye Contact. Making eye contact is extremely important in presenting a positive professional image. Always look directly into the eyes of the person to whom you are speaking, and look at the person when you are listening as well. Direct eye contact indicates that your full attention is being given to the conversation. When your gaze wanders, you suggest that your attention is wandering also.

Avoid wearing tinted glasses indoors, because they cause others to suspect that you are not looking into their eyes. People generally perceive others who do not make eye contact as weak or untrustworthy.

Other elements of body language should also be observed by the person who is concerned with projecting a positive image. For example, you may show interest in another person and in what is being said with body movements. And, of course, you may show disinterest or irritation.

Body language that may show interest in people and in their comments includes leaning toward the speaker, nodding the head, showing pleasant expressions, and even adopting a posture similar to the speaker's. On the other hand, body language that suggests disinterest includes avoiding the speaker's eyes, frowning, drumming fingers, sitting casually, and giving your attention to objects unrelated to the speaker. More overt actions, such as stamping out of a room and slamming a door, or throwing books to the floor, are strong signals of disagreement and anger. (These last very unattractive signals are not recommended for responsible professionals.)

As you become more aware of messages you may send and receive by body language, remember that a specific body action does not always send the same message. Folded arms are a good example of this point. You may fold your arms because you are cold or because you disagree with a speaker. It is a mistake to assume that you can always know what a person is thinking by that individual's body position. But if you are aware of body language you can get clues that will guide you in understanding others, and you can use your own body movements to communicate your interests, feelings, and attitudes.

HYGIENE

Hygiene relates to the care we take in keeping our bodies clean. It involves daily baths, skin care, dental care, and hair care, all of which contribute a great deal to appearance.

General Care. Daily bathing may be a quick shower, a leisurely soak in the tub, or even a sponge bath. Regardless of the method, a thorough cleaning of the body each day is a must. Proper cleansing involves scrubbing the skin with warm water and soap. Use a soap that is right for your skin—people with sensitive skin may choose a different soap from the one chosen by people who have very dry skin. When the body is thoroughly washed, rinse with cool water to close the pores.

Be sure to clean all parts of the body, especially the feet. Washing between toes reduces bacteria and helps to control odors. (Be sure to dry feet thoroughly to avoid athlete's foot.)

Body odors are offensive. Most of them are caused by perspiration or lack of a daily bath.

Everyone needs to use an underarm deodorant or an antiperspirant. If you perspire a great deal, you may choose an antiperspirant instead of a deodorant because an antiperspirant is stronger. Follow the directions for use of the product you choose. Too much of it may stain clothing and irritate the skin. In addition, some people are allergic to certain products. If a rash or pain develops, change brands. Products are also available to control foot odors.

Figure 2-7 All business professionals can benefit from a professional manicure. (From *Milady's Art and Science of Nail Technology*, Milady Publishing Company.)

Nail Care. Well-groomed hands can be a sign of a professional person. Regardless of which profession you choose, your hands will probably be highly visible. Even people who use their hands in rough work can keep their hands well-groomed.

Cleaning dirt from your hands is certainly the first step toward a well-groomed look. Using hand lotions regularly keeps hands from looking red and rough and keeps skin from becoming dry and cracked. In addition, both men and women can benefit from a regular manicure (see Figure 2-7) or special treatment of hands and nails. A manicure may be done at home or by a professional manicurist. A good manicure involves these steps:

◆ Clean nails with a soft brush. Give special attention to removing any soil under the nail.

◆ While the hand is still softened from being washed, or after applying oil, gently push back the cuticles.

◆ Trim nails with clippers and smooth them into a slightly rounded shape with an emery board.

◆ Dry hands thoroughly and apply a lotion.

Toenails require similar care; however, you should cut your toenails straight across to discourage ingrown nails.

Face Care. The correct way to care for your face differs, depending on the type of skin you have. You may have normal, dry, oily, or combination skin.

If yours is normal or oily skin, you will probably use a soap for cleansing; being sure to rinse well after soaping. On the other hand, if you have dry skin, you may prefer a special cleanser instead of soap because soap may cause skin to be even drier. Some people use creams, and some prefer lotions as cleansers. Try various products to determine which is right for you. Remember that most soaps are basically the same, and most cleansers have similar ingredients. Major differences in cost are attributable to added scents, advertising, and packaging.

Clean your face at least twice a day, probably when dressing in the morning and before going to bed at night. Remember that the more you clean your face, the drier it will become. Table 2-1 summarizes the care needed for all skin types.

If you have oily skin, you will want to clean your face frequently. Use soap, and be sure to rinse well. Apply astringent to remove excess oil. If you have dry skin, use a cleaner and follow that with a skin freshener, which is milder than astringent.

Acne, a problem for many young people, is a condition that may be caused by increased hormone production as the body matures. Pimples form when bacteria get into pores that are clogged by excess oil. Although acne usually corrects itself in adulthood, it can be troublesome for several years.

If you have acne, wash your skin frequently, giving gentle care to affected areas. Clean your face often with soap and water to remove oils and bacteria. Apply an astringent after rinsing. Otherwise, avoid touching the acne areas because contact may spread the bacteria, and exerting pressure on the pimples may cause scarring. Use oil-free cosmetics (they are usually clearly labeled) and be sure to remove all makeup at the end of each day.

Healthful habits of regular sleep, exercise, and a balanced diet may discourage acne. In recent years, doctors have found that tension and stress contribute to acne: however, they have also learned that acne is *not* caused by eating certain foods such as chocolate and fried foods, as was once thought. Today, dermatologists (doctors who specialize in diseases of the skin) have very effective treatments for acne. If you have a serious skin problem of this type, visit a dermatologist for advice and treatment.

Skin Care. Skin care involves more than the daily bath. It also involves protection from the sun and wind. Another special skin problem results from overexposure to the sun or to the ultraviolet rays in tanning booths. These rays dry the skin excessively and may produce early signs of aging

TABLE 2-1: STEPS IN CLEANING ALL FACIAL SKIN TYPES

STEP	SKIN TYPES			
	NORMAL	**OILY**	**DRY**	**COMBINATION***
STEP 1	Wet skin with warm water to open pores.	Wet skin with warm water to open pores.	Wet skin with warm water to open pores.	Wet skin with warm water to open pores.
STEP 2	Gently apply soap; lather well.	Gently apply soap lather well.	Gently apply cleanser; lather well.	Gently apply cleanser; lather well.
STEP 3	Rinse well to remove all residue. Blot dry.	Rinse well to remove all residue. Blot dry.	Rinse well to remove all residue. Blot dry.	Rinse well to remove all residue. Blot dry.
STEP 4	Apply astringent with cotton pad or ball.	Apply astringent with cotton pad or ball.	Apply skin freshener with cotton pad or ball.	Apply skin freshener with cotton pad or ball.
STEP 5	Use oil-free skin lotion as desired.		Use moisturizer to help reduce dryness.	Use moisturizer on dry areas or oil-free skin lotion over face.

* Combination is oily around nose and on forehead, dry or normal in other areas.

and wrinkling. You will want to use extra creams and other moisturizers to minimize the effects of these rays on your skin. The best way to avoid this problem is to minimize your exposure to these rays. If you must be outdoors over extended periods of time, use sun screens regularly.

Dental Care. Hygiene also includes dental care. Clean teeth and breath are vital to a professional. Brush your teeth daily and visit a dentist periodically for a thorough cleaning. When dentists clean teeth, they remove stains as well as materials that can be harmful to the health of teeth and gums.

If you are bothered with bad breath, the dentist will treat the condition or recommend that you see another physician who can correct the problem.

Hair Care. Clean hair, trimmed and styled in a contemporary fashion, promotes a professional image. Be sure your hair gets the care it requires.

Healthy hair is a sign of a healthy body. Eating a well-balanced diet, exercising and getting plenty of rest contribute to healthy hair. Some people believe that they improve the health of their hair by the addition of various chemicals. Actually conditioners only temporarily change the appearance of the hair by coating it and sealing split ends.

Shampooing hair regularly is the first requirement for attractive healthy hair. Many people shampoo daily; others do so less frequently. It is important to shampoo often enough to prevent an oily or limp appearance. You may want to apply a conditioner or creme rinse before the final water rinse to make your hair more manageable.

Choosing shampoo/conditioning products that are right for your hair can take time. Although there are many products available and they all have similar ingredients, they will react differently to the chemistry of your hair. Some may even contribute to oiliness or limpness. Purchase small, travel sizes of various products while you are trying to find what works best for you.

Hair can be damaged by overexposure to the sun, by long hours of swimming in chlorine-treated pools, by hair dryers and electric rollers, and by chemical treatments, such as coloring or perming. When you limit these factors you promote healthy hair.

Dandruff is a scale that flakes from the scalp. If you are bothered with dandruff, try the special shampoos that are available to relieve the problem. Severe cases may require special treatment by a dermatologist.

GROOMING

Good grooming begins with cleanliness and basic care of the body. Correct application of cosmetics and attractive shaping of the hair are just as important to your professional appearance. Here are some special considerations for the well-groomed look.

Cosmetics for the Face. Makeup is usually a consideration for women; however, some men use makeup to conceal blemishes or scars. Products are available in colors to blend with natural skin tones to cover pimples and other blemishes. Other products called "bronzers" are designed to make skin tones more even. Usually bronzers come in gel form to be spread thinly and evenly over the face. The result looks like suntan. Perspiration can discolor the effect, so people who use bronzers must take care to blot their faces frequently to prevent perspiration runs.

Foundations are used to cover blemishes and provide a smooth base for skin color. Foundations are available in various forms and a tremendous variety of colors. Some provide a glossy finish and some

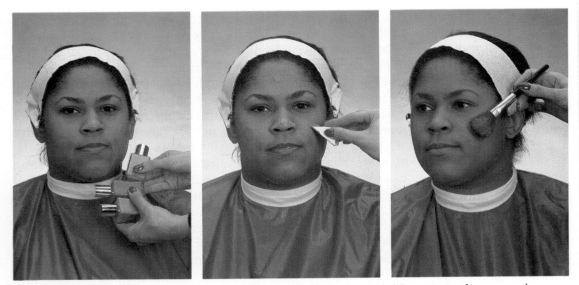

Figure 2-8 (a) Select the right foundation, (b) apply it, and (c) use powder to set it. (From *Milady's Standard Textbook of Cosmetology*, Milady Publishing Company.)

give a "matte" finish. Choose the one that has a texture best suited for your skin in a color that is as near to your natural coloring as possible.

Young women who have few skin problems usually choose a light liquid foundation makeup. On the other hand, women who have more blemishes often choose a heavier cream foundation. In addition to liquid and cream, foundation is also available in gel, mousse, and pancake forms. More moisturizer is necessary as a base when the heavier foundations are used.

All foundation colors have either a rose base or a gold base. If you have warm skin tones, you will want to choose a foundation with a gold base. On the other hand, if you have cool skin tones, you will want to choose the foundation with a rose base. (For more on skin tone and warm and cool colors, see Chapter 3.) When you shop for a foundation makeup, try a small amount of the various shades on your neck or on the side of your face. Look at your skin in good light to select the foundation that blends best with your natural coloring.

Apply foundation with gentle strokes of the fingers (pancake foundation must be applied with a damp sponge), spreading it as evenly as possible across the face. Try not to pull your skin as you apply the foundation. Difficulty in spreading the foundation is an indication that your skin is not moist enough. Some women find that wiping the face gently with a sponge after applying the foundation is a good way to ensure a smooth look. Wiping with a sponge also removes excess foundation. Remember that the goal is a smooth, natural look.

Apply foundation only to the face, but blend it into the neck area, being careful to avoid creating a makeup line at the jaw. Blend carefully into creases of the face to create a smooth look. Avoid foundation buildup.

Thoroughly removing foundation at night is critical to healthy skin and an attractive appearance. Follow the skin care routines outlined earlier in this chapter to ensure a healthy look.

Powder is useful for setting foundation and as a base for color. Powder is available in sheen, matte, or luminescent finishes. Apply it lightly. Many women choose to apply powder with a brush or a cotton puff, brushing away any excess. Pressed powder is convenient to carry in a handbag or to keep in a desk drawer for quick touch-ups.

Cheek color or *blush* may be used to give the skin a healthy glow; however, use it sparingly to avoid looking artificial. Color for the cheeks comes in powder, liquid, gel, and cream forms.

Select a cheek color that is compatible with your skin tones. Again, if you have the bluish white undertones, choose a cool-colored blush, and if you have gold undertones, choose a warm-colored blush. The depth of the cheek color selected should be determined by the intensity of your own coloring.

Liquids, creams, and gels are applied directly over the foundation, with smooth strokes of the fingers. Powdered blush is added after an application of powder and is applied with a soft brush. Place the color in the cheek area above the bottom of the nose and behind an imaginary line falling from the pupil of the eye to the floor. Avoid getting the color

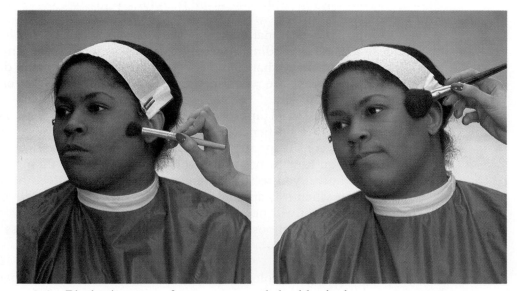

Figure 2-9   Blush gives your face a contoured, healthy look. (From *Milady's Standard Textbook of Cosmetology*, Milady Publishing Company.)

too near the nose or too low on the face. Blending is critical to successful use of cheek color.

Eye shadow may be used to highlight the eyes. Eye shadows should be kept to neutral colors during work hours. Ivory, cream, grey, and soft blues are popular daytime colors. Professional women usually choose eye shadow to even the color of the eyelids and areas below the brow, or they use it to lighten tired eyes. The secret to skillfully applied eye shadow is thorough blending. Never wear frosted shadow at work.

Eye liners in either liquid or pencil form frame and highlight the eyes. Avoid heavy lines that give a "cat eye" appearance. A narrow, even line edging the upper or lower eyelid is effective. Choose a color that is not harsh black or dark brown if you have very dark hair; warm brown if you are a brunette; and light brown if you are a blond.

Mascara is used to separate and emphasize the eyelashes. Again, avoid harsh colors. Apply mascara by brushing the lashes upward and outward. Use it sparingly for a professional look.

Eyebrow pencils are useful for people who have thin eyebrows or little color in their eyebrows. Select a shade of brown harmonious with your own coloring and following the natural eyebrow line, move the pencil in short controlled strokes in the natural direction of the individual hairs in the eyebrow. Avoid trying to redesign your eyebrow line with a pencil. Maintain the natural look.

After you have applied eye makeup, review the effect carefully and closely. Use a cosmetic tip to remove any stray flecks of color. Avoid false eyelashes; they produce an artificial look that is not compatible with a professional image.

Lip color provides the final makeup touch. Its purpose is to highlight lips. Choose a color depending on whether your skin tones are warm or cool. Select a color that is harmonious with your wardrobe for the day. Lighter shades generally are recommended for daywear and darker ones for evening.

The most professional approach to applying lip color is to first outline the lips with a lip pencil and then fill in the defined area with color. A cosmetics consultant at a department store or cosmetics specialty shop can show you how to use a lip pencil to visually alter the natural outline of your lips, if you feel that is needed. Some people feel that lip color lasts longer when it is applied with a lip brush rather than directly from the lipstick. You will need to experiment to discover what works best for you. You may choose to finish this step with a clear gloss or lip conditioner.

Other Cosmetics. Nail color may be added to well-manicured nails; however, it is not necessary to have nail color to look professional. If you choose to wear nail color, select a color that is not overwhelming—

Figure 2-10 Eye makeup highlights your eyes. Eye shadow, eyebrow pencil, eyeliner, and mascara give a complete look. (From *Milady's Standard Textbook of Cosmetology*, Milady Publishing Company.)

Figure 2-11 Lip color is the final makeup to give you a finished, professional look.
(From *Milady's Standard Textbook of Cosmetology*, Milady Publishing Company.)

fluorescent purple would be inappropriate for the office, for example. Avoid wearing chipped polish or nail decorations. Keeping a bottle of nail polish in the desk drawer will help you eliminate chips. Do not apply polish at your desk.

Fragrances such as perfume are also popular grooming aids. If you choose to wear a fragrance, choose a light one and use it sparingly. People around you should get a whiff of something that suggests your good taste in choosing a scent and applying it, not be overwhelmed by a fragrance that they may or may not like. Heavy scents are inappropriate in the work place.

Hair Styles. Hair styles can contribute to a contemporary, professional look. The right hair cut will strengthen your good features and help to minimize your less attractive features. If you do not know a hair stylist, ask friends or acquaintances whose hair you admire for the name of their hair dresser. Then arrange a visit to discuss your own style.

If you have not changed hair styles for several years, give serious consideration to whether you have a "dated" appearance. If a person has an old-fashioned hair style, others may assume that the person's knowledge and skills are as dated as his or her appearance.

If you are considering a change of hair style, take a picture of the style you prefer with you when you visit the hair dresser. Talk with stylist about the texture of your hair, the shape of your face, and the care you

Figure 2-12 A professional man's hairstyle is usually relatively short. (Courtesy of Matrix Essentials, Inc.)

are willing to give to maintain a style. The stylist can help you choose a style that is flattering to you and easy to maintain and can advise you about highlighting, rinsing, or coloring your hair.

Many professional men choose relatively short haircuts; however, men still have to decide about whether to have a layered cut or get a blunt cut; the placement of the part; the length around the ears; and the length at the neckline. These decisions should be based on the shape of the face and individual facial features as well as the kind of hair (see Figure 2-12).

For the professional woman, research suggests that hair should be neither too short nor too long. Avoid an extremely short cut that has a masculine look. Also avoid styles that are extreme or that seem appropriate only for a formal event. Instead, choose a simple style that flatters your facial features and face shape. The style should not require much care during the business day (see Figure 2-13).

Your hair should not overhang part of your face or in any way seem to obstruct your vision or interfere with your efficiency on the job. Also, avoid twisting strands of hair or disturbing the hair during thoughtful or anxious moments. This detracts from a polished, professional image.

An array of hair grooming aids are available including hair spray, mousse, spritz, and gel. All are designed to help the user style and control hair in degrees from gentle hold to extra firm hold. As you interview for or begin a new job, follow this advice with regard to hair control. Less is best. Use just enough to enhance and shape your good hair cut; avoid the "plastered" look. You may find after you begin a job that extensive use of these hair products is accepted, and then you can style your hair accordingly.

Figure 2-13 A professional woman's hair style should not be extreme in any way. It should be simple and flattering. (a) Copyright Spiegel, Inc.; (b) Courtesy of J.C. Penney.

Face Shapes. You may be able to make a more satisfactory choice of hair styles if you relate your choice to your face shape. Generally speaking, the oval face shape is considered the ideal one.

The oval face is slightly longer than it is wide, measuring $1^1/_2$ times longer than its width at the brow. Additionally, the oval face is proportioned in equal thirds—one third from hairline to eyebrow, one third from eyebrows to end of nose, and one third from end of nose to bottom of chin (see the oval face in Figure 2-14).

Many people have other face shapes—round, square, oblong, diamond-, heart-, or pear-shaped. Ask a partner to help you assess your face shape using the illustrations shown in this chapter. When you have determined your shape, you may choose a hair style that will create an illusion of the ideal oval shape. For example, a person with an oblong face may choose to wear bangs to make a face less long and more oval. Or a person with a diamond-shaped face may create a more pleasing look by pulling hair away from the side of the face, leaving it long in the neck area. Analyze the illustrations to see ways in which various styles promote the perfect oval.

Although every person will want to choose his or her own style to complement one's individual uniqueness, here are some guidelines that may be helpful as you make hair style choices:

◆ Consider your age, size, hair color, and hair texture when choosing a personal style.

◆ Choose a style that is compatible with your professional role.

◆ Short, petite figures look most attractive with short hair (long, full styles overpower the figure).

◆ Tall people usually look attractive in longer hair (perhaps shoulder length), which provides a pleasing proportion to the total figure.

Figure 2-14 Find your basic facial shape in these sketches and see which hairstyle is best for you. (From *Milady's Standard Textbook of Cosmetology*, Milady Publishing Company. Illustration by Judy Frances)

- People with gray hair are usually more attractive in short rather than long styles.

- Straight styles are most attractive on young people, and older people usually find soft curls flattering to the face that is beginning to wrinkle.

- Sweep hair up and away from the neck to make a short neck appear longer.

- Wear shoulder length hair to complement a long, thin neck.

- Wear bangs to conceal a receding hairline.

- Choose soft curls to soften a face with wrinkles.

- Soften an angular profile with wavy curls.

- Wear hair pulled back from the face when the hairline is low on the forehead.

Glasses and Hair Styles. If you need to wear glasses, take comfort in the fact that they will give you a look of maturity. And for a new professional, the mature look will promote credibility among clients and customers. However, you may want to take into consideration your glasses as you choose your hair style.

First, choose glasses that complement, not repeat, your face shape. For example, if your face is round, you will not want round frames. Then as you plan your hair style, choose a style that pulls the hair away from the glasses.

Follow the suggestions of specialists to choose glasses and hair styles that are mutually complementary. Specialists in eyeware suggest that you choose glasses for both comfort and attractiveness. Choose a frame for professional life that is a neutral color—one that matches your hair or skin color. Choose a size that allows the frames to follow the brow line. Avoid lenses so large that they rest on the cheek.

When you are ready to choose frames for new glasses, take a tactful, honest friend with you to give you honest feedback about the effect of various frames on your face.

If you feel that glasses are not for you, ask your optician about contact lenses.

Hair Color. Probably you have healthy, attractive hair if you are a healthy person who pays attention to keeping your hair clean and neatly trimmed. If that is the case, you are probably most attractive with your hair in its natural color. However, some people enjoy highlighting their hair or even changing its color completely. And, of course, many people who have gray hair choose to cover the gray with color.

If you choose to color your hair, take into consideration these guidelines:

◆ Any use of chemicals, such as hair color, is drying to the hair.

◆ Select hair color that is compatible with your body pigmentation.

◆ Generally people with cool color tones look best with hair color chosen from ash brown/blonde, blue-black, blue-gray, or frosted with ash tones.

◆ Generally people with warm color tones look best with hair color chosen from frost with golden tones, golden browns, golden blonde, or red.

◆ Follow product directions carefully if you choose to apply your own hair color. Many people feel that investing in hair color by a color specialist is wise.

◆ If you choose to try a hair color, begin first with temporary tints. Later you may use more permanent color methods after you have seen the effect of a new color on your hair.

Facial Hair. Men must decide whether the presence of facial hair helps or hinders then in reaching their career goals. In general, it is best to be clean shaven when looking for a job. Some young men remove facial hair until they are secure in their work. Then they grow a beard or mustache. If you do decide on facial hair, keep it clean and neatly trimmed at all times.

Shavers are available in blade or electric form. For a blade shave, the facial hair needs to be very wet, but not oily. Apply a cosmetic designed for blade shaving, either a foam or gel. Both types of products cause hair to stand up, thus making it easier to remove. Allow the shaving gel or foam to work a few minutes before beginning to shave. Then, use a clean, sharp blade to remove the hair in the direction of the grain of the hair growth. Hair on the upper lip and chin is heaviest, so it will need the longest soaking period. Work gently and rinse your face well. Follow the shave with an aftershave cosmetic—a lotion, skin bracer, or skin refresher. Lotions are recommended for men with dry skin, and bracers or refreshers are for men with oily skin. Some men use an additional moisturizer.

An electric razor is best to use with a dry beard. Follow the cleaning of the face with a preshave to dry the beard and stiffen it. Then use the electric shaver with the same gentleness recommended for a blade shave, and use the same follow-up procedures. (Be sure to clean your razor after each shave.)

Figure 2-15 Facial hair should be clean and neatly trimmed at all times. (Photo by Jennifer Brunson.)

Hair Removal. Although cultures vary in the way body hair is regarded, American culture has long dictated that women have minimal visible body hair. Various methods of hair removal for women are available—blade razor, electric shaver, waxing, electrolysis, and depilation.

Shaving legs and underarms with a blade is inexpensive, but hair regrows rapidly. (Never use a razor to remove excess facial hair.) Use of an electric shaver is quick and easy but the shave is not as close as with a blade. Waxing produces a smooth look, but hair must be long before waxing can be accomplished. Some people think the process is painful.

Electrolysis usually removes hair permanently, but it is expensive; it may be painful; and it must be done by a professional or with special equipment for use at home. Finally, depilation (removal of hair with a chemical preparation) is simple and effective; however, some people experience skin irritation.

A consultant at a full-service beauty salon should be able to educate you about the various methods, their costs, and their advantages or disadvantages. The best answer for you right now will probably be the one that accomplishes hair removal with a modest investment of time and money. Later you may opt for one of the more permanent and more expensive methods.

GROOMING CHECKLIST

DIRECTIONS: Read each statement and indicate how well you think you manage each area of personal grooming by placing a check under excellent, average, or needs improvement.

	Excellent	Average	Needs Improvement
1. Daily baths			
2. Daily use of deodorant			
3. Daily dental care			
4. Clean face morning and night			
5. Care for acne problems			
6. Daily shave (men)			
7. Careful application of makeup (women)			
8. Regular sleep			
9. Balanced diet			
10. Regular exercise			
11. Clean, well-trimmed hair			
12. Attractive hairstyle			
13. Absence of dandruff			
14. (Women) Remove visible body hair regularly			
15. Regular manicures			
16. Appropriate use of fragrances			

REVIEW QUESTIONS

1. What are the eight personal qualities needed for success?
2. Explain why eye contact is critical to a professional image.
3. Explain how posture affects a person's business image.
4. What is the purpose of foundation makeup for women?
5. Contrast skin care for persons with dry and oily skin.

6. What treatment is recommended for a person with severe acne?

7. Is it appropriate for a professional women to wear nail color? Explain.

8. What advice would you give a young professional about the use of colognes and perfumes in the work world?

9. Name three methods of hair removal for women.

10. Would you advise a young man with a mustache to shave it off before going on a job interview? Why?

ACTIVITIES

1. Role play introducing yourself to a stranger in the business world. Give attention to eye contact, firm handshakes, and clear communication.

2. Interview three managers about how the personal appearance of employees affects productivity and promotability. Write a one-page summary of each interview.

3. After completing the personal qualities checklist in this chapter, write a personal goal that will create a more professional image for yourself.

4. Borrow some books of hair styles from a beauty salon. Meeting in small groups, discuss which styles would be appropriate for a job interview and why others would not.

5. Visit the cosmetic department in a store or beauty salon and ask for a lesson in application of makeup. Analyze the suggestions that the specialist makes for you and decide if you want to follow them.

CHAPTER GOAL:

To provide you with skills needed for achieving and maintaining a professional appearance.

CHAPTER OBJECTIVES:

After studying this chapter you should be able to:

1. Recognize appropriate professional dress for men and women.
2. Build your own professional wardrobe.
3. Use effective methods of clothing care to promote a professional appearance.

Clothing may be the single most influential factor in making an impression. Style of dress communicates a great deal about a person. For example, clothing frequently signals the roles people play. People decide what to expect of you based on the clothing you wear. If you wear a nurse's uniform, people feel confident that you can meet their health needs. If you wear a garment with the insignia of a plumber, people feel they can rely on you to fix their sink. Similarly, the business suit establishes a person's authority and position in the business world.

The importance of dressing professionally has been emphasized by

Figure 3-1 You show you are a professional in business by the way you dress. (Copyright © Spiegel, Inc.)

authorities in the business world, in the clothing and textiles industry, and in research. These specialists give the following three reasons for dressing professionally:

1. The person who is appropriately dressed *feels more self-confident,* and such a feeling causes the person to act in ways that create success.

2. *Clients and customers respond more positively* to workers who are dressed in a manner that commands respect.

3. *Superiors perceive workers* who dress appropriately as persons who can be *promoted* to higher levels in the organization.

A professional appearance is based on being well-groomed and appropriately dressed for the occasion. Professional dress differs among professions. For example, the most conservative kind of clothing is expected of people in law, banking, and accounting. On the other hand, people in creative fields, such as fashion merchandising and interior design, may dress less conservatively and still be considered professional. Regardless of the company focus, the message delivered to customers and the world outside is partially communicated by how its employees dress (see Figure 3-2).

Your first concern for a professional appearance will be when interviewing. In contemporary society a professional look is expected of a person interviewing for a position, and it is fairly standard: a business suit. The look may be modified for the work day by the demands of the specific work role.

WARDROBE BASICS

Several factors should be considered when selecting a suit, including fabric, color, fit, and style. The natural-fiber look is preferable in suit fabrics, although in reality, many suit materials are blends of natural and chemical fibers. Natural fibers include wool, silk, linen, and cotton. There are suits made of 100% wool, silk, or linen; however, modern chemical fibers, such as polyester and rayon, have been developed to look like natural fibers. Blends of natural and chemical fibers are often more desirable than 100% natural fibers, because they may be less expensive and more comfortable. Also, a blend may hold its shape better and be easier to care for. Sales consultants in stores should be able to discuss the pros and cons of various fabrics with you. Check the fiber content of any suit you consider purchasing. The garment label will provide this information.

Your choice of suit colors is an important factor. Based on client response to workers and research by designers, recommended colors for business suits are black, dark blue, gray, and taupe (light grayish brown). Brown is recommended less often, and green least of all colors. Some

Figure 3-2 (a) and (b) People who work in professions, such as banking, law, and accounting wear conservative business clothes. (a) Courtesy of Jockey International, Inc; (b) Copyright Spiegel, Inc; (c) and (d) People who work in fields such as fashion merchandising, advertising, or interior design can dress more casually and more individually. (Courtesy of Leslie Fay Companies, Inc.)

FOCUS ON: DRESSING THE PART

Adaire Hall is a high school biology teacher in Baltimore, Maryland. Although she is 23, she looks young for her age.

"I realize how young I look," Adaire explains, "and I can't change my looks, but I knew there had to be a way to change my *image*. It's very important to me to be perceived as a professional in the eyes of my principal and other teachers, and especially by my students."

Adaire decided to consult Suzanne Spurrier, a fashion specialist at Image, Inc., about the role of dress and its impact on her professional image. The consultation lasted for an entire morning, and included an "Image Rating," which included a complete analysis of Adaire's wardrobe and grooming habits.

A savvy professional with over 10 years' experience, Suzanne quickly pinpointed Adaire's problem. "Adaire was wise to come to us," Suzanne said. "She *does* look young. She could easily pass for one of the high school students, if she's not careful about the way she dresses."

Professional image, both for women and men, is largely based on two essential qualities—good grooming and appropriateness of dress. Although the business suit may project the look of a professional, it may not be practical in certain work environments, like the classroom.

Suzanne taught Adaire how to achieve a "non-suited" professional appearance. "Suitability of clothing is important," she stressed. "It is important to appear relaxed and comfortable, especially in a classroom full of teenagers!"

"Thanks to Suzanne, I have completely revamped my wardrobe," Adaire says, obviously pleased with the results. "My clothing now makes its own subtle statement. It lets others know that my work is very important to me. And most important to me, it identifies me as a teacher—not a student."

Suzanne nodded in agreement, saying, "Adaire's clothing was 'too old' for her face and body. It made her look like she had raided her mother's closet. I advised her to wear well-fitted clothes that were modest in design. You don't want to call attention to your body in a classroom. Comfort is an important factor, too. Fabrics should be of good quality and sturdy. Also, I asked Adaire to carefully observe the dress code at her school. What were the other women teachers wearing? Obviously, if no one was wearing slacks in the classroom, this was no time for her to become a trailblazer."

Over the next week, Adaire observed the prevailing dress code among teachers at the high school and reported back to Suzanne.

"I suggested that Adaire fill out her wardrobe with blazers and simple skirts or lined slacks in basic colors, using accessories such as scarves to add a touch of color. Because she's small, I suggested that she avoid big prints and over-bright colors."

"Now I fit in," Adaire said, beaming. "But at the same time, my clothes are fashionable *and* comfortable. I feel that people are taking me more seriously, coworkers and students alike. I *really* knew I was on the right track when one of my seniors remarked, 'Nice threads, Miss Hall!' This happpened just moments after Ms. Jenkins, the principal, had said the same thing, not using the same words."

research suggests that navy blue is the best color choice if you can afford only one suit. On the other hand, some researchers have reported that their clients respond most favorably to professionals wearing gray pin-striped suits.

Color in suits may elicit a specific response from clients. For example, black not only symbolizes your respect for people or events, but it also gives the wearer a look of authority. The darker the suit, the more authority is projected by the wearer, according to researchers. Light blue has been recommended for professionals who want their clients to "like" them right away. Regardless of color, authorities recommend moderate colors and patterns in all business dress.

WEARING THE SUIT WELL

Pattern is only one consideration in selecting a suit. Two other important factors are fit and style.

Fit. A suit is an investment that is greatly enhanced by perfect fit. A well-trained, experienced salesperson can help you achieve the right fit. The well-fitting suit has these characteristics:

Jacket
Hangs straight
Lapels and collar lie flat
Sleeves long enough for $1/2$ inch of shirt or blouse cuff to show
About $1/2$ inch of shirt or closed blouse collar should be above jacket collar
Does not wrinkle when wearer crosses arms
Fits smoothly across shoulders and back; does not bind or gape
Not too tight in front when jacket is buttoned

Skirt
Hangs smoothly over hips with no overlap or appearance of extra material as skirt falls to hem
Just grazes the top of the knees, or falls below the knees, or extends to midcalf, or may be a little longer if worn with boots

Pants
Hang straight from hips
Brush shoe top with slight break in front

Characteristics of a poorly fitting suit are:
Collar too high
Wrinkles at sleeve
Wrinkles where buttons pull
Sleeves too long or too short
Pants or skirt does not hang straight

Pants or skirt too long or too short
Suit too tight

Style. A classic business suit is the style recommended for a professional look. Avoid western, fad, or European cuts. Double-breasted suits are popular, but a double-breasted suit adds weight to the figure. If you want to look heavier, the double-breasted suit may be right for you. However, if you are concerned about looking overweight, avoid this style. Later in this chapter, you will learn more about which styles are best for various figure types.

A style consideration for men is the pants leg. Men may choose cuffed or uncuffed pants; either is correct. The pants should "break" properly at the shoe top (see Figure 3-3).

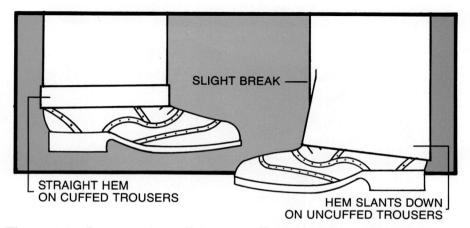

SLIGHT BREAK —

STRAIGHT HEM
ON CUFFED TROUSERS

HEM SLANTS DOWN
ON UNCUFFED TROUSERS

Figure 3-3 Pants can be cuffed or uncuffed and with or without a "break."

Women have a variety of style considerations in choosing a suit, one of which is the length of the jacket. Jackets are available in waist-, midhip-, and lower-hip lengths. All these lengths are appropriate; the selection will depend on the woman's figure. For example, a waist-length jacket is more flattering on a petite woman, whereas a longer, boxy jacket enhances a taller figure.

Skirt length is another consideration. Regardless of fashion, the ability to sit, move briskly, and bend while maintaining modesty should help determine appropriate skirt length. Contemporary practice places the professional length in the knee area. As fashion changes, however, lengths may vary. Many authorities on professional dress say that skirts lengths above the knee have no place in the corporate office.

Wear your suit with only one button of the coat fastened. The shirt or blouse that you wear with a suit may make or break the image you

Figure 3-4 The length of a jacket is one factor a woman should consider when she buys a suit. (Copyright © Spiegel, Inc.)

want to achieve. Wear a long-sleeved dress shirt or blouse (no short sleeves) in a color that coordinates with the suit. To ensure coordination, buy more than one shirt/tie or blouse when you buy a suit. If you wait until later to buy additional shirts, ties, or blouses, be sure to wear or take the suit coat with you when shopping. It is difficult to coordinate from memory.

VARIATIONS ON THE SUIT

Women and men have many options for expanding the suited look. Just as men mix and match with blazers or sports coats and slacks, so women may form many combinations by coordinating skirts, blouses, and jackets. In addition, women may add a jacket to a dress to get the "look" of a suit. Women should be careful not to dress too severely or appear to imitate masculine dress. The goal is for a woman to look professional but retain her femininity.

Some dresses are as appropriate as suits for business attire. Many stores have sections called Career Dresses or Executive Dresses. In general, dresses of a wool or wool blend, silk or a silky polyester, rayon, cotton, or linen blends are suitable. The pattern, or print, and the color should be conservative. To evaluate a dress for its appropriateness for the office, use the following standards:

◆ Fabric that is neither shiny, see-through, nor flimsy (never one that would be chosen for evening wear, such as satin, chiffon, etc.)

◆ A modest neckline

◆ Skirt length that is a professional length, suitable to the proportions of the figure

◆ Sleeves may be of varying lengths, but not sleeveless

Business shirts and blouses are available in many colors and patterns. Most are appropriate business attire if they coordinate with your suit. Remember this rule when making a choice: "When in doubt, white is never wrong!" White is an especially good choice for formal meetings and for events at which you want to show respect. For example, if you were asked to be present at a formal meeting to be attended by upper-level management, you would be appropriately dressed in a white shirt or blouse paired with a dark, solid colored suit.

ACCESSORIES ADD CLASS

Both men and women may effectively vary the look of a suit by wearing shirts or blouses that have subtle stripes or patterns. They achieve even more versatility with ties, shoes, hosiery, jewelry, belts, suspenders, scarves, and handbags.

Figure 3-5 It is acceptable for a professional woman to wear a tailored dress instead of a suit. The addition of a jacket makes the dress more professional looking. (Reproduced by permission of J.C. Penney Company Inc., 1992.)

Ties. The classic, popular patterns in men's ties are the diagonal stripe, the subtle print, and the polka dot, with the diagonal stripe being the most popular (see Figure 3-6). Today paisley, floral and contemporary designs are also popular. Among these patterns, the tie with tiny polka-dots is the most formal. Women's ties are available in a wide variety of flowered, patterned, and solid colors. Silk ties handle easily; however, many people find synthetic fibers quite satisfactory and far less expensive than silk. Examine fibers, fabrics, color, and pattern carefully before selecting ties to accompany business suits.

A man may knot a tie in whatever style appeals to him, but it should

Figure 3-6 Classic, popular patterns in men's ties: (a) solid; (b) pindot; (c) stripes; and (d) foulard. (Courtesy of Lands' End Inc.)

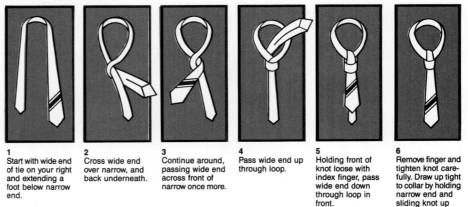

1 Start with wide end of tie on your right and extending a foot below narrow end.

2 Cross wide end over narrow, and back underneath.

3 Continue around, passing wide end across front of narrow once more.

4 Pass wide end up through loop.

5 Holding front of knot loose with index finger, pass wide end down through loop in front.

6 Remove finger and tighten knot carefully. Draw up tight to collar by holding narrow end and sliding knot up snug.

Figure 3-7 When done correctly, the four-in-hand knot yields the proper neck-to-waist tie length.

be tied in a way that yields the correct neck-to-waist length. The four-in-hand tie is probably the most popular (see Figure 3-7). A tie is worn correctly if its tip brushes the top of the belt buckle.

Women may also wear narrow "ties" loosely knotted at the neck. More frequently, women wear scarves shaped into rosettes or tied as loopy bows at the necks of solid or lightly striped blouses.

Shoes. The most conservative business shoe for men is the tied shoe; however, loafers are acceptable in many businesses. Bankers, accountants, and lawyers usually choose tied shoes, whereas others may choose either type of footwear.

The classic leather pump provides the most professional look for women. These are frequently available with accessories such as small buckles or bows. Variations of the basic pump include the sling-back pump and the open-toed pump. Again, choose a comfortable shoe with a heel that provides comfort when walking. Avoid a fabric and style that you might choose for evening (3-inch heels) or a sandal that could be worn to the beach. You should coordinate the color of your shoes with your outfit to a certain extent; however, it is preferable to choose basic colors, such as black, navy, or taupe.

Hosiery. Socks and hose may contribute to or detract from the professional look. Men should wear socks that have tops long enough to cover the portion of leg that shows when they cross their legs.

Sock color is important, too. Coordinate sock color with either pants or shoes. For example, if a man is wearing brown shoes and beige slacks, brown socks would be a good choice. Similarly, if he is wearing black shoes and navy pants, black socks are a good choice.

For women, natural-colored hosiery contributes to a professional look. Authorities recommend that professional women avoid wearing brightly colored hose, lace hose, hose with a back seam, or heavily patterned hose to the office or to business functions. Save these styles for evening wear.

Jewelry. An appropriate amount of jewelry completes the well-dressed look. However, professional women should avoid excessive jewelry in the form of dangling earrings, jangling bracelets, and multiple rings. Again, these accessories have their place, but in the office the emphasis should be on who you are and your abilities, not on how glittery you are or how much noise your jewelry makes.

Belts. Belts add a finished look to two-piece outfits and to some dresses. A narrow, matching belt creates a classic look and neither increases, nor decreases, the image of the body's size. A wide belt accentuates the waistline, and if a contrasting color, it may add an illusion of weight to the body. Belts may be used to change the look of an outfit, and they are useful to give a coordinated look to separates.

Scarves. Colorful scarves add interest to the wardrobe, and they may even expand it. There are endless ways to wear scarves. Salespeople at department stores and accessory shops can provide information about the many ways scarves may be tied and worn with various items of clothing. In cold weather they serve another function, as they are very useful to wear at the neck to keep cold away from the body! A collection of scarves in different shapes, sizes, and colors will enhance your wardrobe.

Suspenders. Suspenders, also known as braces or galluses, are often worn to keep men's trousers in place. The classic look they create is popular in men's fashions today; however, managers in some businesses do not feel that they create the conservative look appropriate for their environment. Observe the dress code where you work before you choose to wear suspenders. When wearing suspenders, leave off your belt; the two should never be worn together.

Handbags or Purses. The professional look for women is created with a conservative handbag or a briefcase. However, a woman should avoid carrying both. The most professional handbag is of modest size and a neutral color. Many women find that two bags in different neutral colors are sufficient for their total professional wardrobe. Well-organized belongings within the bag create an image of order and efficiency.

When a woman travels alone, a briefcase signals her role as a professional person, rather than a person available for social contacts. For efficiency, the traveling woman may carry a briefcase with a small

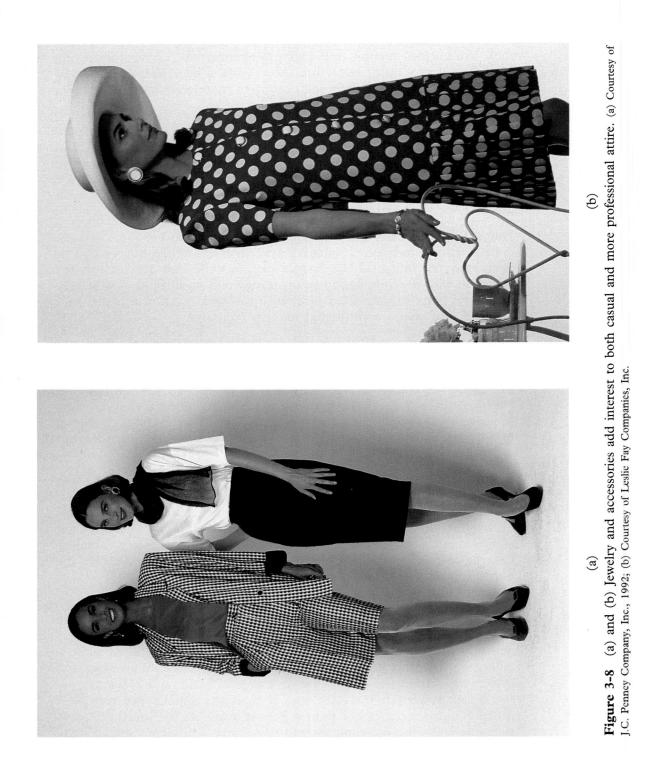

(a)

(b)

Figure 3-8 (a) and (b) Jewelry and accessories add interest to both casual and more professional attire. (a) Courtesy of J.C. Penney Company, Inc., 1992; (b) Courtesy of Leslie Fay Companies, Inc.

clutch bag tucked inside for use when going to dinner, or other places where a briefcase is too heavy or inappropriate.

A STARTING WARDROBE

Any new professional will probably have a limited budget for buying clothes. This section suggests the items needed to establish a good, basic wardrobe, and explains how to expand a few good pieces into a sufficient wardrobe for 2 weeks or more.

A MAN'S BASIC WARDROBE

For the professional man, the following items create a basic office wardrobe:
- One dark suit, tropical year-round weight
- One navy blazer
- One pair tan-colored pants
- One pair gray pants
- Coordinating shirts and ties (3 of each)
- Loafer shoes
- Black leather belt

A more extensive wardrobe might include the following items:
- One navy blue, lightweight suit
- One gray, lightweight suit
- One striped navy blue suit, lightweight
- One navy blazer
- One tan blazer
- One all-weather coat
- Various shirts and ties
- Loafer shoes
- Tied shoes
- Appropriate accessories

Be sure to invest in suits that are of good quality; have them fitted by a menswear specialist. The information on page 72 may help you in your discussions with the tailor. It is better for your professional image to have one good suit, one quality sportcoat, and two well-made pairs of pants than to have twice as many pieces of inferior clothing. These few items can be the basis of a professional wardrobe.

Figure 3-9 A few good, basic items in your wardrobe can provide a number of different outfits. Basics could include a navy blazer or a gray pin-striped suit. (Courtesy of J.C. Penney Company Inc., 1992.)

A WOMAN'S BASIC WARDROBE

For the professional woman, the following items create a basic office wardrobe:

- One black suit
- One gray suit
- One printed skirt
- Four blouses
- Two sweaters
- One dress
- One all-weather coat
- Black pumps

In the beginning, you will want to invest in all-season suit fabrics, such as gabardine or rayon blend. As your budget expands, you will be

(a)   (b)

Figure 3-10 A basic men's wardrobe begins with a classic dark suit, either (a) single-breasted or (b) double-breasted. (Courtesy of J.C. Penney Company Inc., 1992.)

MENSWEAR TERMINOLOGY

Braces	Another term for suspenders
Break	The crease in the front of trousers above the shoe top
Collar: standard	Collar with 3-inch point
Collar: button-down	Points held in place with buttons
Collar: French	Short points; wide spread
Clothing	Suits and coats—not sportswear
Cuffs: barrel	Shirt cuffs that close with buttons
Cuffs: French	Shirt cuffs requiring cuff links for fastening
Drop	Difference between waist size and coat size
Furnishings	Men's accessories—belts, socks, jewelry, etc
Vent	Opening in bottom of suit jacket or sport coat

able to afford wool, or wool blend suits just for winter (depending on your climate, of course).

With a less modest budget the following items provide a comfortable wardrobe:

- One navy blue suit
- One beige suit
- One white skirt
- One white cardigan sweater
- Two two-piece dresses
- One pair navy slacks
- Three blouses
- Two leather belts
- One all-weather coat
- Two pairs high-heeled shoes
- One pair low-heeled shoes

It is best to avoid wearing slacks to an interview or to work. If there is acceptance of women in slacks at your workplace, it will be apparent after you have spent a little time on the job. If there are work days when slacks seem appropriate, wear well-fitted ones that are not too tight, and coordinate them with a jacket.

Professional women on a modest budget may choose to own only one coat. In this case, an all-weather coat with a zip-out lining is a good choice. Fashion experts recommend that women avoid coats with too many pockets, belts, and buckles. It is also important that the coat cover the entire skirt. A skirt showing beneath the coat creates an unattractive appearance.

A wardrobe as basic as two suits, one skirt, and several blouses—all coordinated—make it possible for a person to go to work for several days without repeating an outfit.

Don't overlook the value of accessories in expanding your wardrobe. Accessories are the least expensive way to alter and add pizzazz to a basic wardrobe.

CONFLICTING MESSAGES IN APPEARANCE

It is important to understand that style and manner of dress should vary depending on the situation. Both men and women occasionally use dress to attract the opposite sex. However, the workplace is not the appropriate arena for a pursuit of social interests. Avoid dressing in a manner that sends unbusinesslike or unprofessional "messages" to the opposite sex.

Some styles of dress that may send an inappropriate message are:

◆ Clothing that fits too tightly
◆ Revealing necklines
◆ Western cut vests
◆ Skirts that are too short

PROFESSIONALS AND FASHION

The up-to-date, informed woman or man is aware of the fashion trends that influence professional dress. However, some people feel that dressing in the latest fashion may detract from one's professional image. On the other hand, dressing without regard for fashion, or in fashions obviously out of date, may hinder professional advancement.

Dress within contemporary fashion, but avoid fads and trendy looks. If you wish to wear extreme fashions, save them for your private life. Keep abreast of fashion trends and use this knowledge to your professional advantage. See the following timeless fashion guidelines.

ASSESSING YOUR WARDROBE

Assessing and building your wardrobe are easy tasks.

1. Consider your needs.
2. Evaluate what you have.

Figure 3-11 (a) Separates of the same color give the look of a suit. (Courtesy of J.C. Penney Company, Inc., 1992); (b) Separates of different colors appear more casual. (Courtesy of Leslie Fay Companies, Inc.)

GUIDELINES FOR
THE PROFESSIONALLY DRESSED WOMAN

◆ Choose a suit, classic dress, or skirt with blazer for daily wear.

◆ Base your professional dress on being well-groomed and appropriate for the occasion.

◆ When wearing a sleeveless dress or blouse, add a suit jacket or blazer.

◆ Select fabrics with enough body to hold their shape.

◆ Select shoes, belts, and handbags in basic colors.

◆ Shoes and bags need not match but should coordinate with your outfit.

◆ Avoid wearing slacks to work.

◆ Always wear hose.

◆ Avoid clothes that give mixed social and business messages.

◆ Enhance your femininity—don't try to imitate male dress.

◆ Carry a briefcase or a well-organized handbag, if appropriate for your profession.

◆ When planning your professional dress, work to create an image that expresses your respect for yourself and for those with whom you come in contact.

3. Clean, launder, and repair soiled or damaged items.

4. Plan for additions.

Consider Your Needs. To consider your needs when building a wardrobe, review your job responsibilities and your interests in relation to your clothing. For example, a young man working as a food service manager may review his work responsibilities and decide that he needs work clothing for 5 days each week, casual clothing for bowling and socializing, and dress clothing for important days at work, and for special holidays or events. As he considers his needs in relation to the weather, he may realize that he also needs heavy outer wear for winter days and sweaters for other times of the year.

After a person has reviewed his or her needs, it is helpful to make a written list of needed clothing items. For example, in the case cited above, the young man may decide that he needs six different work-day outfits to have variety, and to accommodate laundering and cleaning.

Evaluate What You Have. Experts recommend that you remove everything from your closet as you begin your clothing evaluation. Examine each garment with these criteria in mind.

◆ Does it fit my body?
◆ Is it suitable for work?
◆ Is it in good condition? Are repairs needed?
◆ Is it clean and wrinkle-free?
◆ Is the color right for me?
◆ Is it still in fashion?

As each garment is evaluated, it should be placed in various groups with these labels:

1. Launder
2. Dry clean
3. Repair
4. Discard
5. Store
6. Return to closet

Before returning anything to your closet, clean the closet thoroughly. Vacuum the floor; wipe off the shelves; remove any trash. If necessary, add storage accessories. Retailers carry a variety of items, such as easy-to-add second rods, designed to expand storage space.

Before you return items to your closet, experiment with new combinations, for example, a jacket with all the skirts you own. Try different tops with different bottoms. In this way you will find new combinations you have not considered before.

Organize your closet by grouping similar items. For example, place all the pants together, all shirts together, all jackets together, etc. This arrangement promotes variety of dress with fewer garments. It will also make items easier to locate as you get dressed.

Maintain or Discard. Never return an unwearable garment to your closet. Place dirty garments in your dirty clothes hamper or in the bag you reserve for garments to be taken to the dry cleaner. Set aside the garments that need mending. The next time you sit down to watch TV, sew on the necessary buttons, repair the loose hem, or make other needed repairs.

If you are not able to make repairs, or if you do not wish to make repairs, take the garments to the dry cleaner and have repairs made by the tailor. This repair service is usually done for a modest fee. In either case, every professional person needs a clothing repair kit for emergencies. Such a kit might contain:

◆ Scissors
◆ Pins

Figure 3-12 Keeping your clothes in an orderly way in your closet or bureau makes it easy to put an outfit together quickly. (Courtesy of Techline Closets, by Marshall Erdman and Associates, Madison, Wisconsin.)

- Needles
- Black, red, white, blue, off-white thread
- Shirt buttons
- Mending tape

Discard clothing that cannot be made wearable. Perhaps you will decide to pass them on to another person, or you may wish to put them in a garage sale. If, however, you cannot bring yourself to part with them, put them in storage rather than in your closet. The time you spend getting dressed for work each day will go more smoothly if you do not have to dig through unwearable clothing to find something acceptable.

ADDING TO YOUR WARDROBE

As you plan to purchase or make new garments (or someone may ask what you would like as a gift), consider the garments and accessories that are right for you in terms of color and style. You will also want to consider how the new item will complement clothing you already own.

LINE

Line is an element in design. It is the path between two points. And in clothing, line is created by the cut, style, and decoration of a garment.

In clothing you will find vertical lines—those which go up and down the body, horizontal lines—those which cross the body from side to side, diagonal lines—those which are placed at an angle on the garment, and curved lines—ones that are circular or wavy. All these lines are produced in clothing by the structure of a garment or by the decoration on the garment. Lines may also be created by the use of color. For example, when contrasting colors are placed side by side, a line is created. This is most often seen in clothing when blouses and skirts, or trousers and shirts, of contrasting colors are worn together. The contrasting tops and bottoms create a horizontal line making the body appear to be shorter.

The human eye moves with the direction of the line it sees. Notice how the lines in Figure 3-13 appear to be different lengths when they take different directions. Notice, too, how the intersection of lines calls attention to a point.

When you understand the illusion each line creates you may use line to create illusions of the body you desire. For example, if you wish to look taller and thinner, choose vertical lines. On the other hand, if you want to look shorter and heavier, wear clothing with horizontal lines. Curved lines soften the figure and usually add the illusion of weight. Diagonal lines create excitement.

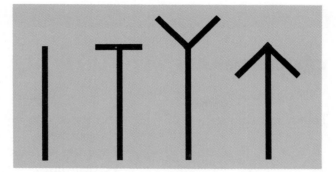

Figure 3-13 Lines can appear to be different lengths, even though they are the same.

Zigzag designs create the most excitement. On the other hand, straight lines project a formal, classic look. Read the chart on page 80 to determine ways you may change the visual image of your body by the use of lines in your clothing.

TEXTURE

Texture is another element of design. And it is especially useful in clothing, because all clothing is made of fabrics that have their own unique texture. Consider words that express the different ways fabrics feel to the touch, and you have words that describe the texture of fabrics.

Various textures may be used in clothing to create special looks. For example, crisp fabrics make the body look larger, while soft, clingy ones emphasize body curves and irregularities. Smooth fabrics do not distort the body image, but rather reflect it as it is. On the other hand, shiny fabrics, which reflect light, add size to the figure, and dull fabrics, which absorb light, reduce the size of the figure.

COLOR

Color may be the most important resource you have for enhancing your personal appearance. Colors that are right for you can give your skin a healthy glow, highlight your natural good looks, and accent your best features.

Warm and Cool Colors. A color system that is easy to follow is the system of "warm" and "cool" colors. A warm color is any color that has a gold undertone or base, whereas a cool color is one with blue undertone or base. Consider the color red. When you add gold to it, it becomes

CREATE IMAGES WITH LINES IN GARMENTS

TO LOOK	WEAR . . . .
Taller and thinner	Outfits of one color
	Narrow belts
	Tapering V neckline
	Vertical lines
	Straight-legged pants
	Vertical stripes
	Tailored garments
Shorter and thinner	Simple lines
	Tailored garments
	Contrasting separates
	Horizontal lines
Taller and heavier	Vertical lines
	Turtlenecks
	Narrow belts
	Light colors
	Fuller garments
Less hippy	Emphasize the upper body
	Dark-colored pants or skirts
	Shirts or blouses in bold colors
Heavier	Lighter colors
	Fuller garments
	Gathers
	Cuffed pants
Narrower in the waist	Accents at the shoulders
	Diagonal lines at hips
	Narrow matching belts

warm red (perhaps you might describe it as orange red). Add blue to the same pure red, and you get cool red (you might describe it as rosy red). Other colors become either cool or warm when blue and gold are added to them as well.

Skin Tone. Skin tones also have undertones of either bluish white or gold. Every person—male or female, young or old, white or black or brown—has these same blue or gold undertones. People with the bluish white undertones are described as people with cool skin tones, and people with the gold undertones are described as having warm skin tones.

If you have the bluish white undertones, you will find that the cool colors are most compatible for you. On the other hand, if your skin has gold undertones, warm colors will be most flattering with your natural coloring.

Warm colors. Among neutrals are brown, beige, off-white, and some grays. Other warm colors are yellows, oranges, some pinks, and some reds.

Cool colors. Among neutrals are black, white, and some grays. Other cool colors are blues, greens, purples, and some reds.

To determine whether you should wear warm or cool colors, look at the inside of your wrist. Does the skin there look as if it has undertones that are bluish white? Or does it look gold? If you cannot decide, ask several people to join you in the analysis. When you look at several wrists together, you can see obvious differences. Be sure to use a good natural light for your experiment.

WARDROBE COORDINATES

Once you have decided whether your best colors are warm or cool, you can make decisions more easily about your wardrobe. For example, if

Figure 3-14 The red in this jacket is warm, while the aqua in the suit is cool. (Courtesy of BeKi Image Color Consultant, from *Creating Images*, by BeKi Kraynak, New York City. Fashion designs by Akira, New York City. Photos by Lucille Khornak, New York City.)

your natural coloring is cool, you will want to choose shirts, blouses, and even makeup, that have the cool base. Conversely, if your natural coloring is warm, you will make choices that have the warm base.

A further advantage of knowing what colors work best for you is having a wardrobe made up of items that coordinate well with each other.

Color may be used as a basis for building a professional wardrobe. To do this, select two compatible colors and use them for all basic items in your wardrobe. For example, a woman may choose navy blue and white (cool colors) or brown and beige (warm colors) as her basic, compatible colors. She could then purchase two suits, one in each color, using the skirts and jackets interchangeably to create new combinations. Her choice of blouses would include those that could be used with either navy blue or white, brown or beige. Other items, such as a print blouse in these colors, could be added. The use of two compatible colors as basics allows the interchange of items to create variety in a limited wardrobe.

The professional person often chooses neutral colors for wardrobe basics. Colors such as black, brown, grey, and beige are common choices. However other basics may greatly extend your choices. To add variety, consider navy, camel, wheat, ivory, khaki, taupe, burgundy, rust, forest green, and blues.

You may use color to your advantage if you wish to appear smaller or larger. Dark colors make a person appear smaller, whereas light colors make a person appear larger. A person who is overweight looks much heavier in a white skirt or pants than in the same garment in black. Try on light- and dark-colored garments and check the image you create with the different colors. The difference is immediately obvious. A suit with the same color top and bottom makes a person appear taller than a suit with contrasting top and bottom.

PATTERNS IN FABRICS

Line, color, and shapes join to create patterns in fabrics. The variety of patterns used in the creation of fabrics is endless: large and small, realistic and abstract; some are woven or knitted into the fabric, and some are applied to the fabric.

Regardless of how pattern is created, it projects certain images regarding the body on which it is worn. For example, large prints make a person look larger; small ones make the wearer look smaller. Subdued patterns produce a formal, classic look, whereas bold patterns create illusions of casual excitement.

A prominent example of the use of pattern in clothing is found in men's suiting. Fabrics for classic business suits are either without pattern

WARDROBE MIX AND MATCH (WARM COLORS)

5 tops + 5 bottoms = 20 outfits

	Dark Brown Blazer	Red Orange Sweater	Beige Jacket	Ivory Sweater	Print Blouse
Dark Brown Skirt					
Print Skirt (red/brown/beige)					
Beige Skirt					
Dark Brown Slacks					
Brown Dress					

Tips: Make one of the sweaters a sweater jacket; then it can be worn with a skirt or dress.
When you can expand your options, get two or three more blouses, in varying styles.
A solid color skirt and blazer bought separately may not match exactly; buy them together as a suit.

WARDROBE MIX AND MATCH (COOL COLORS)

5 Tops + 5 Bottoms = 20 Outfits

	Navy Blazer	Aqua Sweater	White Jacket	Green Sweater	Print Blouse
Navy Skirt					
Print Skirt (Navy/Green)					
White Skirt					
Navy Slacks					
Black Dress					

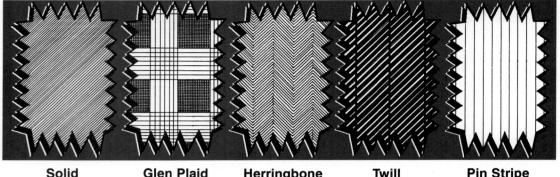

| Solid | Glen Plaid | Herringbone | Twill | Pin Stripe |

Figure 3-15 Patterns in men's suits include pin stripe, plaid, twill, herringbone, and solid.

or have very subdued, muted patterns, whereas patterns such as bold plaids are often used in men's sportswear.

Patterns in men's suiting have names. The most popular ones are twill, pin-stripe, herringbone, and glen plaid. See examples of these patterns in Figure 3-15.

SHOPPING WITH SATISFACTION

In addition to considering which lines and colors are right for you, decide where to shop and how to shop to add to your wardrobe efficiently. Planned shopping benefits you in several ways. It can result in your finding items that perfectly complement what you already have, while getting the most for your money. And, it is less frustrating and time-consuming than shopping without a plan. Additionally, impulse buying is greatly reduced with planned shopping.

Where to Shop. Basically there are three types of retail organizations available to shoppers—discount centers, specialty shops, and department stores. Each of these serves certain needs of the consumer. However, experts often recommend that you begin your wardrobe shopping at a department store, where you can expect to find standard quality, average pricing, and a great variety of choices. After you have reviewed what is available at the department stores, you can better evaluate similar items at specialty shops and discount centers.

Generally, specialty shops feature unique items, and more services than are available from other retailers, which means more individual attention for the customer. Because of these added features, the consumer pays higher prices for the merchandise. There is also less variety.

Discount centers feature lower prices than are available at either department stores or specialty shops. However, the quality of the

Figure 3-16 Experts suggest that you shop at a department store when first building your wardrobe. Department stores offer a wider selection of options. (Courtesy of Leslie Fay Companies, Inc.)

merchandise varies. As a consumer, you will need discriminating skills for shopping at a discount center. You will want to examine with care the items you are considering for purchase at a discount center to ensure that they are of the quality you desire. There is a reason why a designer label dress is in the discount store and not selling for three times more at a department store.

When you shop for a professional wardrobe, your own appearance and behavior as a shopper will affect the help you receive from salespeople. Groom yourself carefully and dress neatly. If you want to purchase garments that coordinate with items you already have, take the item's jacket, sweater, and so on, with you as you shop. Colors are very difficult to match from memory.

How to Shop. It is possible to be an intelligent, discriminating shopper if you follow the guidelines on page 86.

You will find that your shopping experience can be pleasant as well as productive if you observe the rules of shopper's etiquette on page 86.

Many consumers buy clothing and other merchandise from catalogs. There are advantages and disadvantages to catalog shopping. The

GUIDELINES FOR SHOPPERS

◆ Make a list of what you need and carry it with you as you shop.
◆ Take a garment (or a swatch card) with you if you want to match a color or pattern.
◆ Wear appropriate underwear, shoes, and hosiery for trying on garments.
◆ Choose classic styles; fads and trendy styles are shortlived, making their purchase a poor use of your money. Classic styles can be worn for years. Fads quickly date your wardrobe.
◆ Buy accessories to update a classic wardrobe.
◆ Read labels for information on fiber content and care instructions.
◆ Evaluate advertised sales to determine if items are good buys.
◆ Practice courteous behavior as you shop.

SHOPPER'S ETIQUETTE

Be courteous	Speak kindly and politely to salespeople and to other shoppers. Wait your turn for assistance. Avoid bumping. Make sincere apologies if you interfere with others.
Be ethical	Don't ask merchants to redeem merchandise that you have damaged.
Be careful with merchandise	Avoid damaging merchandise when you try on garments. Try not to destroy a display as you search for items you want.
Be businesslike	Be prepared to pay by the appropriate method—cash, credit card, or check—with the appropriate identification.
Be organized	Shop with a plan for what you want, what sizes you need, and so on.

advantages are that consumers can save a tremendous amount of time by not having to shop in person. Also, merchandise from catalogs is often (but not always) less expensive than similar merchandise in stores because the retailer does not have to pay overhead. The two major disadvantages to shopping by catalog are (1) you do not see or touch what you are buying, so colors and fabrics may not turn out exactly as

GUIDELINES FOR CATALOG SHOPPERS

◆ Read the catalog thoroughly to learn about costs, sizes, payment plans, delivery, and return policies.

◆ If possible, choose sizes like small, medium, and large rather than numbered sizes.

◆ Select garments featuring easy fit, such as roll-up sleeves and dropped waists.

◆ Choose basic colors like red, black, or white, rather than sky blue, wheat, spring green.

◆ Never send cash through the mail. Pay by check, money order, or credit card.

◆ Keep a record of your order. If merchandise is not shipped in thirty days, you may cancel your order.

◆ Consider ordering by telephone to be able to talk with a telephone salesperson about your choices. Most telephone ordering requires the use of a credit card.

you expected, and (2) you cannot try on what you are buying. Follow these guidelines if you choose to shop by catalog.

CLOTHING CARE

Have you ever had your white socks turn pink in the wash? Have you ever rushed to get ready for an appointment only to find that the top button is missing from your shirt? Have you found yourself at an important event with a spot on your tie or a runner in your hose? These embarrassing and frustrating moments result from a lack of clothing care.

Routine care involves dry cleaning or laundering, repairing, and storing your clothes. Proper care of your clothing will save you time, money, and frustration, but more importantly, it is essential if you want to create a positive professional image.

CLEANING

Before deciding how to clean a garment, check the care label for the recommended methods of cleaning. Garments cleaned by methods other than those recommended on the labels are often ruined. Follow care label instructions to give your clothing long life. Labels provide terms such as the following:

Label Terms	Meaning
Machine wash and dry	Wash and dry at any temperature.
Dry clean only	Do not launder.
Machine wash in warm water; tumble low	Use warm water only. Set dryer on low.
Hand wash	Wash by hand
Flat dry	Lay garment on towel placed on a flat surface, hand smooth, and allow to dry.
Warm iron	Do not set iron on a high setting; fabric may melt.

LAUNDRY

You may wash your washable clothing by hand or by machine; however, you will have more satisfactory results if you follow care label instructions. Here are basic steps for laundering your clothes:

1. Sort clothing

2. Treat stains

3. Hand or machine wash

4. Dry

5. Fold or press or iron

6. Store

Sort Clothing. Clothing that is to be washed should be sorted twice. The first sort is to separate clothing that will be washed by hand from clothing that will be washed in a machine. The second sort divides clothing by color and weight of fabric. Separate colored clothes from whites, and separate delicate from heavy items. Wash whites separately. (If you wash colors with whites, the color may bleed, causing the whites to take on their colors.) Some people divide colored clothing into light and dark colors, and wash each group separately. Others wash very light colors with whites. Finally, if you have some heavy fabrics—for example, white rugs—you will want to separate those from delicate fabrics such as white lingerie.

Treat Stains. Treat stains before laundering a garment or the stain may be permanently set by washing. Most stains can be removed if treated properly. See the accompanying chart for recommended methods of removing spots.

Machine Washing. Prepare clothing for washing by closing zippers and other fasteners. Also, make sure pockets are empty.

As you machine-wash clothing, it is important to follow the manufacturer's directions for amounts and types of laundry product to use in the machine. Too little laundry powder or liquid will not remove soil, and too much may clog the machine or cause sticky buildup on clothing. Measure laundry powder or liquid accurately.

Select the washing cycle recommended on the garment's care label. For example, towels and sheets are washed on the regular cycle; shirts may be washed on the wash-and-wear cycle; and lingerie is washed on the delicate cycle. Avoid overloading the machine; crowded clothing will not get clean. There should be room for the clothes to swish freely in the tub as they are agitated.

You may dry your clothing by laying it flat, as recommended for sweaters; by hanging it wet, as recommended for drip-dry shirts; or by using a dryer.

Follow the manufacturer's directions for drying clothing. If you leave clothing sitting in a dryer for too long after the items are dry, the clothing will wrinkle. If you can, remove garments and put on hangers in a damp-dry stage to avoid wrinkling.

DRY CLEANING

Clothing labeled "dry clean only" must be taken to a dry cleaner. Shop for a satisfactory cleaner, and when you find one, use it consistently. You will get better service when you are known as a regular customer. Before you take clothes to a dry cleaner, make sure the pockets are empty. Pointing out spots on the garment that need special attention usually ensures more satisfactory results.

REPAIR

To make emergency and routine repairs of your clothing, you will need some basic equipment. See the list provided earlier in this chapter for emergency care. Skills needed for common repairs are hemming, replacing buttons, sewing ripped seams, and mending tears.

Holes or tears in garments may often be mended easily with iron-on patches. Check fabric and notions stores for prepared patches that match your garment in color and weight. Large holes may be repaired by replacing a section of the garment with matching fabric (a sewing machine greatly expedites this process), and tiny ones may be mended by handstitching the edges together with matching thread.

STAIN REMOVAL CHART

Blood	Soak in cold water as soon as possible for 30 minutes or longer. Rub detergent to stain and launder. If yellow stain remains, soak with bleach and relaunder.
Chewing Gum, Candle Wax	Harden gum or wax by placing them in freezer or rubbing with an ice cube. Scrape off as much as possible with a dull knife or fingernail. For wax, place stained area between paper towels and press with warm iron. If stain remains, sponge fabric with cleaning fluid. Launder.
Chocolate	Scrape off chocolate. Soak in cool or lukewarm water. Apply detergent to area and launder. If any stain remains, bleach and relaunder.
Cosmetics	Rub detergent into area and launder. If stain is stubborn, sponge fabric with cleaning fluid.
Grass, Foliage	Rub detergent into area and launder, using hottest water as possible for fabric. If stain remains, bleach and relaunder.
Grease, Oil	Scrape off as much as possible or blot with paper toweling. Rub detergent into area and launder. For grimy grease, place stain between paper toweling and press with warm iron. If necessary, sponge fabric with cleaning fluid and launder, using plenty of detergent.
Ink, Ball-Point Pen	Spray lightly with hair spray or sponge with rubbing alcohol. Leave on for a few minutes and blot off as much as possible. Repeat, if necessary. Rub in detergent and launder.
Nail Polish	Sponge with nail polish remover (do not use acetone on acetate fabric) or cleaning fluid. Launder.
Paint, Varnish	Treat immediately. For latex paint, saturate fabric with warm water and launder. For oil-base paint, saturate fabric with paint solvent, such as turpentine, and rinse with cool water. Launder.
Perspiration	Soak in warm water with presoak product, or sponge with ammonia. For old stain, sponge with white vinegar and rinse. Rub detergent into stain and wash in the hottest water possible for fabric.
Soft Drinks	Sponge or soak in cool water, and launder.

Source: *Clothing* by Weber, Glencoe Publishing Company, Columbus, Ohio, p. 208. Reprinted with permission.

Figure 3-17 Men's wool suits are frequently labeled "dry clean only".
(Copyright © Spiegel, Inc.)

Rips may be repaired by machine or hand stitching. If you do not have access to a sewing machine, use small hand stitches. Backstitching makes a strong seam. A double row of stitches reinforces areas where there is extra stress in wear.

Tighten loose buttons rather than wait and have to replace a lost one. To reattach a button by hand use a double strand of thread. Secure the thread and place a toothpick or heavy pin under the button. Bring the needle up through one hole, over the toothpick and down through the second hole. Repeat for several stitches, then remove the toothpick and pull the button to the top of the thread loop. Wind the thread tightly around the stitches under the button. Secure the thread with several small stitches on the backside of the garment.

Replace hems by hand or machine, depending on the method used for the original hem. Hand hemming is done with small stitches that should not show on the top side of the garment. Care must be taken not to pull the thread too tightly, or the hem will be visible.

Press garments after repairs are made. For more information on repair of garments, write to your County Home Economics Extension Agency for detailed instructions.

STORAGE

Before storing your clothing, brush it to remove loose soil and lint. A good clothes brush is essential for clothing care. Specially designed rollers with adhesive surfaces remove lint with ease. A specially designed roller with tiny blades may be used to "shave" pilling (little knots of fabric) from sweaters.

If garments have odors from smoke or something else, hang them in the air for a time to freshen them. Sweaters and other garments that should not be hung may be laid across a chair for airing.

When you undress, place your garments in laundry bags or on hangers. Those items that do not need cleaning and should not be hung may be folded and placed on a shelf or in drawers or containers. The habit of storing clothing immediately after undressing saves time in clothing care and extends the life of your clothing. This habit also ensures that you will never have unwearable garments in your closet or drawers.

A well-organized closet is an invaluable aid in careful storage of clothing. You may want to add accessories to your closet to use it more effectively. Consider double rods, shoe bags on closet doors, plastic containers for shelves, and hooks for belts. Plastic or wooden hangers give more support for your garments than wire hangers. Pants need padded hangers to prevent marks or creases.

Well-organized drawer space is also an asset. Group similar items together, and consider the use of trays and/or small boxes to organize small items in large drawers.

Seasonal storage is important. When your closet contains only those clothes for the present season, you can dress quickly and easily. Guard against moths and mildew in long-term storage. To do this, be sure all clothes are free of soil before putting them away for a season. You may also wish to add moth balls. Storage in dry places prevents mildew. Remember that leather and fur items need air circulation for long life. Cover such items with cloth for seasonal storage.

1. Name three professions in which conservative professional dress is expected.
2. Write five characteristics of the professional look.
3. What are the criteria for a well-fitted man's suit?
4. Describe the suited look for a woman.
5. Write five guidelines for the professionally dressed woman.
6. List the steps in building a wardrobe.
7. Explain warm and cool colors.
8. Describe the advantages of planned versus impulse shopping.
9. Give five guidelines for shoppers.
10. Describe routine care required for maintaining a professional wardrobe.
11. How may storage space in a closet be expanded?

ACTIVITIES

1. Evaluate your wardrobe, listing those items of clothing that may be used as a part of a professional wardrobe.
2. Plan an outfit you will wear for a job interview.
3. Observe three people in their regular working clothes. Write a description of their grooming and dress; then write suggestions for changes that would give them a more professional appearance. (Avoid the use of names in your report.)
4. Interview a first-year professional for ways he or she adapted a wardrobe to obtain a professional appearance.
5. Assemble a repair kit for use with your own clothing.
6. Shop for an interview suit at retailers in your town. Compare styles, costs, and information you are given by sales personnel.
7. Interview an established professional person about the routine care required for their professional garments.

CHAPTER 4

GETTING A JOB

CHAPTER GOAL:

To plan and execute a job search.

CHAPTER OBJECTIVES:

After studying this chapter you should be able to:

1. Locate sources of information about job opportunities.
2. Prepare an impressive resume.
3. Write appropriate letters for the job search.
4. Interview successfully.

Locating the job that is right for you requires intelligent planning, concentrated effort, and the accumulation of some basic information. You will need to understand employment processes, know how to locate job opportunities, prepare yourself for interviews, and write appropriate communications related to interviews.

Read about these skills in this chapter. Then practice them as you seek the job you want. You will locate a job more quickly, get a more satisfying position, and be able to take advantage of new job opportunities if you master these techniques.

UNDERSTANDING THE JOB MARKET

It is important to know how the job market operates if you are to compete in it successfully. This includes knowing what jobs are available, where they are, and how to favorably impress interviewers.

When many jobs are available in a geographic region, throughout the country, or in a specific career area, the economy is said to be "strong." Employers speak of "abundant job opportunities," or they may say the market is "open" or "growing." On the other hand, if few jobs are available in a career area, employers speak of "limited job opportunities," or they may say the market is "tight" or "closed" or "declining." Sometimes they speak of a job market as either "stable," "growing," or "receding."

If job opportunities in your field are abundant, your job search will be easier than if the market is limited. However, even in a receding job market, there are always openings. Replacements must be hired for retiring employees. In addition, some employees die, resign for personal reasons, or choose to move on, and their positions become available. Experts in labor statistics estimate that almost two thirds of all job opportunities result from the need to replace workers.

Often, especially in a declining job market, jobs are available somewhere in the country, but they may not be available in your area. If you can be flexible about where you work, you may have a much better chance of getting the type of job you want than if you restrict yourself to a certain geographic area. Your willingness to work on a flexible schedule may increase your chances, too. For example, in some work situations new employees are needed to fill late night or weekend working hours. It is also important to be somewhat flexible in your salary requirements. Thinking about your salary in a range, from $15,000 to $20,000, for example, will also help your chances in a declining market.

Learning about the job market also means learning about employers. To get a job, you must impress an employer favorably. Employers know what type of worker they want. The profile they have developed for each employee they seek includes a preferred level of education, specific technical skills, and frequently, certain personal qualities. Employers are increasingly demanding more highly trained workers. In addition, employers understand the "image" their company wants to have in the minds of the customers the company serves, and they look for employees who will fit and help project that image. Fitting and projecting a company image involves the employee's personal appearance, speaking and presentation skills, and evidence of personal qualities, such as enthusiasm and honesty (see Figure 4-1).

Figure 4-1   This job candidate is creating a positive impression by her well-groomed professional appearance, preparation, and enthusiasm. (Photo by Paul E. Meyers.)

LOCATING JOB OPPORTUNITIES

Many job opportunities await you. But how can you find them? And how can you be successful in getting the right one? The answers to these questions depend on your learning where and how to look for jobs. Although at times other people may be able and willing to help you get a job, you need to develop your own job-seeking skills to be independent throughout your professional life. You can find out about job openings from a number of different sources.

SCHOOL PLACEMENT OFFICE

Begin your job search by working closely with the *placement office* at your school. Placement offices provide valuable services, such as available job listings, contacts in local companies, or short courses in resume writing or interviewing. Often employers arrange to interview graduating students at the placement office. Ask about whether this service is available. If it is, get a list of the dates when employers from your field will be interviewing candidates on your campus. Ask to be put on the mailing list so that you can receive information about job openings as they become available. Make a practice of reviewing the placement office bulletin board for information about positions that might interest you.

If your school assigns each student to an *adviser*, this person may play a major role in helping you get a job. Not only can advisers alert you to job possibilities and introduce you to prospective employers, but advisers may speak directly to employers on your behalf. Keep in close touch with your adviser until you have located your first job. In many schools, the placement officer serves as student adviser in matters dealing with job searches.

FOCUS ON:
FASTEST GROWING OCCUPATIONS ARE DOMINATED BY WOMEN

The fast growing occupations are ones traditionally dominated by women. The chart below shows some interesting trends. In the left column you see the eight occupations projected to have the largest number of new positions by 1995. Look at the center column to see how frequently the occupations are dominated by female workers.

These numbers do not mean that all the new employees for the jobs will be women, but these numbers suggest that the percentage of women in the work force will continue to increase.

Occupation	Percentage of Women Workers	New Jobs by 1995
Cashier	83	556,000
Nurse	95	452,000
Cleaner	40	443,000
Truck Driver	2	428,000
Waiter/Waitress	84	424,000
Salesperson	17	469,000
Accountant	44	307,000
Teacher	90	281,000

(Source: Bureau of Labor Statistics)

Figure 4-2 Review the placement office bulletin board regularly for job opportunities. (From Bailey, *The Job Ahead*, Delmar Publishers Inc.)

PERSONAL CONTACTS

Many people get their first job (and later jobs) as a result of *information from friends, family members, and acquaintances*. When you begin your job search, talk to a variety of people about your goals. Ask them to let you know if they hear of a job opportunity in your field. As mentioned in Chapter 3, this process of sharing career-related information is called *networking* and it is an invaluable resource throughout a person's career. If there is a student or community organization related to your field of interest, join it and attend meetings. This is another way to network.

NEWSPAPERS

Local *newspapers* are excellent sources for finding job openings. If you are interested in relocating, get a newspaper from the city of your interest. Read the classified section to understand the experience and skills required and the salary ranges offered in your field. For example, a want ad may tell potential workers that a medical receptionist is needed and that 2 years of experience are required as well as a pleasant personality and references. You can learn what companies are generally paying for someone with 2 years of experience (although a salary is not always listed). You may also use the ads to compare benefits offered by various companies, although usually details are scarce, covered by a simple "generous benefits" or "outstanding perks." For example, some ads may mention that parking is free or that 4 weeks of vacation are offered. Review the want ads on shown in Chapter 2 to see what other benefits are mentioned.

EMPLOYMENT AGENCIES

Professional *employment agencies* can help you locate a job. Some agencies charge job seekers a sizable fee once they become employed; however, most agencies pass the fee on to the employer. Some private placement firms charge you a small fee up front for access to their list of openings. They may not provide the full services of a placement consultant, just information about openings. When you approach a professional employment service, ask about fees and the type of services provided.

EMPLOYMENT COMMISSIONS

State and municipal (city) *employment commissions* exist throughout the country to help workers find jobs. Their services are free and are used by many people. Many state agencies administer a test and give you a grading, or employment classification, such as clerk, secretary, supervisor. If there are no immediate openings for someone with your classification, a state agency will contact you when an opening at your level becomes available.

DIRECT CONTACT

Direct contact with the potential employer has been successful for many job seekers. In midsize and large companies, job seekers go to the Personnel Department for employment information. In a small company, the owner may respond to your letter or telephone call requesting an interview. If your community has a newspaper or newsletter that focuses on the business sector, you can learn about companies that are growing and may be hiring. The Chamber of Commerce may provide you with a list of local businesses.

The most important thing to remember is that most professional people use a variety of approaches in their search for a job. Don't depend only on newspaper ads; only about one third of available jobs are listed there. Try to be thorough. A company may not hire you today but may be so impressed by your initiative and abilities that it will contact you when a job becomes available.

PREPARING FOR THE SEARCH

At first you may feel inadequate and afraid of making mistakes as you contact employers. Those are natural feelings; most people have to work at overcoming natural shyness, a lack of knowledge about the hiring process, and an inability to talk easily about themselves and their skills. Everyone going through this process makes mistakes. It is important that these mistakes become simply a part of your learning process. You have already taken a step toward success in job hunting because you know how to find job opportunities. Next you will learn how to present yourself and your abilities and how to interview effectively.

Before you go after a specific job, you will need a resume and, in addition, you will need to be able to complete an employment application neatly and thoroughly.

YOUR RESUME

A resume (pronounced *reh-zoo-may*) is a written summary of your professional goals, education, and work experience. It may also contain relevant personal data such as participation in community organizations and related volunteer or life experiences. Most experts recommend that a resume be one page in length and that it be professionally typed and printed. Review the three sample resumes in Figures 4-3 (a), (b), and (c). Notice that the three are not set up the same way. Each has information organized in a way that most appropriately highlights the qualifications of each person. You may wish to use one of these samples for your resume, or you may choose to design your own.

JOY JONES

Present Address: Permanent Address:
225 East Street, Apt. 9   110 Main Street
University, TX 77777   Smithville, AZ 66666

CAREER OBJECTIVE: To manage a retail fabric store.

EDUCATION: B.S. degree in Fashion Merchandising,
                     State College, University, Texas
                     Diploma, Smithville High School, 199X

COLLEGE ACTIVITIES: Secretary, Fashion Merchandising Club
                     Member, Interclub Council
                     Volunteer, United Way
                     Honor Roll, two semesters

WORK EXPERIENCE: Salesperson, Brown's Clothing Store
                     University, Arizona, 199X–199X

                     Waitress, Harry's Restaurant, Smithville,
                     Arizona
                     Part-time, 199X–199X

REFERENCES: Furnished upon request

Figure 4-3 Notice that each of these resumes has a different format. Choose one to use as a model for your qualifications or create one of your own.

JOHN STEPHENS
114 West Main Street, Apt. 7,
College, Colorado 78888
(409) 555–8731

CAREER OBJECTIVE

To work as a manager in the food distribution industry

EDUCATION

University of Colorado
Boulder, Colorado 78888
Graduate, 198X
Bachelor of Business Administration
Overall GPA: 3.6

Pleasant High School
Pleasant, Colorado 78888
Graduate, 198X

COLLEGE ACTIVITIES AND AWARDS

*   Vice President, Business Club
*   Dean's Honor Roll, 6 semesters
*   Scholarship from the University of Colorado Alumni Association
*   Member, Phi Delta Kappa fraternity
*   Member, University of Colorado Soccer Club

WORK EXPERIENCE

Salesperson

Butler's Men's Apparel
Pleasant, Colorado
199X–199X

Cook

Western Sizzlin
Pleasant, Colorado
199X–199X

REFERENCES

Furnished upon request

Figure 4-3 Continued

MICHAEL HERNANDEZ

PRESENT ADDRESS: PERMANENT ADDRESS:
408 East Pallings, Apt. 6   622 Clover Street
Campus, New Jersey 91111   Woodville, New Jersey 00181
409/555–9814   214/555–5670

CAREER OBJECTIVE

To teach health education at the high school level

EDUCATION

Graduate, 198X, Browning University, Browning, New Jersey 00181
Major in Health, Second Teaching Field: History
Overall GPA: 3.6
Graduate, 198X, Woodville High School, Woodville, New Jersey 00181

COLLEGE ACTIVITIES AND AWARDS

Dean's Honor Roll, 5 semesters; Scholarships from Browning University
Athletics Association; President, Health Club; Member, History Club;
Member, Browning football team; Southland Conference defensive
player of the year, 198X.

WORK EXPERIENCE

Manager, Spud's Super Gym, Browning, New Jersey, 199X–199X
Supervisor, Harry's Lumberyard, Woodville, New Jersey, 199X–199X

REFERENCES

Furnished upon request

Figure 4-3 Continued

Before you write your resume, think seriously about three major
points and how you will express them:

 Your professional goal or career objective

◆ Your related education

◆ Your work and work-related experience

Career Objective. The *professional goal,* or *career objective,* is a statement
about the career you desire. It may also be a statement about the
particular job you are seeking. Here are some examples of professional
goals or career objectives:

◆ An entry level management position that requires the use of excellent
microcomputer and interpersonal skills.

◆ To assist in the care of children in an early childhood center.

◆ The opportunity to work as an accountant in the oil and gas industry.

Notice that a goal statement completes the phrase, "My goal is . . . ." The three examples above show different ways to phrase your goal, that is, your phrase may begin with a noun that names the work (a management position), or it may begin with the preposition "to" (to teach . . .), or it may begin with a phrase, such as "the opportunity to . . . ."

The objective "to serve as an office supervisor" may be a general one for use on a resume, whereas the objective "to use my word processing and microcomputing skills in a growth-oriented company" may be used when responding to a specific want ad to indicate to an employer that you are flexible about the level at which you are willing to enter the company.

Usually only one goal statement is used on a resume. Make yours broad enough to cover a variety of positions for which you might apply. On the other hand, make it specific enough to explain what work you wish to do. See the sample career objectives shown below.

SAMPLE CAREER OBJECTIVES

1. To work in real estate management using financial and communications skills.
2. A career with a consulting or technology-based firm which combines marketing and strategic planning skills.
3. To work in secretarial services using word processing skills.
4. To work as a caregiver in a health care facility for the aged.

Education. The section of your resume that deals with your education should be thorough. Give the month and year of high school graduation and the name of the school from which you graduated, or the month and year in which you received your General Education Diploma (GED). Give names of all other schools you have attended even if you attended for only one course. You may also enrich the resume by including information about short courses or seminars you have taken that relate to the job for which you are qualified. Interviewers sometimes want to know about your major, or area of skill concentration, your grades, and student activities. However, experts recommend that you omit grade information from your resume unless your grades reflect overall excellence. You may also consider including the names of courses you took that relate directly to the job you want. Also, add specific skills related to technology if you are seeking a technology oriented job.

Work Experience. Work experience is a vital part of the resume. Show all the work experience you have had. Don't be embarrassed if the tenure of a job was brief. As a student, you may not be old enough to have long tenure in the workplace.

If you have not had paid employment yet, list any volunteer work you have done. Perhaps you have served as a scout leader, worked as a volunteer health aide, or served as pianist for a group. You may have done summer work with the aged or at a camp. These and other volunteer work experiences are evidence of responsibility just as paid employment is (see Figure 4-4). People who supervised your volunteer activities may vouch for your performance and skills just as would supervisors on paying jobs.

Figure 4-4 Volunteer work is valuable experience to put on your resume. (From Hegner and Caldwell, *Nursing Assistant*, 6th edition, Delmar Publishers Inc.)

If you have not been either a paid employee or a volunteer, it would be wise to begin building a resume while you are in school by getting some kind of job. Potential employers want to see evidence of some use of your skills in technical areas. They also want proof that you have good work habits, such as promptness and responsibility, and that you work well with others.

Other Sections. After you have planned the three major components of a resume, you are ready to write it. As you make resume decisions, consider these recommendations from experienced professionals:

1. Give your name, present address, permanent address (if different from your present address), and a telephone number where you can be reached.

2. It is not necessary to include a personal data section that provides information about age, health, marital status, or physical build although you may include that information if you desire. When personal data are included, they are usually given as the final entries on the resume. Information about race, religion, and politics is never included.

3. Do not include a photograph unless you are applying for a position as a model or some other job in which appearance will be a factor.

4. A section called "Personal Interests" may provide some information that will help the interviewer know you as an individual. Hobbies and special interests are included in this section. Inclusion of this section is optional.

5. Omit references. You can state that references will be supplied on request. Be sure to take names and addresses of persons you will use as references when you go for interviews.

6. The resume should be produced as neatly and clearly as possible. Many professional services are available to assist in resume preparation. If you can afford professional printing, the investment will be worth it. Particularly where entry-level jobs are concerned, employers see many poorly constructed resumes; hence, a professional-looking one really stands out. If you choose to type your resume and photocopy it, be sure to use a good typewriter or computer printer. Ask someone who is a careful reader to proofread the final version for spelling, clarity, grammar, and appearance.

THE APPLICATION LETTER

Once you have your resume printed, you are ready to make your first request for a job interview. Using a list of potential employers from one or more of the sources mentioned earlier, send letters of application to the person whose name you have as the contact for that vacancy. Be

Ms. Julia Perkins
Personnel Director
Long Print Services
P.O. Box 1000
Phoenix, Arizona 66665

Dear Ms. Perkins:

   Your want ad for a receptionist appeared in Sunday's *Phoenix News*. I am interested in the position.

   I recently completed a course of study for administrative secretaries at The Phoenix School of Business. As you can see on my enclosed resume, I took several courses which were designed to prepare me for a position such as yours. My grade point average supports my ability to be a productive worker.

   Although I have never had a full-time job, I worked in part-time positions while I was in high school and since completing high school. I can supply names of former employers who will provide references for me.

   I will be available for an interview after May 20. Please call me at 111-2020 to arrange a time that will be convenient for you. Thank you for this consideration.

                                                 Sincerely,

                                                 Gretchen Russell

                                                 Gretchen Russell

Enc.

Figure 4-5 Use these letters of application as a guide to write your own.

certain you know the person's title within the company. If possible, try to learn the person's preferred form of address: Mr., Dr., Mrs., Miss, or Ms. If you do not have a name, send your letter with an attention line: Attn: Employment Department (or Personnel Director).

   Your letter of application or inquiry may be the first contact you will make with your potential employer. Be sure it provides a positive image of you as a professional person. Use all the letter writing hints found in Chapter 7 and review the letters of application or inquiry in Figure 4-5. Note the content of the letters.

   The following parts are found in the body of such a letter:

◆ Paragraph 1 tells the reader that you are interested in a position available in the organization, and how you learned about the position.

◆ Paragraph 2 gives a brief overview of your qualifications for the position.

Dr. John Jones
Dentistry Clinic
220 Main Street
Miller City, TX 77002

Dear Dr. Jones:

   Miss Smith, my high school counselor, has told me you have a vacancy for a part-time file clerk. I am interested in a part-time job, and I believe I can work successfully in an office such as yours.

   In May I will finish my junior year at Miller City High School, and I will be available for employment all summer. During my senior year, I will have afternoons from 3:00 to 5:00 available for work.

   In high school, I have had several responsible positions. I am secretary of the junior class. Last year I was a committee chairperson in the history club. I have worked as a babysitter in my community for four years. My overall grade average is 84.6. Mrs. Wright, my English teacher, has offered to speak with you about my ability to work as a clerk.

   I am available for an interview each afternoon after 4:00. Please call me at 555–0011 if you would like to consider me for the job.

                                        Sincerely,

                                        Mary Katherine Smith
                                        Mary Katherine Smith

Enc.

Figure 4-5   Continued

◆ Paragraph 3 tells enough about your experiences to create an interest in your application.

◆ Paragraph 4 asks for an interview. (You might also ask for materials describing the organization.)

   Type your letter of application on white or off-white business paper. Limit the letter to one page and enclose a resume with it in a neatly typed matching envelope.

COMPLETING JOB APPLICATIONS

Most organizations require candidates for employment to complete a standard job application form (see Figure 4-6). You may be asked to do

Computer PLUS   **Employment Application**

An Equal Opportunity Employer
Computer PLUS Policy and Federal Law Forbid Discrimination Because of Race, Color, Religion, Age, Sex or National Origin.

Date_____

Personal Data

Applying for position as _____ Salary required _____ Date available _____

Name: _____
           (Last)   (First)   (Middle)   (Maiden)

Present address _____
                        (Street)   (City)   (State)   (ZIP)   (How long at this address)

Permanent address _____
                           (Street)   (City)   (State)   (ZIP)   (How long at this address)

Telephone number _____ Social Security number _____
                          (Area code)

Are you either a U.S. citizen or an alien immigrant?   ☐ Yes   ☐ No

Check appropriate box for age: Under 16 ☐, 16 or 17 ☐, 18 through 69 ☐, 70 or over ☐

Do you have or have you had any serious or prolonged illnesses?

☐ Yes   ☐ No   If "Yes," explain _____

_____

Person to be notified in case of emergency:

   Name _____ Relationship _____ Telephone _____

   Address _____

How were you referred to Computer PLUS?

   ☐ Agency ☐ School ☐ Advertisement ☐ Direct contact ☐ Computer PLUS employee ☐ Other

Name of referral source above: _____

Activities

Do not name organizations that will reveal race, religion, age, sex or national origin.

School and college activities _____

Special interests outside 1. _____   Indicate the amount of 1. _____
of business.   time devoted to each.
                           2. _____   2. _____

                           3. _____   3. _____

Skills

List any special skills you may have _____

                                     ☐ Speak   ☐ Speak   ☐ Speak
What foreign languages do you: ☐ Read _____   ☐ Read _____   ☐ Read _____
                                     ☐ Write   ☐ Write   ☐ Write

Business machines you can operate _____

Typing speed _____ words per minute   Steno speed _____ words per minute   Method _____

Educational Data

Schools	Print Name, Number and Street, City, State, and ZIP Code for each School Listing	Type of Course or Major	Graduated?	Degree Received
Grade School		/////		/////
High School				/////
College				
Graduate School				
Trade, Bus., Night, or Corres.				
Other				

Approximate scholastic average: High school _____ College _____ Class rank: High school _____ College _____

Percent of college expenses earned _____ How earned? _____

Employment Data Begin with most recent employer. List all full-time, part-time, temporary, or self-employment.

		Mo-Yr	Mo-Yr
Company name		Employed from	To
Street address		Salary or earnings Start	Finish
City	State	ZIP code	Telephone (Area code)
Name and title of immediate supervisor		Your title	
Reason for terminating or considering a change			

		Mo-Yr	Mo-Yr
Company name		Employed from	To
Street address		Salary or earnings Start	Finish
City	State	ZIP code	Telephone (Area code)
Name and title of immediate supervisor		Your title	
Reason for terminating			

		Mo-Yr	Mo-Yr
Company name		Employed from	To
Street address		Salary or earnings Start	Finish
City	State	ZIP code	Telephone (Area code)
Name and title of immediate supervisor		Your title	
Reason for terminating			

Permission is granted to Computer PLUS to verify all statements contained in this application. I understand that my employment will be contingent upon the accuracy and acceptability of such information. My present employer will not be checked until after I accept an offer of employment with Computer PLUS.

I have read the above paragraph and accept the same as a condition of my employment by Computer PLUS.

Date _____   _____
                                                                                              (Signature of applicant)

Personnel Relations Interviewer _____

Figure 4-6 This is a standard employment application you might be asked to fill out when you apply for a job.

```
                          POCKET RESUME

NAME _____    ADDRESS _____
SOCIAL SECURITY # _____    DRIVERS LICENSE _____
TELEPHONE _____      PLACE OF BIRTH_____
SCHOOL_____    DATES _____    ACTIVITIES _____
      _____          _____              _____
      _____          _____              _____
      _____          _____              _____

WORK EXPERIENCE _____ (Names, Addresses, Telephone Numbers)____
                  _____
                  _____
                  _____

REFERENCES: Name _____   Address _____
                 _____   Tele. No. _____
            Name _____   Address _____
                 _____   Tele. No. _____
            Name _____   Address _____
                 _____   Tele. No. _____
```

Figure 4-7 Create your own pocket resume to take with you when you go for an interview.

this either before or after the interview. In either case, it will provide the employer with necessary information about you. It will also provide the employer with another image of you as a person and as a possible employee.

Be sure your application is filled out completely. If some sections do not apply to you, use the response "NA" (not applicable) to indicate that you have not carelessly forgotten to complete something on the form. Be sure that the application is neatly written (print, if necessary) and not marred by erasures or crossed out words.

Carrying certain basic information with you to all interviews and inquiry visits will make filling out applications easy. You will need a list of schools you have attended with addresses and the years you attended. You will also need your Social Security number; a list of names, addresses, and telephone numbers of all previous places of employment (you may also need the name of the person you reported to); and a list of names, addresses, and telephone numbers of people whom you are using as references.

References are people who know about you as a worker. Employers want to verify the information you provide by checking with people from your work history. Be prepared with the names of three to five people who can speak on your behalf. Supervisors at previous places of employment and managers of community endeavors you have been a part of make good references. If you have no work history, teachers make good nonwork references. Be sure to contact the proposed reference before using the person's name. Your conversation with possible references will signal them to begin thinking about what they would say if an employer were to call them about you. After you have obtained a job, remember to thank people for help they provided.

Some job seekers carry a pocket resume with them for ready access to pertinent information.

INTERVIEWING

The interview is often the most critical element in the employment process. You will want to plan your interview strategies carefully. The interview process can be divided into three parts: preparation for the interview, the interview itself, and the follow-up. Each of these parts is presented separately to make them stand out in your mind.

PREPARATION FOR THE INTERVIEW

First, *learn all you can about the company* where you are interviewing. Sources of information may be materials the company sent to you as a result of your letter of inquiry or materials you obtained from a placement office or employment agency. You may want to visit a local library to read about a company, or you may talk with other employees or people who have knowledge of the operation.

Get the name of the person who will interview you, if that is possible. Addressing the interviewer by name as you enter the room shows that you give attention to details. You may know the name of the person from a communication you received when you were setting up the interview. Or, when you are contacted to arrange for an interview, ask the name of the person who will be interviewing you. You may need to arrive early for the interview to get the name of the interviewer from the secretary at the interview site.

As you gather information, *prepare a list of questions* you want to ask when, at some point during the interview, you are invited to ask questions. A common question is to request a description of the organization. For example, you may ask how many salespeople represent the company, or how large an area is served by the business, or what level of support the community gives the organization. Other common questions might relate to the company's expectations of workers. The following are examples of other questions you might ask:

EXAMPLES OF QUESTIONS AN INTERVIEWEE MIGHT ASK

1. What kind of computers does your division use?

2. Do you provide training to keep your workers updated on the use of new computer programs?

3. How many people are employed by your word processing division?

4. Do you provide incentives for further education of your employees?

5. Please tell me something about your company benefits.

6. What do you see as the future of your organization?

7. Are your employees ever transferred to other parts of the country?

Take your list of questions to the interview. This will ensure that you are prepared when the interviewer asks what you want to know about the organization. Your having given prior consideration to specific questions will increase your self-confidence. Don't worry about needing to refer to the written list. The interviewer will be impressed that you did your "homework."

Next, *analyze yourself*—your personal qualities, your education, and your work experience. Consider how these qualify you for the position being filled. Everyone is a salesperson at this point—"selling" the employer on *you*. You will want to convince the interviewer that your experience makes you the best person for the job.

Then, prepare to *present a professional appearance* at the interview. Your posture, dress, and grooming will create the first, powerful impression long before you answer the interview questions.

Many career counseling experts recommend wearing a suit to an interview. A suit in a neutral color (taupe, navy, gray, etc.) with a white or well-coordinated blouse or shirt and appropriate accessories would be appropriate. A well-groomed appearance is equally important. Apply the chapters on personal appearance and professional dress in this book. In addition, see the list below for questions most often asked of specialists on professional dress by students preparing for interviews.

QUESTIONS FREQUENTLY ASKED ABOUT PROFESSIONAL DRESS AND GROOMING BY INTERVIEWEES

Question	Answer
1. What about wearing a sports coat and slacks (or blouse and skirt) for interviews?	The full suited look with matching fabric and color gives the desirable professional look.
2. What color suit is best?	Neutral colors like blues, grays, khaki, or taupe, are fine choices. Avoid bright colors such as reds and yellows.
3. Should a woman choose suits made of menswear fabrics?	No, it is important for a woman to avoid the impression that she is imitating the male look. She can look professional and feminine at the same time.
4. What kind of shirt should a man wear?	Any long-sleeved shirt coordinated with the suit. The conservative nature of law, banking, and accounting may suggest a white shirt as the best choice for those interviewees.
5. Should a man wear jewelry to an interview?	A modest amount of jewelry is all right. Avoid jewelry that calls attention to itself.
6. Should women wear makeup?	Certainly. Makeup adds a look of maturity, which is an asset for the new professional. Visit a makeup specialist for help in getting the right cosmetics for your skin and for learning correct application techniques if you are unsure about your appearance.
7. What about nail color?	Well-manicured nails are a must. If you choose color, be sure it is in harmony with your skin tones and your clothing. Avoid glaring colors and excessively long nails.
8. What do you recommend about hair length?	Men's hair should be trimmed and shaped in contemporary fashion, as should women's. A dated hair style may prompt an interviewer to wonder if your knowledge is as dated as your appearance! Experts recommend that women's hair be neither too short or too long.
9. What about hosiery color?	Men match sock color to pants and/or shoe color and women choose hose in neutral colors harmonious with suit and shoe color.

THE INTERVIEW

People who interview successfully arrive early; they look professional; they project self-confidence; they are prepared; and they communicate effectively. How can you do that?

Plan your schedule so that you are sure to arrive at the interview site at least 10 minutes early. Plan the route you will take to the interview so that you have no trouble finding the building and office. Perhaps you will need a city map to travel to a new place with confidence. You may be asked to arrive early to fill out the application form before the interview.

Give your name to the secretary, then wait patiently. You may spend the waiting time reviewing your list of questions, or you may read materials in the waiting room or something you brought with you. Use good posture and be courteous even as you wait. It may surprise you to learn that the success of some interviewees is based on the impression that the secretary receives and passes on to the interviewer.

Be sure to go alone. Don't take a friend or family member even if that person waits outside. This suggestion is important, because if you take someone with you, you project a lack of independence and confidence.

Be professional not only in your dress and grooming but also in your behavior. Do not smoke even if offered a cigarette and do not chew gum because many people find both of these habits irritating. Do not wear tinted glasses because people cannot see your eyes. The eyes carry much of a person's expressiveness, and interviewers are taught to rely on "reading" the eyes and evaluating eye contact.

Your body language will communicate self-confidence, or lack of it, to the interviewer. Use good posture; stand straight and sit erect. Establish eye contact as you speak and listen. When you enter the interview scene, extend your hand to give a brief but firm handshake. Do not sit until you have been asked to do so.

Then, sit back in your chair with feet flat on the floor and hands in your lap. Crossed legs and arms show tension, and mannerisms such as fingering a strand of hair or swinging a crossed leg indicate a lack of self-confidence.

You can feel confident because you have prepared well for the interview. You know you are appropriately dressed, you are prepared to explain your training and experience, and you have a list of questions to ask. Your positive attitude will show.

A Lively Discussion. Approach the interview discussion with enthusiasm and alertness. Be friendly, but businesslike. Listen carefully to the questions you are asked and respond directly. When you are asked, tell what skills you have developed, explain your abilities, and discuss what you have learned in past experiences. Most importantly,

Figure 4-8 During an interview, body language can speak as loudly as verbal language. What do you think this job candidate's body language is saying? (Photo courtesy of Clairol)

show the relevance of your education, training, and experience to the job for which you are being considered. Remember that people are hired because interviewers believe they can make contributions to the organization. Explain how you can meet the needs of the company.

Being able to relate your work and volunteer experiences to the job under consideration is extremely important. For example, if you were interviewing for a position as a hospital emergency station receptionist, you might say, "While I was in school, I worked summers at the community health clinic interviewing patients for their health histories; I gained a lot of experience dealing with people who were in pain."

Exhibit good conversational skills by speaking clearly and distinctly, neither too loudly nor too softly. If the interviewer asks you to repeat an answer or indicates that he is having trouble hearing you, for whatever reason, turn up your volume. Adjust to the needs of the situation. Be serious and businesslike, but use a tone of warmth, and try to interject humor when it seems appropriate.

As you talk, avoid criticizing former employers. Being negative is not useful in attaining your goal. Furthermore, interviewers have no way of knowing whether your criticisms are justified or not; they only know that you have negative feelings that may affect future job performance.

Interview Questions. Questions asked by the interviewer will have been planned to encourage you to talk enough to give him or her a strong impression of you as an individual. Questions generally relate to your education, your experience, and your expectations for a career. Following are the most commonly asked questions:

QUESTIONS FREQUENTLY ASKED AT INTERVIEWS

1. What type of position interests you?
2. In what school activities did you participate most often?
3. How do you spend your spare time?
4. Are you interested in sports?
5. Why do you think you might like to work for our company?
6. What jobs have you held?
7. What courses did you like best? least?
8. Why did you choose your major?
9. Do you prefer any specific geographic location?
10. How did you spend your vacations while you were in school?
11. What do you know about our company?
12. Do you have a good general education?
13. What qualifications do you have that will make you successful in the career you have chosen?
14. What extracurricular offices have you held?
15. What salary do you expect?
16. How do you feel about family?
17. Can you begin learning from scratch?
18. Why did you leave your various jobs?
19. What plans do you have for further education?
20. What can you do for our company?

As the interview progresses, be a good listener. Never interrupt the interviewer, and always think about the question before answering it.

If the interviewer has requested a transcript of grades, he or she may need help in interpreting course titles, grades, or special symbols. Be prepared to explain what knowledge and skills you developed in courses related to the job. For example, you might say to a person interviewing you for a position in clothing retailing, "Please notice that I took Marketing 301 in which we learned effective approaches to customers as well as how to extend sales. I also took Fashion 402; we evaluated garments for quality and specific features."

It will be to your advantage to be thorough and honest in your responses to questions. Be careful, however, not to state your opinions as facts. You will not want to seem to be a closed-minded person.

Occasionally an interviewer will ask a questions that you do not understand. In that case, feel free to ask for clarification. For example, you might respond to the question, "Do you have experience in using computers?" with "Do you mean using business software or programming?"

Sometimes interviewers ask questions that you may feel are inappropriate. A number of questions legally cannot be asked in an interview. See the list of inappropriate topics below. You need to know how to respond if you are asked one of these questions.

INAPPROPRIATE INTERVIEW TOPICS

1. Previous name
2. Race
3. Marital status
4. Number of dependents
5. Age or date of birth
6. Religious preference
7. Membership in political or religious organizations
8. Willingness to work any particular religious holiday
9. Place of birth or national origin
10. Arrests
11. Type of military discharge
12. Citizenship status of parents
13. Pregnancy
14. Credit rating
15. Sexual preference
16. Health

Some interviewers do not know that certain questions are inappropriate, and some simply want to see how you will respond. Turn an inappropriate question to your advantage. For example, if an interviewer were to ask you whether you have children and about your child care arrangements, you might say, "My husband and I have found an excellent day care center, and we have agreed to share the responsibilities for any emergencies that arise." As a single parent, you might say, "I have my children in an excellent day care setting, and I have other people lined up to help me with emergencies," or you might say, "I'm sorry, and I may be wrong, but it is my understanding that your question is not a legally approved one in an interview." Try to say it matter of factly, not defensively; you may be on shaky ground already by pointing out to an interviewer an unethical or unlawful practice.

If you simply do not know the answer to a question you are asked, don't be afraid to say that you do not know. It is better to be truthful than to fumble with an answer.

Avoid asking questions about salary in the initial interview. You do not want to give the impression that money is your primary concern. However, as the interview draws to a close, if the interviewer has not mentioned salary at all, you may initiate a conversation about it by saying something like this: "What can you tell me about company benefits?" After all, the issue of salary may determine whether another interview is even necessary, from both your viewpoint and the employer's.

Ending an Interview. The interviewer will indicate by his or her actions that the interview is about to close—looks at watch, stacks papers, or says something like, "I believe that is all for today." At that point, ask any question that remains of concern to you. You may want to ask the interviewer when you can expect to hear the decision about the position or when you will be notified of a second interview. Then thank the interviewer, stand, shake hands, and leave with confidence.

AFTER THE INTERVIEW

As soon as you are alone, make notes about your impressions of the interview, including the pros and cons of the position as it was described. If you still want the job, make a list of your follow-up strategies, and place on your personal calendar the date when you can expect to hear from the organization.

Send a letter of thanks to the interviewer as soon as possible. The follow-up letter need not be long, but it should exhibit all the characteristics of a well-written letter. Use white or off-white business stationery. Be sure the letter is sincere and error-free. See a sample follow-up letter in Figure 4-9.

TABLE 4-1: INTERVIEWING SUCCESSFULLY

BEFORE THE INTERVIEW

1. Learn all you can about the business.
2. Learn the name of the interviewer.
3. Plan questions to ask.
4. Analyze yourself and plan how to explain how your education and experience qualify you for the job.
5. Groom yourself carefully and dress appropriately for the interview.
6. Plan the route you will take so that you have no trouble finding the location.

DURING THE INTERVIEW

1. Arrive on time or early.
2. Go to the interview alone.
3. Do not smoke or chew gum.
4. Wait patiently and quietly.
5. Shake hands firmly; use good grammar.
6. Be enthusiastic and alert.
7. Have a positive attitude. Be friendly, but business-like.
8. Sell yourself:
   —Tell what *skills* you have developed.
   —Explain your *abilities*.
   —Discuss what you *learned* from past experiences
9. Avoid:
   —Critizing former employees
   —Saying "I like to work with people"
   —Saying "I like your product."
10. Take a resume or information card with you. Be sure you have your social security number and a list of 3 people who may be used as references.
11. Thank the employer for the interview. Be courteous and gracious.

AFTER THE INTERVIEW

1. Send a thank-you letter to the interviewer.
2. Don't be discouraged if you are not chosen for the job; most people are interviewed several times before they are hired.

Route 2, Box 100
Cumby, Nebraska 88899
December 30, 199X

Miss Laura Peterson
Meredith and Vance Inc.
2000 Main Street
Cumby, Nebraska 88800

Dear Miss Peterson:

   Thank you for the interview with Meredith and Vance. It was interesting to hear a firsthand account of the work your organization does. The accounting division was of particular interest to me. I feel your company is one in which I could be a productive worker.

   I look forward to hearing from you in the future.

Sincerely,

Lynn O'Brien

Lynn O'Brien

Figure 4-9   A follow-up letter after a job interview can help you in three ways: (1) It shows the interviewer that you are thorough and courteous. (2) It indicates that you are interested in the job. (3) It helps refresh the employer about your qualifications.

The follow-up letter can work for you in several ways. First, it places your name in front of the interviewer for a second time; it serves to refresh his or her memory of you as an individual apart from the other interviewees. Second, the follow-up letter reveals that you are thorough and courteous. Third, it is another opportunity for you to say how interested you are in the job.

Signs of Interest in You. You may not be able to determine if an interviewer is seriously interested in you as a potential employee. However, the following clues are encouraging signs.

◆ A request for another interview. Often the first interview is with a person from the personnel office. If you get through that one successfully, you will be interviewed by the person who will be your manager, and then, perhaps, by that person's manager.

◆ A request for further references, transcripts of grades, or other supporting data.

◆ A request for you to take certain tests to show your specialized skills, abilities, or aptitudes.

Dealing with Disappointment. As you begin your career, you will probably interview unsuccessfully for more than one job. In fact, most professional people receive several rejections before they are offered a position. Remember that there are many applicants for almost any job that becomes available in today's job market, so it is logical to assume that you will experience some rejections as you look for work. Try not to be discouraged, rather see the rejection as part of the process of applying for many positions to get one that is right for you.

Use what you learn at each interview to prepare yourself to do better at the next one. Here is a list of reasons for interview failures.

The applicant . . .

. . . arrived late.

. . . failed to make eye contact.

. . . dressed unprofessionally.

. . . had a limp handshake.

. . . smoked.

. . . used poor grammar.

. . . criticized former employers.

. . . had no questions to ask except about salary.

. . . talked too much.

. . . knew nothing about the company.

. . . could not explain how his or her abilities related to the job being considered.

. . . answered questions with only yes or no.

See Table 4-1 for a summary of the steps that lead to successful interviews.

REVIEW QUESTIONS

1. Explain the meaning of the term "declining job market."
2. Name three sources of information about job opportunities.
3. Outline the major parts of a resume.
4. Write five career objectives for yourself.
5. Describe the basic components of a letter of application.
6. Give five suggestions for success in a job interview.
7. Name five reasons for failure in interviewing.
8. Describe body language that a person should not exhibit in an interview.

9. Name five questions you might ask of a person who is interviewing you.

10. Why is it important for you to ask questions during the interview?

ACTIVITIES

1. Develop and prepare a personal resume. Submit it to your instructor for comments or constructive criticism.

2. Write a packet of sample letters:

   a. A letter of application to two different types of jobs that appeared in the newspaper (attach the ads on a separate sheet of paper)

   b. A letter of application to a local company whose success you have been following and who might have openings

   c. A follow-up letter to a recruiter you met at the placement office

   d. A thank you letter to an interviewer

3. Prepare a list of references with addresses and phone numbers that you may use when interviewing (at least three names).

4. Research and write a three-page paper on the changing nature and importance of employee benefits.

5. Visit your school's placement office and fill out an application for a permanent file (submit a copy to your instructor).

UNIT 2

WHO YOU WANT TO BE: BEGINNING A JOB

CHAPTER 5

UNDERSTANDING THE BUSINESS YOU JOIN

CHAPTER GOAL:

To help you understand and appreciate the environment of the organization you join and help you determine how you fit into the organization.

CHAPTER OBJECTIVES:

After studying this chapter, you should be able to:

1. Define organizational culture.
2. Read clues to a specific organizational culture.
3. Describe how a specific job fits into the total operation of an organization.
4. Identify clues that define a specific worker's place in an organization.

Years ago most businesses in the United States were small. Owners started the businesses, and they were the primary managers. The objectives of the owner were the objectives of the business. The owner knew all the employees and often supervised them. Thus, the owner had opportunities to gain personal knowledge about each employee's values and motivations. Employees were close to the heart of the business. The owner and employees usually shared the goals and objectives of the organization. Those employees who did not share the vision usually did not stay.

Today, in a society of complex and often very large corporations, unions, government agencies, and health care facilities, the situation is very different. Instead of having one owner/manager who knows all employees, many businesses have hundreds of managers. Yet, organizations still try to find employees whose values and motivations match those of the organization. The organization is still interested in finding an employee that "fits" (see Figure 5-1).

The fit between you as an individual and the organization is a most important factor in your success. This fit has a great deal to do with whether or not you receive a job offer, whether you will be considered as an outstanding worker, and whether you will be promoted at appropriate intervals.

Your success in any new job depends on your ability to quickly recognize, understand, and fit into the organization you join. This chapter will help you do it.

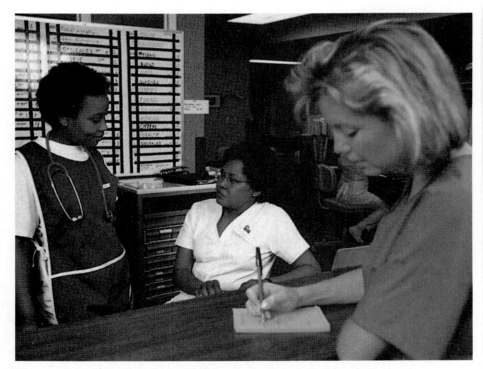

Figure 5-1 To "fit" into the job of admitting clerk/receptionist in a hospital, you should enjoy working with a variety of people in a fast-paced environment. (From Hegner and Caldwell, *Nursing Assistant*, 6th edition, Delmar Publishers Inc.)

ORGANIZATIONAL CULTURE

Organizational culture is the set of key values, beliefs, and goals that are shared by members of an organization. *Sharing* is the key word in this definition. A sharing or grouping of values and beliefs is central to organizations. This does not mean that all employees' individual values are the same but that their attitudes toward company matters are in sync.

THE IMPORTANCE OF ORGANIZATIONAL CULTURE

Organizational culture helps define the basic activities of the organization, while communicating to employees the *individual behavior and procedures that are acceptable to the company.*

Look carefully at the words that are in italics in the last sentence. Consider how important it is to your success in a job to understand *quickly* the signals that communicate to you how things should be done. For example, is it ever appropriate for you to call the president's office directly with a question, or should you convey the question to a superior who will get the answer for you? Is it acceptable for a long personal phone call to be substituted for a break period? Must customers be dealt with politely no matter how rude they get? Are there "last straw" situations?

Each of us has personal values, goals, skills, and abilities. Who we are results from many influences: cultural heritage, our personality, educational background, and a vast array of conscious and unconscious influences. The person each of us is may be very different from the "person" of the business we join. The corporation, like the individual, is the result of many influences, shaped in part by its business goals, its leaders, and its history. These differences may cause problems for us as workers and for the organization as our employer. To minimize conflicts and to take advantage of the opportunities that result from such differences, you can identify and learn to work in harmony with the culture of the business you join.

Figure 5-2 illustrates how becoming a part of a company's culture can affect a worker's success on the job. Managers evaluate workers on the basis of their ability to perform required job activities. Managers also evaluate employees on how well they fit in and adopt the company's values, beliefs, and attitudes. Therefore, someone who does not adapt will not receive a good evaluation and will not succeed in the job.

In our country, the Marine Corps is a good example of a well-defined organizational culture. Think about how the Marine Corps handles a new recruit. During boot camp, drill instructors teach recruits the "Marine way." The training attempts to strip the recruits of some ideas they previously held as individuals and give them a new way of

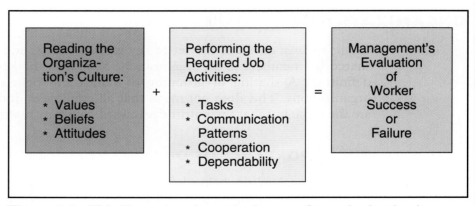

Figure 5-2 This illustration shows the impact of organizational culture on a worker's success or failure.

thinking, which will enable them to work as a team with other Marines who are their "brothers" and "sisters." The recruits are taught to think and act like Marines.

In a much less dramatic way, organizations today try to convey a certain way of doing things—the organization's way. To be successful in an organization, workers must quickly identify and adapt to the culture of the organization.

THE CREATION OF ORGANIZATIONAL STRUCTURE

Organizational culture is seldom dictated by top management in large organizations. Rather, it usually develops by an evolutionary process. For you, this means that your orientation or early job training in an organization will not be enough to allow you to understand the organizational culture. If culture were something dictated by top management, a portion of your orientation could be, "Our Company's Organizational Culture." Few companies include this topic in orientation sessions! You must be alert enough to learn the organizational culture of your new company for yourself.

To learn about organizational culture, consider how it grows and develops. It is reflected in the language, ceremonies, and history of an organization.

Language. Language is a unique feature of every profession or organization. The language of an organization becomes the means through which the values, beliefs, goals, and attitudes are communicated. Language can communicate messages about characteristics of the people who are doing the communicating as well as the messages contained in the meaning of the words used.

For example, the Navajo language does not contain words for superior, subordinate, boss, and hierarchy. Navajos have never been concerned with such organizational relationships. If the Navajos had been concerned with these relationships, they would have developed words to express the concepts. The absence of these words says something important about the Navajo culture. The absence of words such as boss and subordinate reflects the Navajo's belief that all people should receive similar degrees of respect.

Just as the Navajo language reflects its culture, most organizations develop their own jargon, abbreviations, and slogans that reflect basic values and beliefs. For example, in some companies, managers are always called "Mr." or "Ms." In other companies, managers are always addressed by their first names. Some company manuals always use the words superior (manager) and subordinate (worker). Other companies always use manager and team or staff. The words chosen express the attitude that the company chooses to communicate to all its workers and to the outside world.

Many company slogans also carry important cultural meanings. For example, AT&T's slogan, "AT&T is the right choice," is not only a catchy advertising phrase, but it also symbolizes AT&T's message to its workers. Similarly, John Deere's slogan, "Nothing runs like a Deere," reflects the company's deep commitment to quality workmanship in its parts, products, and services. Employees at John Deere must identify with quality, just as employees at AT&T must identify with their company's concept of being first and best.

Ceremonies. Ceremonies also help establish organizational culture. Ceremonies are planned events that celebrate significant occasions in an organization. Ceremonies celebrate and at the same time convey symbolic meaning to employees and to others. Ceremonies give managers an opportunity to reinforce values and beliefs of the organization.

Often ceremonies are built around particular "heroes" of the corporation. For example, McDonald's conducts a nationwide contest to determine the best hamburger cooking team. Competition starts at the local level, works its way up to the national level. The awarding of the title, "best team," is a special event. What does such a ceremony communicate to the employees of McDonald's? Perhaps it communicates these messages:

1. Quality preparation of hamburgers is important.

2. Employees who strive for quality will be recognized and rewarded.

Ceremonies are also an important part of the Mary Kay Cosmetics operation, one of the most successful companies in the cosmetics industry and a company largely made up of women. The founder of Mary Kay believes strongly that success can be achieved through hard work and positive motivation. Achievement, recognition, positive motivation, and hard work are part of one of the best examples of organizational ceremony and ritual in America.

At their annual meeting in Dallas, Texas, Mary Kay saleswomen meet to celebrate the past year's successes. The annual meeting is not unlike a beauty pageant, with employees and others in the audience dressed in glamorous evening clothes. Awards, gifts, and prizes ranging from gold and diamond pins to pink Cadillacs (a Mary Kay trademark and much-valued award) are presented to workers for sales successes.

This ceremony acts as a motivator by publicly recognizing outstanding performance. In addition, the ritual reflects the personal determination and optimism that enabled the real Mary Kay to overcome personal hardships, start her own company, and achieve great financial success. It conveys to her salespeople that reaching their sales quotas is important and that through hard work they can achieve success and be handsomely rewarded.

History. You can see from this example that history also influences organizational culture. The stories of a company's past, which are passed along within an organization, have a profound impact on organizational culture. Often these stories involve the beginning of the company or the founders. Whether a story is true or legend, it symbolizes and preserves a past that is important to the organization.

For example, many organizations have historical stories in their culture that emphasize the need to follow rules and regulations. One of the most famous of these comes from the IBM Corporation. A story is told about Thomas Watson, Jr., the founder of IBM. At the time the incident took place, Mr. Watson was chairman of IBM's Board of Directors and perhaps the most powerful man in the corporation. He was taking a tour of one of the firm's plants. When Mr. Watson toured plants he did not go alone; secretaries and assistants accompanied him on the walking tours. On one occasion as he moved through a plant, the group came to an area requiring security badges for admission. At the entrance to the area stood security officer, Lucille Burger, 22 years old and 90 pounds. She felt, naturally, extremely intimidated by all these managers in the group, but she stopped Mr. Watson and said, "I'm sorry. You cannot enter. You do not have the appropriate security badge."

One of Watson's aides whispered, "Don't you know who he is?" Watson immediately raised his hand for silence and sent one of his party hurrying off to get him a badge.

You can see the values and beliefs that underlie this story. They are: (1) Every employee is expected to do his or her job in the best way possible. (2) Even the most powerful manager is to treat employees with respect. (3) All employees—even managers—need to know and follow the rules and regulations.

Figure 5-3 Employee awards give workers recognition and allow them to feel good about being part of the organization they work for. (Courtesy of IBM.)

FUNCTIONS OF ORGANIZATIONAL CULTURE

Culture performs a number of functions within an organization. By knowing and recognizing these functions, you can increase the quickness of your acceptance by coworkers and managers.

CULTURE DEFINES BOUNDARIES

Have you ever thought about organizations having boundaries? They do. In a sense the boundaries are the distinctions between one organization and another. Some boundaries are tangible, like products or buildings. Others are intangible, like attitudes and values. For example, one homeowners' insurance company may cover total cost to a home for hail damage; another pays only 75%. The former company places greater value on retaining its customers over the long term than on the extra dollars it pays out now (short term) for damages. This aspect of its culture distinguishes it in the minds of customers. A pizza chain may advertise that if your luncheon order is not served to you within 10 minutes, it's free. They are promising exceptional service and challenging you to try it. Their culture distinguishes them from other pizza parlors.

FOCUS ON: PREVENTIVE HEALTH CARE BENEFITS

Faced with spiraling medical costs and insurance premiums, more and more companies are adding preventive health care to their employee benefits package. This may include health screening for employees, educational seminars and workshops, and opportunities for physical activity.

Here is how the program operates at one large corporation. The program, called "Live for Life," offers classes on stress management and how to quit smoking. It teaches employees the importance of blood pressure testing, weight control, and exercise. The company has a fitness center on site.

In the center, an aerobics instructor leads exercise classes before and after work and at lunch time. Free laundry service is provided. The company distributes a monthly newsletter on fitness and sponsors regular seminars on good nutrition and other topics.

The program is voluntary, but incentives to participate are provided. For every 20 minutes of exercise, employees get $1 of "play money." They can use it to purchase jogging suits, ankle weights, and other health-related items. About 60% of the company's 30,000 employees participate.

Research has shown that fitness programs such as this pay off. There are fewer illnesses and accidents, reduced absenteeism, and a more vigorous, creative, positive workforce. In one company, it was found that the average yearly medical cost for exercisers was less than 50% of that for nonexercisers. Some companies even share the reduced medical costs with employees.

Adapted with permission from Larry Bailey, *Working Skills for a New Age*, copyright 1990 by Delmar Publishers Inc., page 406. All rights reserved.

CULTURE CONVEYS IDENTITY

Organizational culture helps to identify employees as members of the organization. Dress, attitudes, and behavior communicate to outsiders that certain people are associated with a certain organization. For instance, in some large retail operations and restaurants the employees wear badges. Other companies depend on the attitudes and behaviors of their employees to identify themselves as givers of service.

In the early 1980s, William Ouchi's book, *Theory Z: How American Business Can Meet the Japanese Challenge*, pointed out the importance of organizational culture. Many American managers have studied Ouchi's book to learn how the successful Japanese systems are different from their own—and how the U.S. firm might successfully modify its culture. In particular, seven characteristics differentiate the approach used by the Americans (Theory A) and that used by the Japanese (Theory J), according to Ouchi. Ouchi's Theory Z is a combination of those two theories designed to modify the American organizational culture and help firms compete more effectively.

CULTURE FACILITATES COMMITMENT

Workers who identify with the values, ethics, and goals of a company's culture are most likely to develop a commitment to the organization. Often the commitment results in high work standards and strong company loyalty. Pride generated by shared values results in quality products and services produced by workers.

CULTURE ENHANCES SOCIAL STABILITY

The organizational culture helps hold the organization together by providing appropriate standards for the behavior of employees. Regardless of whether a person fits into small groups, the culture promotes a sense of belonging to the larger and most important group.

READING ORGANIZATIONAL CULTURE

Your first involvement with a company is as an outsider and you will "read" its culture from this perspective. It is important for you to make an evaluation at this early state so that you can be ensured of joining a company that has values you *can* support and that will support *you* in your professional growth. For example, if you learn during job negotiations that the company provides lavish bonuses and an extravagant holiday party for its executives yet chastises a secretary for an emergency absence, then consider well whether this company's values and priorities are compatible with your own.

ACTIONS SPEAK LOUDEST

Usually you receive your first impressions of a company when you have a first interview. If you have a chance to talk with a current or former employee, ask these types of questions: Does the company allow time away from the desk for training? (Does it value professional growth of its employees?) Does it give supervisors the discretion to overlook an employee's unavoidable lateness by balancing that against an employee's

ORGANIZATIONAL CULTURE

Characteristics:	Theory A (American)	Theory J (Japanese)	Theory Z (Modified)
Employment with a firm	Usually short-term; layoffs are quite common.	Especially in some of the large firms, it is for life. Layoffs are rare.	Fairly long term; this will help develop a loyal semipermanent workforce.
Evaluation and promotion of the personnel	Very fast; individuals who are not promoted rapidly often seek employment elsewhere.	Very slow; big promotions are generally not given out for years.	Slower; more emphasis is given to training and evaluation than to promotion.
Career paths	Very specialized; people tend to stay in one area (accounting, finance, sales, etc.) for their entire career.	Very general; personnel are rotated from one area to another and become familiar with all areas of operations.	More general; emphasis is on job rotation and more broadly based training to give the person a better feel for the entire organization.
Decision-making	Carried out by the individual manager.	Carried out via group decision-making.	Carried out with more emphasis on group participation and consensus.
Control	Very explicit; people know exactly what to control and how to do it.	Very implicit and informal; people rely heavily on trust and good-will.	More attention to informal control procedures coupled with explicit performance measures.
Responsibility	Assigned on an individual basis.	Shared collectively by the group.	Assigned on an individual basis.
Concern for the worker	Organization is concerned primarily with the worker's work life only.	Organization is concerned with the whole life of the worker, business and social.	Organization's concern is expanded to include more aspects of the worker's whole life.

overtime? Does it allow flexibility in a work schedule when personal circumstances require it—without making the employee feel guilty?

On the basis of the first interview consider these: Was I treated with the respect I deserve for opening myself up to scrutiny, or was I treated as just another face in a long list of applicants? Was I given plenty of time to ask questions and were the answers thorough and forthright? Was everyone I saw expensively dressed? (Is this me—or could it be?)

As an outsider, perhaps you have heard about the firm's products or services or you have formed an impression based on your own experiences with them. There are other sources of "outside" clues.

The Physical Setting. A company's investment in its building, parking area, and facilities says something about its culture (see Figure 5-4). For example, if you were to drive into the headquarters of Tandem Computers' Corporation in Cupertino, California, you might think you were driving into a country club—not the place of business for an international corporation. It has walking and jogging trails, a basketball court, open acres for exercise classes, and a large swimming pool for the employees' use. This informal layout for a company headquarters conveys top management's values of openness and equality.

Contrast Tandem Computers' physical setting with that of General Electric's corporate headquarters in Fairfield, Connecticut. General Electric's structure is a strong statement of the value the corporation places on stability and strength—communicated by its fortresslike structure. Each company is proud of its image, and its physical environment reflects that pride (see Figure 5-4).

Ask yourself these questions as you look for cultural clues in a company's physical setting:

◆ Who has a reserved parking space?

◆ Is there a security gate? Guards?

◆ Are the structures old or new in appearance?

◆ Are some offices much nicer than others?

Company Statements and Publications. Read the company's statements about the organization to see what they communicate. Annual reports, quarterly statements, press releases, and company newspapers reveal a great deal about the values and beliefs of a firm. Look closely at statements and publications for answers to these questions:

◆ What types of employees are shown in pictures? Are a variety of jobs represented?

◆ Is the statement or publication written clearly?

◆ What are the important themes in the publication?

◆ Is a common theme found in publications?

FOCUS ON:
EMPLOYER-SPONSORED CHILD-CARE ASSISTANCE

About 70 percent of women between the ages of twenty and fourty-four are employed. This number is expected to increase to 80 percent by 1995. Over half these women are mothers. This has led to child-care assistance becoming the hot new fringe benefit.

The number of employers offering some type of child-care service has increased about 500 percent since 1982. More programs are on the way. In San Francisco, an ordinance was passed recently requiring developers in that city to include space for child care in new downtown office buildings. In Monterey Park, California, Union Bank opened a new service center in 1986. The office included a separate 5,000-square foot child-care facility with a staff of twelve located just 200 feet from the main building. The AFL-CIO has passed a resolution backing employer-union sponsored child-care centers.

The major reason that companies offer child-care assistance is to attract and hold good employees. For instance, one department head turned down a job across town that offered a large salary increase. She put it this way: "I spend the lunch hour with my six-month-old son. They couldn't put a price tag on having my child within a few minutes of me."

Child-care assistance is an expensive undertaking. Very few companies pay 100 percent of the costs. Usually, employees pay tuition that amounts to about one-third to one-half of the cost of private, community child-care. Experts predict that more employers will offer child-care assistance in the future.

Reprinted with permission from Larry Bailey, *Working Skills for a New Age*, copyright 1990 by Delmar Publishers Inc., page 119. All rights reserved.

Company Treatment of Outsiders. Your first exposure to an organization will be in its reception area. Is it formal or informal? Relaxed or busy? The reception area reflects the company's values.

In a service-conscious company the receptionist may take your coat and offer you coffee. On the other hand, in a security-conscious company, you may be given a security badge, and you may see guards, gates, and escort personnel.

(a)

(b)

Figure 5-4 (a) and (b) What do these two different kinds of corporate exercise and fitness facilities tell you about the culture of the organizations that support them? (a) Courtesy of Bally's Health and Tennis Corporation; (b) Courtesy of Toyota Motor Manufacturing, USA.

THE INSIDE SCOOP

Once you have been accepted for employment, your real test of reading the culture begins—from the inside. You will be expected to fit in quickly. At the same time, people are saying things like, "Oh, you are new, aren't you?" or "You are the new one in the office," or "Let me tell you how things are done around here." They want to help initiate you to the culture, the "way things are done in this office." Here are some clues to help you learn the unique culture of your new organization:

1. Pay attention to the stories that are told. When people want to share how things are done, they often relate them through stories. When several people tell the same or similar story, you will know that the message of the story is significant.

2. Notice how employees dress. The manner of dress is important to most organizations. These patterns may reflect safety considerations, work habits, or just important beliefs and values about the organization's image. Be sure to look for the normal rather than the extremes in attire.

3. Read newspaper and magazine articles written about your new company and the industry in general. Go beyond just reading and listening to stories. Be ready to talk in an informed manner about the issues related to your business. *Remember* this word of warning about media stories. Often they tend to be negative—reporting only the "bad" that has happened. Even when other employees are repeating negative news, as a beginning employee you will want to focus on positive aspects of your organization, defending your company and its practices whenever possible. Build a reputation for yourself as someone who "bends over backward" to support the company. If, however, the tone of your coworkers and the media is overwhelmingly negative, being a Pollyanna will not be well received from a new employee. It would be best to digest all information and simply say that you are still forming an opinion about the issues at hand.

4. Develop an understanding of the primary or core products and/or services of your company. The task may be complex, but it is important for you to know the product from its beginning to its finished state.

5. Understand the career path for employees in your organization. Learn who is considered promotable and why, and take steps to get yourself on that path, if possible. For example, if all important positions are filled by ex-salespeople, then it is fairly clear that the organizational culture values salespeople or the sales function. You could take some courses in sales or marketing or perform a volunteer sales task to improve your skills. The attitudes of a culture are partially shaped by people's perceptions of what it takes to get ahead in the organization.

6. Determine how long people remain in a job before being promoted. The length of time one stays in a job is critical in assessing some aspects of an organization's culture. Short tenure means people are motivated to meet promotion criteria quickly. Organizations that tend to have short tenure sometimes hire a larger number of new employees than will be retained in the long run. Employees that meet the promotion criteria quickly are retained, and others are released.

The organizational culture also affects an employee's interpersonal relationships, as you will learn in Chapter 6 in the discussion of job norms and the roles played by coworkers.

REVIEW QUESTIONS

1. Write a definition of organizational culture.

2. List three functions of organizational culture. Explain each.

3. Explain the relationship of language to organizational culture.

4. Describe how ceremonies emphasize organizational culture.

5. Describe two clues that a person outside a company may pick up about its culture.

6. Explain two clues that a new employee may get from inside as he or she reads company statements and publications.

7. Describe the products or services of a particular company to a classmate. Use language and attitudes that show support for the company.

8. Why it is important to study a company's organizational culture (both before and after being hired)?

ACTIVITIES

1. Interview an experienced worker, asking him or her to describe the organizational culture in his or her company. (Be prepared to define organizational culture for this worker.) Write a two-page report.

2. Obtain at least three publications of a specific business organization. Read them, and describe three values that are reflected in the publications.

3. Describe in writing the reception area of a business that you have visited. List three values that you believe the company holds, based on what you saw in the reception area. Then, if possible, interview a worker from that company to see if your perceptions are on target. (If not, don't blame yourself; the company may be inaccurately portraying itself.)

4. Work with a group of three other students to make a list of guidelines for a new employee to use to learn quickly what is expected of workers in a specific company.

5. Describe some ways that a new employee may learn about his or her company's products or services.

6. Photocopy a negative report in the media about a local company (product or services). Role play an office discussion about the issue between a new employee and veteran employees.

CHAPTER GOAL:

To develop behavior that creates a professional image at work.

CHAPTER OBJECTIVES:

After studying this chapter, you should be able to:

1. Evaluate aspects of physical surroundings in a productive work environment.
2. Set priorities and manage time efficiently.
3. Establish and maintain positive relationships with coworkers, managers, subordinates, and clients.
4. Understand how professionals work effectively in groups.
5. Deal with concerns about special relationships that may occur when men and women work together.

As you read this chapter, you will sense the realities—the "flavor"— of the business environment (see Figure 6-1). For many, that environment is an office; however, it may be elsewhere, and the behavior discussed here applies to many environments other than the office.

(a)

(b)

Figure 6-1 Every job has its own atmosphere that is created by the type of work being done and the people who work there. (a) A modern "modular" office automated through computer and communication technology. (Courtesy of NCR Corporation.) (b) Wal-Mart employees put prices on new merchandise. (Courtesy of Wal-Mart Stores, Inc., 1988 Annual Report.)

As you think about the contemporary office, you will realize that you know a good deal about it already. You may have worked in an office; you have probably visited offices; and you have seen photographs and movies or television shows depicting all sorts of workplaces. This chapter goes beyond surface descriptions of offices to examine the most important aspect of them—the professional behavior of the people who work there.

Three major factors contribute to your professional image in the office:

◆ How you manage your physical surroundings
◆ How you manage your priorities and your time
◆ How you handle your work relationships

MANAGING YOUR WORK STATION

Your work station is the place where you perform your work duties. It contains all the equipment and furnishings necessary for you to do your job. Your work station is the part of your physical surroundings over which you have some control. There are two reasons why having a neat, organized work station is important. First, your work station is a reflection of you, and others may make assumptions about you based on how it looks. Second, you cannot perform your job duties effectively if you are disorganized or messy.

THE DESK

You should organize your desk so that everything you use frequently is readily at hand. Both the desk top and the desk drawers should be organized for maximum efficiency.

The Desk Top. The desk top is the most visible part of your desk. The items you keep on top of your desk should be those that need to be handy. These may include the following:

Pens and pencils. These should be kept in easy reach. Pencils should be sharpened and pens should be of high quality.

Telephone. If you are right-handed, keep the telephone at the left side of your desk so that you can reach it easily with your left hand. If you are left-handed, position the phone at the right. Be prepared to take notes or messages every time you make or receive a call. Always have a note pad or telephone message pad handy. Be sure that you understand how to use your phone correctly. Most modern phone systems provide user's instruction manuals to help you learn how to perform the necessary functions on the phone. If you do not have a manual, ask a coworker.

Calendar. Keep your calendar current with your own meetings and appointments scheduled. If you are responsible for making appointments for your supervisor, keep those appointments on your calendar as well as on his or hers.

In/out box. Keep the in/out box on the outside corner of your desk so that mail can be delivered to you easily. Check through the in box at regular intervals during the day so that you do not miss important messages or correspondence that may have inadvertently been buried.

If you choose to keep other items on the top of your desk, such as an address file, paper clips or a stapler, establish a specific spot for them on the desk and keep them there when they are not in use.

To maintain order, the papers on the top of the desk should relate to the work you are doing at the time. Keep other papers elsewhere. You may put them in folders or in a file tray.

The Desk Drawers. The inside of your desk should be as neat and orderly as your desk top. Organize the drawers so that you can find things easily. If you maintain files in your desk, make sure that they are organized in a way that will enable you and others to find things without difficulty, since someone may have to retrieve something from your desk in your absence.

EQUIPMENT

Your work station may contain equipment, such as a computer or typewriter. Always make sure that your equipment is kept clean and is well maintained. Keep coffee cups and other liquids away from equipment. If you have a computer, keep software stored safely and be sure that nothing that is magnetized is ever close to the computer or the software. Be sure that you understand how to operate the computer and the software before you use it. Some companies provide training for new employees in computer and software operations. User's manuals are provided with most computers and software. If you are uncertain of how to use the computer or the software, talk to your manager.

SHELVES AND WALLS

You may have shelves on the walls of your work station. Items kept on the shelves should be neatly arranged and clearly labeled.

If you notice that other workers have hung business-related items on the walls, such as the office telephone list, you may feel comfortable in doing so. However, be sure that you affix items to the wall in a way that

Figure 6-2 A neat, well-organized desk is an outward sign of a professional approach to the job. (Courtesy of VARCO Incorporated)

will not damage the wall. Some office walls are metal, and magnets can be used to affix things to the wall. If you use magnets, be sure to keep them away from computer-related items. If you are not sure of what to use, ask someone for advice.

MANAGING YOUR WORK TIME

The work of most professionals is characterized by frequent interruptions, by varied tasks and activities, and by meetings. Your task is to "manage" yourself under these conditions. Here are suggestions for successfully managing your work time.

SET GOALS

People who manage their time effectively know what they need to accomplish within a general period of time. All good time managers make a "To Do" list. This is a list of actions that must be taken or work that must be completed. Some "To Do" lists are made up for one day's worth of work; others are for a week or longer. As a new employee, you should make up a daily "To Do" list. The list also means that you do not have to rely only on your memory to be in the right place at the

Figure 6-3 Items on the shelves near your desk should be neatly arranged and clearly labeled. (Courtesy of UARCO Incorporated.)

right time, and to do those things that contribute most to your company's business. The "To Do" list is one piece of paper on which all your daily tasks are listed rather than multiple slips of paper with various notes written on them.

PRIORITIZE TASKS

Prioritizing means planning to work first on the task that is most important or most urgent. Notice in Figure 6-5 how the items shown in Figure 6-4 have been prioritized. Each level of priority has been assigned a value:

    A . . . Don't go home until it is done
    B . . . Do today if possible
    C . . . Can wait until tomorrow

SET DEADLINES

Try to set realistic target dates before you begin a project. You want to develop a reputation for completing work on time. If you generally meet deadlines, a manager may be more willing to give you extra time when a job takes more time than was originally expected.

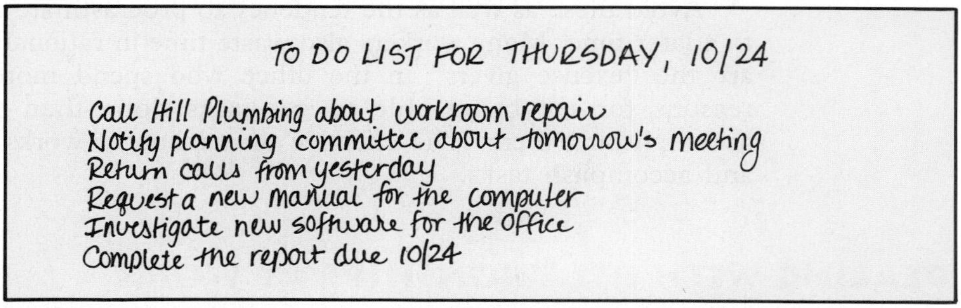

TO DO LIST FOR THURSDAY, 10/24

Call Hill Plumbing about workroom repair
Notify planning committee about tomorrow's meeting
Return calls from yesterday
Request a new manual for the computer
Investigate new software for the office
Complete the report due 10/24

Figure 6-4 Use this model to create your own daily "To Do" list.

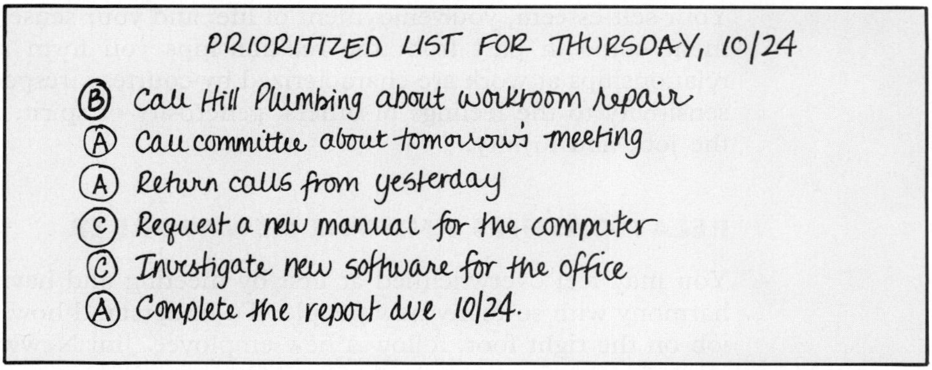

PRIORITIZED LIST FOR THURSDAY, 10/24

Ⓑ Call Hill Plumbing about workroom repair
Ⓐ Call committee about tomorrow's meeting
Ⓐ Return calls from yesterday
Ⓒ Request a new manual for the computer
Ⓒ Investigate new software for the office
Ⓐ Complete the report due 10/24.

Figure 6-5 Prioritize your daily "To Do" list. You should put the most important tasks first and the least important last.

AVOID TIME WASTERS

Here is a list of common time wasters:

◆ Telephone interruptions and lengthy conversations
◆ Drop-in visitors
◆ Lack of objectives
◆ Lack of specific plans for reaching objectives
◆ Poor organization
◆ Poor communication
◆ Inability to say no
◆ Poor health and overwork
◆ Lack of understanding about individual responsibilities
◆ Extended coffee breaks
◆ Lateness
◆ Lack of information needed to complete a task

Avoid these as well as the tendency to procrastinate or put tasks off to a later time. Many workers also waste time in rationalizations. These are the "excuse givers" in the office who spend more time finding reasons for *not* being able to get tasks done than they spend in accomplishing them. The effective time manager works to reach goals and accomplish tasks.

DEALING WITH RELATIONSHIPS AT WORK

Professional relationships are important to your success on the job. These relationships are with managers, coworkers, and subordinates. Your self-esteem, your enjoyment of life, and your sense of accomplishment come in part from the relationships you form at work. Good relationships at work are characterized by courtesy, respect, helpfulness, sensitivity to the feelings of others, generosity of spirit, enthusiasm for the job, and loyalty.

RELATIONSHIPS AND THE NEW WORKER

You may feel overwhelmed at first by meeting and having to work in harmony with so many new people. To understand how to begin a new job on the right foot, follow a new employee, Jim Neww, as he goes to work for the first time in Anyfirm Company.

Jim sees the need to establish good relationships with the people in his office quickly. What should he do, what can he expect in establishing relations with his new manager, coworkers, and subordinates?

As the newest employee, Jim will be the subject of curiosity for a while. He knows that he must be patient and cautious in establishing relationships. After considering the situation, Jim has decided to follow these suggestions:

1. Listen and observe as much as possible. Listen more and talk less during the first week.

2. Be equally nice to all employees. Since Jim does not know the informal relationships within the group, he will be extra careful to speak to every employee with courtesy—from the security guard, who does not affect his job directly, to his manager's secretary, who does.

3. Avoid quick judgments about who is powerful, who will make a good friend, and who is trustworthy. Jim needs to keep an open mind, waiting until later to make these decisions.

4. Ask questions about the job, not questions about people. It is best for Jim to avoid asking personal questions about coworkers. Open curiosity about other people will give him the reputation of being a gossip.

Figure 6-6 Your relationship with your manager is a very important factor in your professional life. (Copyright Roger Tully, 1992.)

5. Jim, as assistant to the sales manager, needs to understand the importance of, and show respect for, all other members of the support staff. Avoiding unreasonable demands, thanking them for their work, helping when he can, and praising them for their accomplishments are first steps in making friends.

With these actions, Jim is off on the right foot as a new worker. Now he needs to give attention to developing good relationships with selected groups.

RELATING TO SUPERIORS

Jim knows that the most important person in establishing his success is his immediate manager. Jim has some excellent guidelines in mind for dealing with his manager:

1. *Discover your manager's goals.* Ask questions, visit with your manager, and be sure to listen to the answers. Understanding your manager's goals will help you to understand the business and, more importantly, will help set priorities in your own work.

2. *Accept your dependence on your manager.* Employees frequently, and mistakenly, think that their contributions make managers dependent on them. Jim recalled a story one of his friends told about leaving a job. At the end of the story, Jim's friend said: "I once thought that

I was so important that my boss could not get along without me. But I left him 10 years ago, and he's still there—going strong."

3. *Find out how your manager likes to work.* Does he or she like written reports? Short meetings? Detailed briefings? A formal relationship? Subordinates do not always agree with the way the manager works; nevertheless, good relations require that a subordinate be sensitive to the way the manager works and adjust to that work style.

4. *Keep your manager informed.* Send your manager copies of all your memos, giving him or her bad news as well as good news; provide information between the formal reporting periods; never assume that the manager will ask for all the information needed. In short, "Never surprise your boss."

5. *Be dependable and honest.* Jim recalled an office manager at another job who told him: "Dishonesty is about the worst trait a subordinate can have. I cannot keep people on staff unless I can depend on them and their work." Most subordinates are not intentionally undependable or dishonest, but some promise things they cannot deliver, let deadlines slide without explanation, or are absent from work with flimsy excuses. When employees are gone from their desks for long and unexplained periods of time, spend time in personal calls, or stock their closets at home with company stationery and supplies, they are being dishonest. These practices are thefts of the company's time and resources. Jim developed a short checklist—to keep himself honest. Look at Jim's checklist in Figure 6-7 and prepare one for yourself.

A CHECKLIST FOR HONESTY IN MANAGING COMPANY RESOURCES

I maintain these standards	YES	NO
1. Arrive at work on time	____	____
2. Never miss a work day without good reason	____	____
3. Do not abuse coffee breaks or lunch hours	____	____
4. Do not leave work early	____	____
5. Never take office supplies for personal use	____	____
6. Keep personal phone calls brief	____	____
7. Complete assignments on time	____	____
8. Carry through on promises	____	____
9. Maintain company loyalty	____	____
10. Abide by company security regulations	____	____

Figure 6-7 Prepare a checklist like the one above and answer the questions by putting a checkmark in the "yes" or "no" column.

RELATING TO COWORKERS

Jim learned early in his new job at Anyfirm the importance of his relations to coworkers. From the very first, Jim noticed coworkers doing things in certain ways. For example, when he drove into the parking lot, he noticed people parking their cars in a pattern, almost as if a police officer were directing. People greeted one another and formed small groups as they walked into the building. (No one greeted Jim the first day. He thought to himself, "How long will it be before I will know someone to talk to about Sunday's football game?")

What Jim observed are *patterns of behavior*, which are important for all of us. In every area of our lives, we develop patterns or comfortable habits. Patterns in the way we do things and behave free us from having to think about every action and social exchange each time they occur. The acceptable patterns of behavior in an organization, taken together, form a larger pattern, or culture, as discussed in Chapter 5. Company culture is reflected in such things as acceptable standards of dress, the formality or informality of meetings, standards for promotability, and so on.

Patterns are reflected in your coworkers in two important ways: norms and roles.

Norms. Norms are best defined as rules for behavior made by any group of people. Norms are the ways people are expected to behave in a group. Norms are unwritten rules that reflect the shared beliefs of most of the coworkers about what behavior is appropriate. Behind every norm is this sentiment: "Follow this norm because if you do not, someone will suffer for it." For example, common norms in many companies are these:

◆ Don't try to impress, or "get on the good side of" the manager in ways that are not work-related. For example, don't develop a sudden interest in gourmet food because cooking is the manager's hobby.

◆ Do your fair share of work. Volunteering too quickly to do the extra work may be frowned on. So may shirking work.

Can you see from these examples how other group members might be threatened if a member of the group did not follow the unwritten norms?

These unwritten rules are never clear to the new member of the group. Frequently, the new worker finds out about a norm by breaking an unwritten rule and then seeing the negative reaction of coworkers. These reactions may be surly looks, humor at the expense of the offending person, or avoidance. Sometimes a coworker will help the offender. The coworker may slap a new worker on the back and laughingly say, "Come over here and let me tell you how things are done around here." Such

FOCUS ON: LEARNING A ROLE

Maureen Lang began a new job only 10 days ago as a purchasing agent in a small office products company in Duluth, Minnesota. Since her background was as a secretary in another department, she found that she had much to learn about purchasing.

"My duties here at are not at all the same," she said. "Purchasing supplies for the various departments is demanding, and I have so much to learn. So many forms and vendors! But in concentrating so hard on my new job, I learned an important lesson. In fact, I got a real scare!"

The entire purchasing department had been moved to a different floor at the time of Maureen's transfer.

"The whole area was a mess, with no order to it at all," Maureen said. "Boxes and furniture were piled everywhere, both in my area and in adjacent ones. On my second day in the new department, I had arrived for work a half hour early, because I knew the area would need some organizing before I would really have a workable station."

Alone in the department, Maureen rearranged some equipment and furniture that did not belong in her immediate area.

"I moved a lot of stuff and the newly exposed area needed vacuuming. I was anxious to begin my work day, with many orders from the previous day that needed processing. Usually, when I arrived—I'm an earlybird by nature—someone from the cleaning crew was vacuuming. I saw that he was vacuuming and organizing another department. I didn't feel right asking him to stop what he was doing to come and vacuum my area. So, when he was finished, I got the vacuum and did it myself."

Without giving the matter a thought, Maureen began processing purchase orders, but midway through the morning she was told to report to the president's office.

"I still had no idea that I'd done anything wrong," Maureen said, shaking her head, "but I soon found out. I was told in no uncertain terms that I was not to move furniture or do the vacuuming ever again!"

Maureen had tried to explain that she had not meant to interfere with the work of the cleaning crew. "I thought I was helping out by not bothering anyone. I had no idea that the cleaning crew would object to my using their equipment—or lifting and moving things without proper training. Boy, was I wrong! I will never forget that lesson. I felt as if I'd done something horrible. I was only trying to help!"

What should Maureen have done differently?

an action is an example of the way coworkers help new workers learn the norms.

Norms tend to reflect those things that have the common interest of the group members. Norms in an office frequently govern work output, the amount of effort workers show, when to arrive and depart from the office, how to dress, and where to eat lunch. Often the norms define what *not* to do rather than what to do.

Roles. Roles are the positions that people play in relation to others. We all know people who act like "big sisters" or "cheerleaders" or "movie stars." We all fill a variety of roles at work and at play.

Roles allow us to fit comfortably into the work environment. To some degree, our roles are based on our job responsibilities, although there are other factors as well. For example, the person who is the manager of your department has a managerial role. It is part of that role to express displeasure when someone is late. If you arrive at 10 a.m. rather than 9 a.m., you can safely predict your manager's behavior. The worker's behavioral role, on the other hand, involves taking directions and contributing a fair share of work. It may involve satisfying customers.

There are other behavioral factors. For example, if one person in a clerical group has been with the company some time while all others are relative newcomers, the veteran assumes the role of adviser, historian, and unofficial orientation giver, even though her job title may not differ from the others.

Roles are also affected by individual personalities and by skills or talents. Within an office group, someone may have the role of peacemaker or social chairperson or problem solver. These unofficial roles (not purely job-related) complicate the newcomer's task of understanding how coworkers interact.

You see why it may take a little time to sort out the relationships around you. In the meantime, be aware that some work habits will jeopardize your relationships with coworkers, no matter what their roles are. See the list below for work habits to avoid.

IRRITATING WORK HABITS

Using coworkers supplies
Working in coworkers' spaces
Bragging, exaggerating
Selling fund-raising products at work
Taking all the credit
Gossiping
Being insensitive to others
Talking loudly while others are working
Dirtying common work or break areas
Taking or making too many personal phone calls

Figure 6-8 Each employee at this meeting has an important role in the group effort. (Courtesy of Young & Rubicam.)

RELATING TO SUBORDINATES

Your relationship with subordinates can be as critical to your success as any other working relationship. It is essential that you develop mutual respect and loyalty. Keep the following guidelines in mind:

◆ Always be courteous, polite, and respectful.

◆ Request rather than command.

◆ Never criticize a subordinate publicly. Always do this in private and only when it is absolutely necessary.

◆ Criticize only work that is poorly done.

◆ Praise a job well done.

◆ Don't surprise subordinates with work at the last minute. If you know that a big job is coming up, let subordinates know so that they can plan ahead.

◆ Don't "pass the buck." If something is not done correctly or is late, the ultimate responsibility is yours.

◆ *Never* ask subordinates to perform personal errands or personal tasks for you.

If you follow these simple guidelines, you will have a loyal, dependable staff, who, in the long run, will help to enhance your professional reputation.

Figure 6-9 A good working relationship with subordinates is important to a manager's success. (Photo by Paul E. Meyers.)

RELATING TO WORKERS IN GROUPS

At his new job, Jim Neww needs to know how to get along with his manager and his coworkers as individuals. He also needs to know how to work well with others as a member of a group—people brought together for particular business reasons. Offices within the company are also groups of people working to achieve the company's business goals. Groups are powerful forces in the professional world, and they strongly affect individual workers.

Effective groups function in predictable ways. They have a well-defined purpose that is clearly known to the entire group in terms of beliefs, expectations, values, and standards. The group has a leader. The members allot sufficient time for sharing; they operate in a comfortable physical arrangement; and all members participate. Members respect each other, believing that every person can make a valuable contribution. Every group has a system of leadership, power, communication, and operation.

Members of a group contribute in positive or negative ways. Obviously, the negative members reduce productivity; positive ones contribute toward reaching the goals of the group. Review Figure 6-10 to understand both the productive and nonproductive roles of members of a group.

ROLES IN GROUPS

PRODUCTIVE ROLES

1. *Leader*: Directs group work.
2. *Recorder*: Keeps a written record of group work.
3. *Worker*: Accepts responsibility for a fair share of the group's responsibility.
4. *Clarifier*: Asks questions that promote understanding.
5. *Summarizer*: Summarizes group discussion.
6. *Encourager*: Responds to contributors in positive way.
7. *Compromiser*: Offers an option for agreement.
8. *Standard keeper*: Upholds standards for the group.

NONPRODUCTIVE ROLES

1. *Monopolizer*: Dominates meeting.
2. *Follower*: Passively agrees with any opinion.
3. *Blocker*: Resists any solution to problems; responds negatively; does not propose solutions.
4. *Egotist*: Seeks personal attention and credit.
5. *Destroyer*: Works to prevent success of others and the group.
6. *Comic*: Refuses to take seriously the task or efforts of others.

Figure 6-10 Every employee has a special role in an office. Which roles would you want to play?

When people work in groups, either as a department or at a specific meeting, group work usually proceeds in this order:

1. Ciarify the task.
2. Investigate all aspects of the task.
3. Analyze available information and obtain additional information that affects the task.
4. Identify possible courses of action.
5. Agree on one course of action.
6. Assign responsibility for the action.

To be an effective group member, whether in everyday departmental life or at a meeting:

◆ Be an active participant.
◆ Use good communication skills, both listening and speaking.
◆ Avoid monopolizing the group.
◆ Stay on task.

◆ Complete your assigned tasks.

◆ Build good relationships within the group.

Leaders of groups use special skills to enable the group to be its most productive. See the following list for the ways that leaders direct group activity.

WAYS LEADERS DIRECT PRODUCTIVE GROUP WORK

1. Prepare for the task. Notify members. Send information prior to the meeting when appropriate.
2. Provide a physical setting conducive to productivity.
3. Welcome participants and seek rapport with each.
4. Clearly outline purposes and tasks.
5. Share responsibility.
6. Delegate responsibility.
7. Accept ideas and other contributions as valuable.
8. Give recognition.
9. Listen to members.
10. Communicate effectively.
11. Move group into action.
12. Provide instruction where needed.
13. Encourage.
14. Summarize, clarify, motivate, praise.
15. Monitor follow-through.

SPECIAL BUSINESS RELATIONSHIPS

There are some other interpersonal situations that you may encounter as part of your job.

RELATING TO CLIENTS OR OTHER OUTSIDERS

Your contact with people from outside the company may be by telephone or in person. In either case, you must know how to handle the situation.

Relating to Outsiders by Phone. You will probably use the telephone when you want to:

◆ Get information quickly

◆ Give feedback

◆ Generate ideas through discussion

Although the telephone, like face-to-face conversation, is a good way to discuss a problem or an issue, you should not expect that a solution or decision will necessarily come from a single telephone conversation. Sometimes correspondence will need to be exchanged before a telephone conversation can produce a solution, commitment, or final decision.

Policies regarding telephone use for personal reasons, long distance charges, and greetings will be set by management. In addition to following those policies, you may find these guidelines helpful when using the phone.

1. Give callers your full attention. This moves the conversation rapidly to the purpose of the call. Avoid lengthy sessions of small talk. Never chew, eat, or smoke while on the phone.

2. Consider the situation before making business calls to a home telephone. Avoid calling someone at home unless the person works at home or prefers the use of the home number. Calling a client or supervisor at home for any reason, except in emergencies, is ordinarily not done.

3. When you need to transfer a caller, explain the reason and give a name, if possible, and a number for the caller in case the caller is disconnected.

4. Update any caller you put on hold about every 30 seconds. For example, you may say, "I am sorry I do not have that information yet. Would you like to continue to hold, or may I return your call as soon as I have the facts you requested?"

5. When you take a message for others in your office, ask for the caller's name, telephone number, company name, and the message. Record the information carefully and add the date and time of the call along with your initials.

6. Respond to angry callers with care. If your job is such that you receive frequent angry callers (customer service or collections, for example), your company may provide specific training to assist you in handling the calls effectively. However, all workers occasionally receive an irate caller. The most important rule for dealing with angry callers is: "Never respond with anger." Professional behavior requires a response without anger, regardless of how abusive the caller may be. One appropriate response may be to suggest that the caller talk to someone at a higher level in your company; transfer the call or give the name, title, and telephone number to the caller. You may ask the caller to repeat slowly the particulars of the complaint so that you can write it down for appropriate action. Tell the caller that you want to have the problem resolved and that you will resolve it or will get help with it.

7. Keep a telephone log for business calls so that you have a record of promises and agreements made on the phone but not confirmed in writing. Trusting your memory for all the particulars of business agreements is risky when you are a busy professional worker. Written records serve not only to refresh your memory but also as reliable evidence of discussions and agreements.

Relating to Outsiders in Person. There may be any number of reasons for you to deal with people from outside the company. Take Jim Neww, for example. His job at Anyfirm requires that he meet frequently with people from other organizations. These are usually people to whom Jim would like to sell Anyfirm's products. Sometimes they are trying to get Jim to purchase their products, or they are people checking on the performance of products previously purchased by Anyfirm.

Jim knows that each of his meetings with his company's clients is important to his success and to the company. His manager often talks to him and his coworkers about the importance of presenting a professional image toward the clients. This professional image can be established by conducting business according to the following guidelines:

1. *Establish the purpose of a meeting.* It may be one of three basic types: to secure information; to give information; or to influence someone's opinion or behavior. For example, Jim's manager may schedule a brief meeting with him to learn his progress with a new account (secure information). Or, Jim's manager may call a meeting to explain new procedures to the workers (give information).

2. *Plan the agenda.* This is a critical activity before a meeting so that people come away from the meeting feeling that their time was well spent. It is important to plan the environment as well as the activity. Have your office or work space ready for visitors. Remember that opinions are being formed from the moment the client walks into your office building. The part of the environment you control must be presentable if you are to give a positive image of your company. Think critically about what you want to accomplish in the meeting. Be familiar with all aspects of the client's activities with your firm. You should review and organize past records and any information you have about the client.

3. *Conduct yourself professionally.* Keep a balance between making the client feel like a guest and being very businesslike. Usually a one-on-one business meeting proceeds like this:

   ◆ Greeting
   ◆ Brief exchange of informal pleasantries
   ◆ Business deliberations
   ◆ Closing

Figure 6-11 Good office communications skills include good phone skills. One of these skills is the ability to give the person at the other end of the line your undivided attention. (Designed and produced by Liberia and Associates; photography by Pete Saloutes.)

4. *End a meeting effectively.* A meeting may be closed with words and with body language. Express thanks for the client's coming. Some discussion about future business prospects or meetings may be appropriate in the closing conversation. In addition, use body language that suggests the meeting is coming to a close. For example, gather up papers, push back your chair, and stand. Shake hands and walk the client to the reception area.

5. *Maintain security of the office environment.* Security is extremely important to many organizations. A company may deal with sensitive information or may wish to guard plans and projects from competitors. Perhaps you have noticed the presence of a security force in most office buildings. It is not uncommon in some organizations for each employee to be issued an identification tag. In security-conscious organizations, it is courteous as well as important to your company's security that you escort clients to and from the reception area.

MEN AND WOMEN WORKING TOGETHER

In business today, male/female equality in the workplace is legislated and applies to everyone. Companies, and all the workers within companies, are required to treat everyone with fairness, courtesy, and consideration regardless of gender. No longer are men and women expected to perform traditional or stereotyped male/female jobs. Rather, each worker is expected to be productive at whatever task is his or her responsibility. Men and women are expected to work both independently and cooperatively as the job demands.

At times it may be difficult for men and women to work in close professional relationships without allowing the relationship to become personal. Professional relationships that become personal cause many problems in the workplace. The good working order of a department depends on businesslike, professional relationships. This kind of professionalism ensures that extra considerations are not given to one person, that confidential or sensitive information is not shared by only a few people in the group, and that everyone in the office has equal access to a shared social and sociable atmosphere. To avoid disrupting the workplace and endangering your career (and sometimes your reputation) think about these tips:

1. Be careful not to spend too much social time—breaks, lunches—with just one person.

2. Do not share personal information—romantic problems, family matters or feelings and emotions—in long conversations with just one person.

3. Do not tease, joke, dress, or behave in a way that invites someone to think that you are seeking a personal rather than a professional relationship.

4. Think before you speak. If you would feel uncomfortable saying what you are thinking in the presence of a third person, or in a group, don't say it. It is probably an inappropriate personal statement or question.

SEXUAL HARASSMENT

Human resources managers report that sexual harassment is a major problem. Surveys show that from 42% to 88% of women workers feel that they have been victims of sexual harassment at some time. Courts have awarded employees claiming sexual harassment judgments ranging from back salary to large amounts of compensating dollars. Harassment is a serious problem, but what does it mean?

Sexual harassment is behavior with sexual overtones that is unwanted by the person to whom it is directed. It can take many forms. At one extreme, harassment may be direct threats. On the other hand, it may

Figure 6-12   Men and women can work together as a successful team.
(Courtesy of Westinghouse Electric Corporation.)

be as simple as a suggestive look or an insensitive joke. A number of years ago, such things as deliberate touching, suggestive looks, and sexual remarks or jokes may have been considered part of the work world, but attitudes have changed. All these actions may now be considered sexual harassment by the law and by men and women who are the victims.

Sexual harassment is evident in two types of behavior; one is *quid pro quo* harassment (something given in order to receive or retain something else), and the other is *hostile work environment harassment. Quid pro quo harassment* is evident in this threat: "If you don't have sex with me, you don't get the promotion." Such behavior threatens the employee with the loss of some job benefit. People who use this kind of threat do so not only because of sexual desire but because of the misuse of power. The greater the difference in power between the two employees, the stronger the threat. Such behavior is illegal in the work environment.

Hostile work environment sexual harassment exists when an employee feels degraded because of unwelcome flirtation, lewd comments, or sexual joking. The unwanted behavior does not have to result in a threatened loss of job to be harassment. Not only can actions of supervisors and managers contribute to a hostile environment, but coworkers and employees may contribute to a hostile environment.

Pictures on warehouse walls, pats on the hips at the water cooler, remarks in the hallway—all contribute to a hostile work environment.

Of course, not every joke amounts to sexual harassment. Courts recognize that antidiscrimination laws are not intended to mandate clean language. When do sexually aggressive words, touching, or display of sexual posters cross the line to harassment? That answer is left for the courts to decide. However, there is a rule of thumb for on-the-job actions. It is: "Decide how you would feel if the action were directed to you." If you find it offensive, then it may be offensive to others. To determine if behavior toward you is inappropriate, ask yourself these questions: Is unwelcome sexual innuendo more than trivial or occasional? Does it color the work environment? Is a pattern of behavior built on sexual comments? If your answer is yes to these questions, then you need to seek help to remove the actions, behavior, and language that creates this unwelcome and illegal environment.

If the harassment comes from coworkers, report the matter to your manager. If it comes from your manager, report the matter to your personnel administrator. It is important that you take this action in confidence and that you not make your charge the subject of conversation with anyone other than the company representative with whom you have chosen to discuss the matter. If the charge cannot be proven or if the company treats it lightly, you will have damaged working relationships and reputations. You must think long and carefully about the advantages and disadvantages of dealing with legal authorities if your charge is dismissed within the company. Self-interest dictates that you balance discomfort and monetary loss against your career opportunities and possible embarrassment.

REVIEW QUESTIONS

1. Name three parts of a work station.
2. Discuss five ways that people can manage their time more effectively.
3. List three tips for beginning a new job that set the stage for good work relationships.
4. Define the term "role" and explain how you may determine what role to play in a new job.
5. Outline the manner in which a meeting with a client may progress.
6. Demonstrate how a worker may effectively end a meeting.
7. Describe three positive group roles.
8. Define sexual harassment in the work place.
9. Recommend an appropriate response to sexual harassment.

1. Role play handling telephone callers to an office when these actions occur:

   a. The caller is angry.

   b. The caller must be placed on hold.

   c. The caller must be transferred.

2. Interview a successful professional about how he or she manages work time to be most productive. Write a two-page report.

3. From periodicals at the school library, gather information on claims of sexual harassment and outcomes of the claims. Report your findings to the class.

4. Refer to Figure 6-10, Roles in Groups. Role play a group meeting in which class members take on the specific roles mentioned. Be sure that each person in the class has an opportunity to perform one of the roles. Then switch roles if there is time.

CHAPTER 7

COMMUNICATION: PERSONAL AND PROFESSIONAL

CHAPTER GOAL:

To guide you in becoming an effective communicator.

CHAPTER OBJECTIVES:

After studying this chapter, you should be able to:

1. Introduce yourself and others.
2. Listen effectively.
3. Converse well in professional situations.
4. Write appropriate letters of praise, thanks, and condolence.
5. Understand how a professional image is created through written communication.
6. Analyze various forms of business communication.
7. Write effective business communication pieces.

Communication is the key to success for professional people. Through communication you reveal yourself to others, you develop relationships with others, and you conduct the business of your profession.

Your appearance, your speech, and your written words are all factors in communication. Understanding what others are saying and being understood by them are equally important in your personal and professional life. Personal communication begins with introductions and includes conversation and letter writing. Skills in these personal activities promote both personal and professional relationships.

PRESENTING YOURSELF

It is always appropriate to introduce yourself to a stranger whom you wish to meet if there is no one present to introduce you. To make a positive impression, follow these steps:

♦ *Look directly at the person to whom you are speaking.* Eye contact is an important way you show strength of character and interest in the other person.

♦ *Give your full name clearly and distinctly.* Be sure to give your surname as well as the first name, and be especially careful to give your last name clearly because it is often the one most difficult to understand and remember when it is first heard.

♦ *Shake hands firmly.* One shake of the hand (rather than several pumps) is sufficient. Firmness in the handshake also suggests strength of character.

♦ *Tell something unique about yourself at an appropriate time.* This will help others remember you. Make it something interesting, not information that sounds like bragging or phoniness. For example, it might fit the conversation to say that you are one of 12 children, or that you have just recovered from a broken leg, or that you are studying to be an aerial photographer. This type of information will not only give you a sharper identity in the listener's mind but also may open up new channels of conversation. However, try to keep the conversation from dwelling only on your activities.

♦ *Speak with pride about the place from which you come.* Often a self-introduction includes telling a person where you are from—your hometown, the city where you last worked, or the school you attended. Regardless of the size or location of your hometown or college, speak of it with pride and with some description of its attributes. You should be able to tell others the approximate size of your hometown, its economic base, and about something of interest in the area.

For example, Ann Johns replied to a question about where she is from in this manner: "My home is in Miller Grove, a small rural community in Hopkins County. We are, however, the largest milk-producing area in the state."

Similarly, you will want to be able to tell others the size and major focus of the college you attended. For example, "I attend Georgetown

School of Business in Capitol City. It is a large, private business school with a special program for part-time students. The school is proud of its placement record for graduates."

INTRODUCING OTHERS

Everyone needs to know how to introduce people to each other (see Figure 7-1). It is a frequently used skill in business. Although there are guidelines that will help you do it with ease, the only serious error you may make with regard to introductions is to make no introduction when one is needed. An introduction is always needed when two people in your presence know you but do not know each other. Here are helpful guidelines for making introductions:

◆ *When you want to give honor or respect to one person more than to the other, say the name of the person you wish to honor first.* You may wish to show such deference to distinguished people, to your boss, or to the elderly. (In social situations only, you may wish to show deference to women.) For example, you may say, "President Wang, I would like you to meet George Brown." Or similarly, "Grandmother Rodriguez, this is my roommate, Anna Lee." It is also polite to show deference to outsiders over family. For example, you might say, "Mr. Johnson, I would like you to meet my parents, Mr. and Mrs. Polinkas."

◆ *Use the name that you expect each person to use.* For example, if you introduce your mother to a friend you may say, "This is my mother, Mrs. Jones," indicating that the friend should refer to her formally. On the other hand, if you introduce her to a person her own age you might say, "This is my mother, Helen Jones."

◆ *Use of titles is important* when speaking with business superiors, distinguished people, and elderly people. Use a title in such cases unless the individual specifically asks that you use first names. (When asked to use first names, do so.)

When uncertain about which title is appropriate for an individual, you may safely use "Mr." for any man and "Ms." for any woman. On the other hand, when you do know a person's title, use the highest one. For example, you would always use "Dr." rather than "Mr.," "Bishop" rather than "Father," and so on.

Never give yourself a title in conversation. That is, a knowledgeable person would not say in a telephone call, "This is Mr. Anderson," but rather, "This is Joseph Anderson." Exceptions to this guideline occur when you are addressing young students, small children, or workers who are expected to use a title when speaking to you.

Figure 7-1 Making proper and graceful introductions is an important and pleasant professional skill. (*Photo by Robert J. Capece/Mark-meyer Press Photo*)

◆ *If possible, add a comment about common interests the two may have.* This will give them some topic for initial conversation. If you wonder what they have in common, remember that they both know you!

Business people always shake hands when introduced. Appropriate responses to an introduction are "How do you do," "Hello," "I am so pleased to meet you," and similar phrases of salutation.

CONVERSATION

Talking to others with ease, graciousness, and effectiveness is an important skill for successful people. Talking comfortably seems to be natural for some people, but is more difficult for others. Skills for effective communication can be developed with conscientious practice. Check your own conversation habits for effectiveness, for suitable topics, and for improper or annoying mannerisms. Even people who feel they have no conversational weaknesses may be wise to review their speech habits to check for practices that need improvement.

Effective conversation has two parts: listening and talking. Both are essential for the good conversationalist. Being able to listen effectively is important because listening is a major way to gain information, to show respect, and to give support to others. Conversely, when you talk with others you share information (often about yourself), honor others, and gain support from them.

GUIDELINES FOR LISTENERS

Some people are not good listeners. Either they talk too much or they are thinking about other things while someone is talking to them. Here are some tips for improving your listening skills.

◆ *Sit or stand near the other person* (but not too near; we all like to have a "safe" space around us). Adopt a facial expression and posture that says you are interested in what you are hearing. For example, to make a child feel important, an adult may kneel near the child so that their faces are on the same level. Older people feel honored when young people sit beside them for conversation. With both the elderly and the very young, extra patience is often required of the listener. You may need to repeat words to an elderly person who cannot hear well, or you may need to rephrase your message for a child who does not seem to understand some language that you used the first time.

People perceive that you are listening to them by your body language and by your verbal responses. Body language includes facial expressions, posture, and eye contact.

◆ *Look at the speaker.* Visualize a secretary and a clerk talking together. Imagine that the secretary asks a question and as the clerk answers, the secretary checks the time and glances out the window. How do you think the clerk would feel? The answer is obvious, of course, because the body language of the secretary communicates to the clerk that the secretary is not interested in what the clerk is saying. On the other hand, if the secretary had looked at the clerk and avoided distracting activities, the conversation could have progressed with the clerk feeling that the secretary had genuine interest.

◆ *Make appropriate responses when the talker pauses.* When you respond with a comment on the same subject, the listener believes you are interested. For example, if a person has been discussing software available for a new computer, a careful conversationalist might answer with a statement such as, "It's good to know about that software; I'd like to review it." The poor conversationalist might respond with another topic entirely unrelated to computer software. A comment like "Oh, the budget hearing is this afternoon—I must review my notes immediately," leads the talker to believe that the other person has no interest in the software just mentioned.

◆ *Avoid interrupting.* People are irritated when they are interrupted as they talk. People who interrupt are considered discourteous and uninformed in the art of conversation.

FOCUS ON: STEREOTYPING AND COMMUNICATION

When we stereotype people, we put a label on them. That is, we decide what kind of people they are before we get a chance to find out. Such judgments about people may be based on the way they look, their membership in an organization, their level of schooling, their economic status, and so on. Having labeled them with others (as a bunch of losers, radicals, or troublemakers), we are unable to see their individual qualities that set them apart.

A journalist once stereotyped a group with the following words: "Politicians are like a bunch of bananas—they stick together, they are yellow, and there is not a straight one among them." Those words are clever and funny, but unjust. Journalists are not the only ones who fall into the trap of communicating with stereotyped images. Try the following exercise in basing conclusions on fact:

Five volumes of Mark Twain's writings are on a shelf. The pages of each volume are exactly 3 inches thick. The covers are exactly one-half inch thick. A bookworm started eating at page 1 of volume 1 and ate through the last page of volume 5. What is the distance the worm covered?

Your instructor will give you the correct answer and the explanation. If you did not answer the problem correctly, you are not alone. Only 10% of the people who try answer correctly. By the way, do you see how stereotyping affected your answer?

◆ *Never correct the speaker's grammar.* Most people are embarrassed when they are corrected.

◆ *Avoid finishing stories and completing sentences for others.* Speakers are frustrated when others complete their sentences, and they are irritated when someone takes away the ending of their stories.

◆ *Remember first names and use them in the conversation.* When you hear a person's name for the first time, associate the name with a catchy phrase or someone else you know with a similar name. This will help you to remember. Another helpful technique for remembering information is writing it on note paper as soon as possible. The careful business person always has a pencil and paper handy.

An exchange of business cards often takes place during a business introduction, helping you to remember the new acquaintance. Most

Figure 7-2 One of the signs of a good listener is to look directly at the person who is talking to you. (Photo by Paul E. Meyers.)

companies issue standard business cards to staff members who have contact with the public or clients. You may exchange cards as part of the initial small talk or offer yours as you leave a person. (You may also use your card as a quick and informal device for messages. Attach the card when you write a letter or leave a written message in someone's office.)

SPEAKING WELL

Participation is essential to conversation. Most people can speak with ease to family and friends, but successful business people must be able to talk with everyone—clients, coworkers, and management—even the unfriendly and the uninterested. Occasionally you will be asked to talk with angry people as well. You will find that you can talk with anyone about anything if you have sources of information, tact, a pleasing voice, and an adequate vocabulary.

Sources of Information. You can always have topics for conversation if you read, study, and listen. Successful people work to obtain information that will make them current in their chosen careers and interesting to talk to. They read and listen for information about current events in the world.

Local and city newspapers, magazines, and radio and television news programs provide useful information for all types of conversation. Busy people recommend these techniques for being prepared to make conversation that is interesting and timely:

- *Read the front page of the daily newspaper each day.* Sometimes you may only skim the headlines, but at least you will know the major issues in the news.
- *Read at least one editorial daily.* Such reading helps you understand various opinions on current issues.
- *Keep the car radio tuned to a station that gives news every hour.* This practice will keep you updated on the latest events in your community.
- *Watch the national news on television once each day.* Radio and television keep people up to date on local and world events. Remember that you have a choice as a listener. As you shave or apply makeup each morning, you can listen to the top ten hits or you can choose to listen to 15 minutes of local news. Choose wisely with your career in mind.

You may also wish to keep a book or magazine with you in your briefcase or car for reading when you must spend time waiting. Well-informed people use time spent in airports, dentist offices, and other waiting areas to read for information and for pleasure.

Sometimes people are uncertain about what topics to mention to strangers or to people considerably older than they are. Some topics are always safe ones for general conversation. Suggested topics are listed below. Included are examples of ways to introduce each of the topics.

Topics that are best avoided in normal conversation are those related to finances, personal misfortune, or personal characteristics that might be unpleasant or embarrassing to one of you. See the list below for topics to avoid.

Topics to Avoid
The cost of purchases
A person's romantic life
A person's weight or age
Salaries
Grades
Gossip
Your health

Tact. Speaking tactfully means that you speak in ways that avoid being offensive. Tone of voice is a component of tact as are the words you use. A tactful person might respond (with a pleasant voice) to something she thinks is untrue with this statement, "I'm sorry to hear that; I wonder if it could be a mistake," whereas a person who speaks without regard for tact, might say (in a loud, harsh voice), "That's a big lie!"

Quality of Voice. The quality of your voice is more important than you may realize. Think of people you know who speak in a high, nasal,

SUGGESTED TOPICS FOR CONVERSATION

Occupations: "Ms. Brown, what kind of training is required for people in your field?"

Leisure: "Mr. Hernandez, how do you think the college football team will do this year?"

Local Issues: "Tell me, what do you think about curbside recycling?"

National Events/Trends: "I understand that network television viewership is declining. What do you think might be the cause?"

Hometowns: "Mr. Francis, tell me about your hometown."

Local History/Activities: "Mrs. Murdock, when was the local fort established?" "Have you been to the new art museum?"

Any Question: (Notice how any *question* will allow you to begin a conversation.)

or whining voice. You probably find conversation with them somewhat unpleasant. It is often difficult to concentrate on *what* such people are saying because the unpleasantness of the voice is so distracting. To evaluate your own voice, make a tape recording and listen for qualities that you like and qualities that you wish to improve. Ask for input from someone from whom you can accept criticism.

Professional people cultivate a pleasant voice, trying to adjust volume so that they speak neither too loudly nor too softly. They avoid colloquial phrases and try to overcome heavy regional accents. Often people have to work hard at changing their voice and speech patterns. A speech course or visit to a speech therapist may help you reach goals for your own voice and speaking habits.

Grammar. You will benefit from following the recommended practice of using standard vocabulary. Some common grammatical errors are:

Wrong	Right
Where is it *at*?	Where is it?
He *don't* care.	He doesn't care.
Me and Kay went to the mall.	Kay and I went to the mall.
She gave it *to Kay and I*.	She gave it to Kay and me.
I *seen* the show.	I saw the show.
She commutes *back and forth*.	She commutes.
He *ain't* here.	He isn't here.
Yeah!	Yes.

Many people find that to correct habits of poor grammar they must force themselves to repeat each of their statements in which an error was made. For example, when they hear themselves say, "Where is it at?" they immediately say something like, "Oh, I mean where is it located."

Professional people also avoid excessive slang and the latest buzz words. Overuse of slang suggests that the speaker has a limited vocabulary. Also, speakers who use words that are not generally familiar to others are not effective communicators.

Consider how confusing this conversation could be to a person not familiar with the speaker's company vocabulary. "Please bring the new Wordstar manual ASAP. The first one was accidentally put in file 13, and we need to use if for DIP." Translated to more understandable language, the conversation would sound like this: "Please bring the new software manual to me as soon as possible. The first one was accidentally put in the wastebasket, and we need to use it for the Developmental Instructional Program project."

RESPONDING SKILLFULLY

Naturally, during the course of conversation, people will make statements to which you must respond. Some statements may make you feel awkward or uncomfortable, which shows in your response. Statements that may make you uncomfortable are compliments, angry statements, false statements, and harmful gossip.

Compliments. When a person gives you a compliment, respond with genuine pleasure. A simple "Thank you" is sufficient; however, you may want to say more. If you do, a statement such as, "I am so pleased you think so!" or "How good of you to notice," or "Thank you for telling me," are good choices.

Avoid negative responses to compliments. Comments that put down what was complimented exhibit poor manners toward the person who made the compliment. Negative responses such as, "It really was not my best effort," or "This old thing!" reflect insecurity and lack of con-

Figure 7-3   Knowing how to accept a compliment graciously is a good social and professional skill to have. (Courtesy of Hilton International—Caribe Hilton.)

fidence on the part of the person being complimented. They are also a put-down to the person who gave the compliment.

Another common response to a compliment relates to the cost of the item. For example, a person may respond to a comment about the beauty of a shirt by saying "Oh, I got it on sale." Such comments leave the complimenter with nothing positive to say, and the conversation comes to an awkward pause.

Anger. Respond to people who are angry with acceptance of their feelings. Usually people who are angry simply need to be heard. Therefore, when a person makes an angry outburst, respond with a comment such as, "I am sorry that you are upset," or "I understand that you feel strongly about this matter." Then offer to help if you can, or suggest something that might be helpful. You do not, however, have to agree with the angry statements, and you certainly do not have to express strong emotion yourself.

Falsehoods. Responses to false statements should be made calmly, with tact and with facts. For example, if a person says, "The Brown Company closed last week," and you know for a fact that it did not, you might respond with, "That word is widespread, but I was pleased to read in last night's paper that the closing did not occur as expected."

Gossip. Being able to respond appropriately to gossip is vital for the professional person. Experienced business people often simply change the subject or leave the room when gossip begins. Others seek to diffuse it with comments such as, "I am sorry to hear that, but maybe we need more information to really understand the situation." Another response might be, "I am sorry to hear that he is having trouble; he has been a valuable employee." Choose a response that relieves you of the appearance of participating in a gossip session.

ADDITIONAL GUIDELINES FOR CONVERSATION

The careful conversationalist uses several other rules of etiquette to improve the quality of his or her communication. You will probably find that you already follow may of them in your own conversations.

- Avoid being argumentative. Many people enjoy discussing both politics and religion, and these are certainly important topics for conversation. However, because many people have very strong opinions on both subjects, tact may be needed to avoid arguments as they are discussed.
- Avoid overemphasizing your own interests, your family, and your activities. Others are seldom as interested in your activities as you are. Share them, but leave time for others to share as well.
- Avoid telling dirty jokes. Remember, there is always someone in the crowd who finds them offensive.
- Avoid making commands or responding to a serious remark with flippancy.
- Discuss pleasant topics. Avoid those that relate to personal misfortune, your health, finances, or gossip.
- Don't try to top the last story told.
- Don't pry. When you feel a need to question friends or colleagues about a matter, choose your words carefully to suggest that you are concerned about their well-being, not just being nosy.
- Keep group conversation moving. Speak up to fill a conversational void. Include shy people by directing a question to them.
- Be cheerful and positive. If you are positive, the response you get from others will most likely be positive as well.
- Be generous with compliments. A person with a strong self-concept is comfortable and happy to compliment others. However, do not overdo compliments or people will think you are insincere.
- Avoid "talking down" to people, that is, using language that suggests they are inferior intellectually. Sometimes we are tempted to talk down to the very old, the very young, or people who are new in a position.

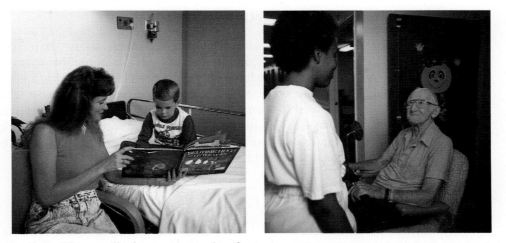

Figure 7-4 Never talk down to people of any age. (From Hegner and Caldwell, *Nursing Assistant*, 6th edition, Delmar Publishers Inc.)

◆ Look around the group when you are speaking so that you do not seem to be talking to only one person in the group. Some people appear to be talking only to their boss or to a special friend as they speak to a group that includes those people.

◆ Be specific. Remember that people hear what you say from their own perspective. The story of the three blind men who describe the elephant illustrates the fact that everyone receives information based on their own experiences. (The first blind man touched only the elephant's trunk and described an elephant as long and rough like a huge rope. The second touched only the side and said an elephant is like a huge leather wall. The third blind man felt only a leg and said an elephant is like a tree trunk.) Saying clearly what you mean improves communication.

PERSONAL LETTER WRITING

Some written business communications are more personal than businesslike in nature. Letters that fit into this category include letters of praise, letters of condolence, and letters of thanks. Writing these skillfully is important because of the goodwill they create.

These types of letters must carry a tone of sincerity. As with any professional communication, you will want to check it for clarity, neatness, and errors. Letters of praise and letters of thanks may be handwritten if you choose to make them more personal. Letters of condolence should always be handwritten.

LETTERS OF PRAISE AND CONGRATULATIONS

Written compliments are often appreciated even more than spoken ones, because the receiver knows that the writer took the extra time to put it on paper—and perhaps shared it with others (as in a copy to the manager). Plan to write a note of congratulations or praise when a colleague has received a promotion, made a spectacular presentation in a committee, or has done something noteworthy at work. Such letters may be brief, but they must be sincere. See an example of a letter of praise and congratulations in Figure 7-5.

LETTERS OF CONDOLENCE

Letters of condolence are sent when someone has died who is an important person in the life of one of your colleagues. Sending a letter of condolence is a courteous gesture. Many people do not write sympathy letters because they do not know what to say in the face of death. The letter can be very short. A good sympathy letter has three parts:

◆ A statement that you are sorry to learn about the death
◆ A compliment for the person who died
◆ An offer to help if you are needed

Sympathy letters are greatly appreciated by friends who have had a death in the family. Sending such letters shows that you take seriously the task of supporting your colleagues at work and beyond work hours.

LETTERS OF THANKS

Thank you letters or notes are in order when a person has done something helpful for you in your professional life or when you have received a gift. The successful professional sends thank you letters often. Here are some of the many times that you may want to send one:

◆ For a Christmas gift from your boss
◆ For a letter of recommendation from a former employer
◆ For help with a project from a colleague
◆ To thank employees for a job well done

A well-written thank you note is composed so that what you are expressing thanks for is named in the first sentence. Be specific in naming gifts or actions. For example, say, "Thank you for the fine letter of recommendation that you sent to the Miller Construction Company on my behalf," not "Thank you for helping me get a position with the Miller Construction Company."

November 3, 199–

Dear Earl,

Your presentation at yesterday's committee meeting was outstanding. The statistical report you put together was especially impressive. I am pleased to be your colleague.

Sincerely,

Mary Francis

Mary Francis

November 3, 199–

Dear Anna,

I am so sorry to hear of the death of your mother. Although I never met her, I know that she must have been very special to have such a gracious and successful daughter. Do call on me if I can help in any way during this difficult time.

Sincerely,

Augustine Montgomery

Augustine Montgomery

November 3, 199–

Dear Mr. Rodriguez,

Thank you for sending the letter of recommendation to the Snelling Company. As a result of the help that you and others gave me, I was chosen as Assistant to the Personnel Director. I will be working hard to justify your faith in my abilities.
Please call on me if I may be of help to you at any time.

Sincerely,

Sam Sanchez

Sam Sanchez

Figure 7-5 Use these letters as models when you write a letter of congratulations, condolence, or thanks.

BUSINESS WRITING

In addition to personal communication, written business communications are an important component of the professional person's skills. Writing is as important in your professional life as your dress, conversation, and actions. In fact, writing may be more important, because once something is written, it has a permanence that actions do not have. Once your name is on paper, the words become *yours*, even if someone else drafted them for you. If the writing is confused or full of mistakes, the reader forms a negative opinion of you and, of course, of your company.

The written word is a permanent record, and you have no way of knowing what will be done with your letter or memo or how long a life it will have. You do not even know how many people will read your correspondence. Although you may write your manager a short status report about your work, you will probably never know what your manager does with it. Will he or she simply read it and throw it away? Will the memo be placed in a file for review next month? Or, will your manager read it and ask a higher level executive to read it?

PROFESSIONAL IMAGE IN WRITING

It is difficult to specify how your professional image is reflected in your writing. It is like the story of an old man who conducted a lifelong search for a secret gold mine. Someone asked him what the gold mine would look like, and he replied, "I don't know, but when I see it, I'll recognize it." A professional image in writing is like the gold mine; it is difficult to describe, but easy to recognize. Figure 7-6 is an example of a letter that projects a professional image.

This letter was important for the corporation. It was sent to all the bank's customers. In addition, the corporation purchased full-page space in major newspapers to print this letter. You see why the letter has to be a good one. You should feel the same need as the bank when you are writing business letters and memos. Your correspondence needs to be impressive.

Examine the letter in Figure 7-6. What are its characteristics? First, the letter looks good. It is clean and neat in appearance. For example, it has no strikeovers. The format is attractive to the eye, inviting to the reader. Appearance is important because readers never get to the message unless they are attracted by the visual appearance of the communication.

Now, reread the letter and notice how easy it is to read. You have no difficulty in understanding the purpose of the letter. You don't have to reread or search for the purpose.

Correcting misleading stories is the purpose of the first paragraph. The three supporting ideas—merger rumors, deposit safety, and deposit activity—are developed in a logical order. Finally, the last three

UNIVERSITY STATE BANK

900 West Main
Dallas, Texas 93939

March 1, 199X

Frank Anderson
999 Windsor Drive
Dallas, Texas 55555

Dear Mr. Anderson:

The purpose of this letter is to correct the ideas presented during the past several days by articles and news stories about our bank. Several of these news stories have presented misleading or incorrect information. Let me explain.

I want to respond to three specific pieces of information in the news stories.

1. MERGER RUMORS:
Our bank has *no* plans to merge with another institution.

2. DEPOSIT SAFETY:
Your deposits are backed by more than $4 billion of total capital in the state's largest financial institution. We continue to have a weil-diversified funding base, with about 80% of the company's assets funded through core deposits, regional sources, and other non-interest bearing funds. These funds are gathered through the work of 189 banking centers in our state. And as you know, deposits are insured up to $100,000 by the FDIC.

3. DEPOSIT ACTIVITY:
Several stories presented misleading information about our deposit activity. Through the first two months of this year, the bank's average total deposits have only declined by approximately $3^1/2$% for the year. More than half of the reduction was an expected decline in foreign deposits with the remainder due primarily to normal seasonal factors.

These are not the best of times for any of us in our state. But our bank is totally committed to serving your needs and contributing to your success. We are here for the long term. And as we all know, tough times bring out the best in each of us.

Mr. Anderson, one additional thought needs to be communicated to you. If you have any concerns or questions that we have not covered in this letter, I want you to call or, better yet, come by for a visit with your bank officer.

Thank you for your trust,

Jim Franklin

Jim Franklin

Figure 7-6 This is an example of how a professional letter looks and reads.

paragraphs give you additional information. As a customer, you would feel confident in the bank after reading this letter. You have been invited to ask questions or to come and visit the bank. You have been asked to think of the staff at the bank as friends, and you have been thanked for your support.

Each of us would be proud to sign our name to a letter as well written as this one. Any company would be pleased to have this letter appear on its letterhead. (A letterhead is the company name printed at the top of the stationery.)

In summary, these two ideas are important to professional correspondence:

1. An image of professionalism that is reflected when the piece of writing simply looks good—is clean, neat, attractive.

2. An image of professionalism that is reflected when the message is communicated clearly and fully in a way that makes readers feel they have received the company's best efforts.

STEPS IN THE WRITING PROCESS

Most writers go through the same steps each time they write until, with experience, they gain confidence to write effectively. Here are the steps:

1. Define the problem.
2. Determine the audience.
3. Gather the facts.
4. Plan the layout or format.
5. Write the draft.
6. Revise, edit, and proofread.

Each time you write, you may place less or more emphasis on one or another of these steps, depending on your knowledge, skill, experience, and the importance of the writing task. For example, an important letter, like a letter of job application, may demand that you follow each step carefully. Other writing projects, like a letter to a friend, will only require a moment's thought about each step.

Define the Problem. To define the problem, it is necessary to answer the question, "What is my purpose in writing this letter?" Establishing a clear purpose is always a critical part of effective writing. To be sure that you have established a clear purpose, ask yourself, "What do I, as the writer, want the reader to do after receiving this correspondence?" For example, as a writer, do you want to:

◆ Provide or request information?
◆ Alter feelings or opinions?
◆ Initiate a course of action?

Determine the Audience. With whom are you communicating? Will the reader share your communication with others? What is the reader's position? When you write something for your manager to read, try to be aware of his or her position and needs. Keep the tone of your writing respectful. If it sounds flip or demanding when you read it aloud, try again. Focus on concrete results and solutions to problems. When you share information with or make requests of coworkers, be direct, understanding, and enthusiastic. Here is an example of a wrong tone in a communication to coworkers: "The conference will be at 2:00 p.m.; be there!" A more appropriately worded communication is: "The conference is scheduled for 2:00 p.m. Please make every effort to attend this important meeting."

How much does the audience know about the topic? Ideally your message contains only information your audience needs and does not have. Use words the reader knows. For example, does your reader know that "BCIS" stands for "Business Computer and Information System" or do you need to spell out the words? On the other hand, do not repeat facts that your reader already knows unless you repeat for emphasis.

Gather the Facts. Be sure to have accurate and specific facts, figures, and information before writing a memo. Read the two memos in Figure 7-7 (a) and (b), noticing how Figure 7-7 (b) presents the facts more clearly and how the presentation made it easy to find the necessary information.

NTSU
DEPARTMENT OF MANAGEMENT
MEMORANDUM

TO: Al Jones, Superintendent
         for Building A

FROM: Jackie Evens, Building
         Services

DATE: December 17, 199–

SUBJECT: Monitors for the Heating System Survey

Please appoint someone from your department to monitor the effectiveness of the heating system between now and January 5. This survey will take place between January 15 and the end of the month.

Please call me (extension 3147) if you or your monitor have any questions about the survey.

Figure 7-7   (a) This memo is an illustration of one that does not have all the necessary information.

```
                    NTSU
          DEPARTMENT OF MANAGEMENT
                 MEMORANDUM

TO: Al Jones, Superintendent        FROM: Jimmy Hinds, Building
    for Building A                         Services
                                    DATE: December 17, 199–

SUBJECT: Monitors for the Heating System Survey

Al, please appoint someone from your department to monitor the
effectiveness of the heating system between now and January 5. During
the period of January 15–31, Burley and Coward Inc. will be reviewing and
balancing the system in Building A.

The person you appoint to monitor the system will have the following
duties:

1. To survey employees at least three times a day to determine their
satisfaction with room temperatures.

2. To contact Burley and Coward with questions and completed surveys.
(TELEPHONE NUMBER 555–1111)

3. To take an hourly log of temperatures from devices provided by Burley
and Coward. NOTE: Burley and Coward will provide instructions at a
meeting with you and your monitor on December 28 in your department.

Please call me (extension 3147) if you or your monitor have any questions
about the survey.
```

(b)

Figure 7-7 (b) This memo has all the necessary information.

Plan the Layout or Format. The physical appearance of your written communications is important. To decide how to set up your communication, you need to determine whether your audience is inside or outside the company. This knowledge often dictates what stationery you should use.

If your audience is outside the company, a business letterhead, as in Figure 7-6 would be appropriate. On the other hand, if the audience is within the company, you would probably use a memo form, as in Figure 7-7.

Your choice of stationery is usually limited to the stationery supplied by the company. This most often includes letterheads and memo forms. If you do not have a support staff to handle your correspondence, check previous correspondence in the department to see how letters and memos are formatted. You may also refer to a secretarial reference manual if one is available.

Write the Draft. Effective writing often takes more than one attempt or draft. A *draft* is the version of what you have written before you edit, proofread, and finalize your work.

Directness in writing is valued. Place your main ideas first so that the reader sees them quickly and easily. Arrange your message in a pattern similar to this one:

◆ The main idea or primary purpose first. For example, "We have not yet received your check in payment for our services."

◆ Add additional explanations, details, or instructions. For example, "We understand that sometimes other obligations may prevent prompt payment."

◆ Add a goodwill statement. For example, "We appreciate your confidence in our services."

If you are typing or using word processing, prepare the draft double-spaced, so that you will have room to make corrections.

Revise, Edit, and Proofread. After you have prepared a first draft, reread it, looking for ways to improve it. Search for mistakes, and decide whether changes in the wording or in the order of sentences and paragraphs are needed.

FIVE CHARACTERISTICS OF EFFECTIVE WRITING

Effective writing has certain characteristics. Make a habit of including them in your writing practices.

The Writing is Concise. For writing to be concise it must be direct and uncluttered. Unnecessary words and phrases should be avoided. Reread the letter from the bank (see Figure 7-6). Notice how it begins with a direct statement. *Avoid* wordy opening statements in a letter or memo; reference phrases may follow in a subsequent sentence.

◆ "This is in reference to your letter of . . . "

◆ "This letter confirms our conversation of . . . "

◆ "Reference is made to the questions asked . . . "

◆ "As per your letter of . . . "

◆ "This letter will confirm our telephone conversation of November 1 with reference to the installation of a gas transfer line that is supposed to . . . "

Read the revision below and notice how the first sentence moves directly to the main idea. "Please install a gas transfer line from the Denton plant to the plant at Southridge. This letter confirms our telephone conversation of November 1."

Conciseness also applies to sentence structure. The construction of this sentence makes it too wordy. "It is requested that each supervisor review . . . " A better sentence would be, "Each supervisor should review . . . "

The Writing is Clear. If your writing is clear, you should be able to answer "yes" to these questions:

◆ Have you used words the reader will understand?

◆ Do your sentences state precise ideas?

◆ Are your paragraphs organized to help the reader understand the problem?

Words are building blocks in writing. To write clearly, you should use only those words whose meanings you understand. You should also feel confident that the reader will understand them as well.

It is important that ideas are clearly presented. For example, when a writer says, "Please contact us . . . " does he or she mean the individual, the company, or someone else?

The connotation, or hidden meaning, associated with words also affects clarity. Think about what happens when words are not clear or when they mean something different to the reader from what was intended by the writer. For example, an airline should not announce a "crash program for lowering ticket costs." Crash is a poor choice because of the different meaning associated with it. A better statement would be: "Limp Wing Airlines will implement immediately a program to lower ticket costs."

Many words have multiple meanings. Always be as specific as possible to avoid lack of clarity and misunderstanding. Examine the examples in the following list:

USE SPECIFIC LANGUAGE

AVOID	USE
At the last meeting . . .	At the February 1 meeting . . .
He makes good money.	He makes $20 per hour.
There is low markup.	There is a 20% markup.
I can try to send something this week.	I will send you three chapters this week.
When the audit is complete, we'll let you know.	When I have completed the audit, I will send you the results.

The Writing is Correct. As you revise your writing, ask yourself these questions:

◈ Is the information accurate?

◈ Have all spelling and grammatical errors been corrected?

Accuracy is critical for the business communicator. Business letters and memos carry information used by managers to make business decisions. Your own manager is likely to make decisions based on information you provide. Be sure you provide accurate information, checked and double-checked. For example, if a coworker gave you a schedule for a meeting that is to take place next week, check with someone to be sure there has not been a change.

Eliminate spelling and grammatical errors through careful proofreading. Many software packages scan for spelling errors, grammar, punctuation, and style problems. Although these packages cannot guarantee perfection, they can help identify problems. Keep a reference manual on hand to look up questions about rules of grammar, punctuation, and spelling.

The Writing is Conversational. The tone of your written communications should sound like your conversation. It may help you to visualize the person to whom you are writing. To check conversational tone, read your first draft aloud. If it sounds normal to you, it probably has the correct tone.

Use active voice sentences. An example of active voice is found in this statement: "Our company produces more fine office furniture than any company in the country." Conversely, the statement in passive voice is: "More fine furniture is produced by our company than by any other in the country." Use active verbs to provide action in a sentence. Passive verbs lend distance and formality to communications.

The Writing is Complete. Have you made all the essential points? Judge the completeness of your writing by asking yourself these questions:

◈ Have I given the reader all the information needed to accomplish the purpose of this communication?

◈ Can I provide an extra help for the reader by adding a suggestion or an additional piece of information?

◈ Is this communication ready to be placed on my company's letterhead?

REVIEW QUESTIONS

1. Name the most serious error made regarding introductions.
2. Explain how to show deference to a business superior as you introduce him or her to someone.

3. Describe how one "communicates" while listening.

4. How may you improve your ability to remember names and other new information?

5. List three sources of general information that are easy to obtain and are available daily.

6. Suggest five topics that would be useful in conversation.

7. Name two features of a letter that produce a good first impression.

8. List the steps for writing an effective business letter.

9. Give five characteristics of effective writing.

10. Suggest two questions you may ask to determine if your writing is clear.

11. Why should a writer read the first draft of a letter aloud?

12. Cite examples of active versus passive voice.

ACTIVITIES

1. Draft a memo to your coworkers Marsha Dunn and Brad Lutz asking for their impressions of new office procedures.

2. Write a brief request to your manager for an additional software package for your computer.

3. Role play introducing your manager to a client.

4. Role play introducing yourself to a classmate at a reception for students, a friend of a friend, and a student counselor.

5. Role play appropriate responses to an angry client.

6. After listening to radio or television news or reading a daily paper, list five timely topics that would be good conversation openers. Role play using them with classmates.

7. Discuss in small groups or as a class how to cope with these situations:

   ◆ Someone in your group is telling dirty jokes. You are not offended but you can see that others in the group are offended.

   ◆ A friend whom you like very much has the habit of talking down to people. You feel it may hinder his career advancement.

   ◆ You have taken a couple of personal days off work to have medical tests. The office gossip comes to you right away and asks what your problem is.

CHAPTER 8

AWAY FROM THE OFFICE: REPRESENTING THE COMPANY

CHAPTER GOAL:

To provide knowledge needed to create a positive professional image away from the office.

CHAPTER OBJECTIVES:

After studying this chapter, you should be able to:

1. Use strategies for traveling with ease.
2. Create a positive image when eating in restaurants.
3. Create a positive image in other public places.
4. Describe the ways that workers can represent their professional organization effectively.

When you travel, eat out, or participate in public events as part of your work, you always want to project a professional image. Certain guidelines for travel can make the experiences both personally and professionally rewarding. Certain table manners add to your positive image as a professional person. In addition to being concerned about your behavior when you travel for your company and when you eat out, you may be concerned with your total public image as you represent your company outside the office.

TRAVEL

Traveling as a representative of your company may involve activities as simple as hand-delivering papers from your office to an outsider or as complex as attending a conference in another city for several days. You may have opportunities to attend training sessions or you may be asked to represent your company in a promotional or fact-finding role. Whatever the reason, you can travel with ease if you develop certain skills.

Travel is less frustrating and more satisfying if it is planned carefully. To plan well, use the services of a travel agency and learn all you can about your destination before the trip begins. The services of a travel agency are free of charge to the traveler (agencies are paid by the carriers they patronize). Often businesses choose one travel agency to handle all of their arrangements. Some businesses have their own travel departments, which operate the same way as travel agents. A travel agency will obtain the most favorable rates for travel and hotel accommodations according to the schedule that you desire. The agent can provide information about travel opportunities and about points of interest in cities you will visit.

Gathering information about a location you plan to visit will aid you in making the most of the free time you have during your stay. In addition to the resources of travel agencies, you can learn about specific locations from the encyclopedia and from travel guides available in bookstores. Talking with people who have previously visited an area may also be helpful.

TRAVEL DOCUMENTS

When you travel to Canada or Mexico, you will need an official copy of your birth certificate. Some travelers are able to substitute a voter registration receipt or an affidavit of citizenship for the birth certificate; however, that substitution may not always be accepted.

You will need a passport to travel overseas, and 2 to 3 weeks may be required to obtain one. First, obtain an application from the district clerk in your county, who can also tell you the location of the nearest passport office (they are found in all major cities). Two passport pictures and a birth certificate (an original, not a photocopy) are needed to obtain a passport. The photos may be taken at the passport office.

Visas are documents of permission to travel to countries with restricted entry. Visas may be obtained from the consulate or embassy of the country that you wish to visit. A passport is required to obtain a visa. Again, a travel agent should be able to tell you the proper procedure for getting travel documents.

Figure 8-1 Airline personnel can also help you make travel plans. (Courtesy of American Airlines.)

TRANSPORTATION

Business travel can involve any kind of transportation. For some trips you may need more than one—a plane and a car, for example.

Traveling by Car. When you are traveling alone by auto, make sure that your car has been thoroughly serviced before you begin the trip. Also be sure to take along highway maps and maps of cities you will be visiting. It is important to keep an accurate record of mileage to file for reimbursements of travel costs when you return to the home office.

When a group of workers travel by car or van, it is the prerogative of the superior to decide whose vehicle is to be taken and who is to drive. Although a company car is often used, if the superior chooses to use a personal car, that is the superior's choice to make. On the other hand, if you as an employee wish to offer to drive your own car for the group, you may do so, allowing the superior to accept or reject the offer.

Traveling by Rental Car. Your travel agent can arrange for car rentals at either your departure point or your destination point. The car can be made available when you arrive by plane at an airport. You may choose to make your own arrangements for car rentals by calling an 800 number (toll-free) found in the telephone book under listings for the largest rental companies. Be prepared to tell the car rental company what size car you will need. Remember that larger models are more expensive than smaller models.

Traveling by Plane. Make plane reservations as early as possible to get the most desirable schedule and the best rates. A travel agent can greatly simplify this process by using a computer that ties into all airline schedules. The agent can also quickly explain the many restrictions that apply to special rates. Arrive at the airport an hour in advance of a domestic flight and 2 hours in advance of international flights. Check your bags and confirm your reservations as soon as you arrive at the airport. When you have obtained your boarding pass, you will be free to relax until your flight is called.

Cooperate with security personnel and in security checks that are a part of air travel. You will pass through an X-ray point, and your carry-on luggage will be scanned by a device that detects concealed weapons and bombs. *Never* make jokes about having dangerous concealed items or you may be taken seriously and detained.

Free meals are served on most flights. Snacks may be provided on very short flights. Most airlines try to accommodate special needs of passengers, so be sure to tell the travel agent if you have any dietary restrictions.

Airlines have several classes of travel. First class is the most expensive. In first class, the seats are wider than in other classes. Services, such as drinks and movies, are free. Most companies have policies that do not allow travel in first class, so never make a reservation for first class without clearing it with your manager. Business class is another option for travelers. In business class, you will encounter other professionals, many of whom will be working in flight. For this reason, business class may not show movies. The third and most common class of air travel is tourist class. In tourist the seats are smaller than in first class or business class and services such as movies and drinks must be paid for in cash. Most of your business travel will probably be in tourist class because it is the least expensive.

Most airlines permit you to carry onto the plane one piece of luggage that is small enough to fit under the seat or in the overhead compartment. Anything too large to fit must be checked when you arrive at the airport.

Figure 8-2 Before you board a plane, go to the reservation desk of the airline you are flying to confirm your reservation and seat assignment and check any luggage that you are not carrying on the plane with you. (Courtesy of American Airlines.)

Garment bags, although fairly large, can be hung in plane closets or can fit in overhead compartments. For this reason, many professional travelers prefer garment bags to more solid types of luggage.

It is often possible to obtain your seat assignment when you make your reservation. The travel agent will ask you whether you have a preference for a window or an aisle seat. Although you may not always get the seat you prefer, you should be prepared with an answer.

Delays, canceled flights, overbooking, and lost luggage may cause frustrating delays when you travel. Often you will be unable to do anything but accept these irritations of travel. However, you may take certain actions to alleviate some of the problems. First, make reservations as soon as possible after you know you must travel to a destination by air. Plan to arrive with time to spare before your responsibilities begin. For example, if you are departing from an area that is often fogged in, leave on the day before you must be at a specific location rather than risk being late by leaving just in time to attend your meeting.

Pack essential cosmetics, and perhaps a change of clothing, in carry-on luggage in case your luggage is lost or delayed. Travel in clothing that will not cause you embarrassment if you arrive at your destination without your clothing bag.

Negotiate with reservations clerks if your flight is cancelled or delayed. Often you will be able to get another flight in time to keep your commitments.

Traveling on Trains and Buses. Occasionally a business person may choose to travel by train or bus. The AMTRAK system is available in many parts of the United States for train travel, and bus service links almost all towns and cities. Although these forms of travel are more time-consuming than air travel and less convenient than personal auto travel, they are low in cost and you may use the time to work or to freely enjoy the countryside. In addition, they (especially buses) may be used to get you to remote areas where air service is not available.

HOTEL/MOTEL ACCOMMODATIONS

Overnight accommodations can be arranged through your travel agent or by you personally. Be specific about the type of accommodations you want. For example, what location do you want—a facility adjoining the convention center or less expensive accommodations that may require a walk or cab ride to your meetings? Determine what quality of hotel/ motel you desire and can afford. Are you simply interested in a clean, comfortable, secure place to sleep, or do you want luxurious surroundings? Hotel/motel costs vary considerably according to their services and their furnishings.

Most hotels will hold a reservation until 6 p.m. If you plan to arrive later, you may want to secure or guarantee your reservation by supplying the hotel with your credit card number. Check-out times vary, so you will want to ask about it when you check in. Check-out times are usually provided somewhere in your room, as well, often on the door.

When you are making room reservations, you may be asked whether you prefer your room to be on a high floor or low floor. Some hotels have rooms in which smoking is not permitted. You may be asked your preference about this as well. Be prepared with answers, even if your answer is that you have no preference.

Some hotels in scenic locations charge more for a room with a view. If you are asked whether you want a room facing the mountains or the ocean, find out whether the rates for such a room are the same as for others before you give an answer.

It is more expensive to order food from room service than to eat in the hotel restaurant or coffee shop. It is also more expensive to make long distance calls from your room than to use a pay phone. Check company policy to learn what costs your company will pay when you travel. If, for example, you have a daily food allowance and you only eat one meal a day, then you may well order a full room service meal and still be within your daily allowance.

Figure 8-3 When you arrive at your destination, you should go immediately to the baggage claim area. (Courtesy of American Airlines.)

You may get to your hotel from the airport by taxi, by airport limousine, or by a hotel courtesy vehicle. These vehicles are usually parked just outside the airport nearest the exit at the baggage pick-up station. Telephones for courtesy vehicles are usually found near the baggage pick-up station as well.

If a courtesy vehicle is available, the cost is less than the cost of a limousine or taxi. However, some people prefer the speed and convenience of a taxi.

If you have arranged for a rental car to be available at the airport, locate the correct rental car company counter after you have retrieved your luggage. Car rental services are located in the baggage retrieval areas. Be sure that you have identification available as well as any written confirmation of the rental reservation that might have been issued. Picking up rental cars can take a while. You may have to travel by bus to the parking area and then wait until your car is delivered to you. Be sure to include this extra time in your travel plans, especially if you are arriving and planning to conduct business on the same day.

Before you drive out of the airport, make sure that you know how to get where you are going. If you are uncertain, ask the person who delivers the car to you.

CLOTHING FOR TRAVEL

Plan your travel wardrobe carefully so that you will have the necessary garments with few excess pieces to carry. Even if you plan to be involved in professional activities the whole time, pack something casual and something dressy for unexpected leisure time.

Travel clothes need to be versatile for wearing more than once, wrinkle-resistant for the well-groomed look, and soil-resistant for a neat appearance. Often travelers plan their wardrobe for a specific trip around one color so that separates may be used interchangeably and so that only one set of accessories is needed.

Before you can make final decisions about what clothing to take on a trip, you need to know the climate of the location you will be visiting. If you are traveling from Minnesota to Florida in midwinter, you will have to pack spring or summer clothing because your cold weather wardrobe will be inappropriate and uncomfortable once you reach your destination.

Here is a travel wardrobe for a woman who is going by plane to a nearby city for a 3-day conference. She will travel on the evening preceding the conference and will return on the morning following the conference. She will wear a gray skirt, plaid blazer, white blouse, and black low-heeled shoes. She will carry an all-weather coat and a briefcase. She has packed these items:

- One black suit
- One small-print blouse
- One red silk shirt
- One sweater
- One red dress with small print
- One pair black slacks
- Black pumps
- Small clutch purse
- Jewelry accessories
- Underwear and sleepwear

Similarly, the following items may be chosen by a man traveling to the same conference. He will wear gray pants with a white pullover shirt, a navy blazer, and black loafers, and will carry an all-weather coat and briefcase.

- Gray pin-striped suit
- Khaki pants
- Three shirts with ties

- Underwear and sleepwear
- One pair black dress shoes

Many business travelers always take a small travel iron or a travel steamer with them on trips. A travel steamer is a device that heats water until it boils. The steam escapes through an opening in the top of the steamer. Clothes are hung up and the steam is directed at the wrinkles, which are eliminated. Both travel irons and steamers are small and light weight and can be obtained at relatively little cost. These devices ensure that you can maintain a well-groomed, professional image away from home. It is also possible to borrow an iron and ironing board from the housekeeping department in most hotels.

PACKING FOR TRAVEL

Often people who fly on short business trips pack in a garment bag and a carry-on bag so they do not need to check any luggage. Others find that packing everything in one bag that may be checked makes for lighter and easier travel. They do not mind waiting a few minutes to retrieve checked baggage. For extended travel, you will probably use an assortment of large and small suitcases and bags, some checked and some carried on to the plane.

For the worker who must attend a meeting immediately on arriving from a flight, it is wise to carry essential toiletries and one change of clothing in a carry-on bag in case baggage is delayed.

Guidelines for packing efficiently and for preventing wrinkles include the following:

- Place heavy items and items that do not wrinkle easily at the bottom of the bag.
- Leave hanging clothes on hangers; cover with plastic bags and fold gently to prevent wrinkles.
- Place all spillable products in sealed plastic bags.
- Place shoes in bags or in socks to protect items they may touch.
- Alternate directions of collars on shirts and blouses so they will stack well on top of each other.
- Roll undergarments and place them between folds of other garments to reduce wrinkles.
- Use a suitcase that is neither too large nor too small for the amount of clothing you are taking.
- Pack toiletries and other small loose items along the sides of the suitcase or in the pockets if your luggage has pockets.
- If you want to leave room for items you may purchase on your trip, pack a folding or tote bag for that purpose.

Figure 8-4 There are many types of luggage to meet different traveling needs. You should pack as lightly as possible for business trips. (Courtesy of Lands' End.)

If you find that you will be traveling often, you may want to consider making a few purchases that will make packing easier and quicker. Many stores carry small travel bags and cases that are designed to hold makeup and other small items, jewelry, ties, and so on. You can also find plastic containers for your toothbrush (you won't want to pack it wet), your own soap, and your comb and brush, just to name a few.

You may also buy travel sizes of items such as toothpaste, talcum powder, hand lotion, and shaving cream. For convenience, you can keep the special travel cases and the travel-size items in your suitcase when you are home. Then when you have to pack, you will be able to find these small items easily.

If you wear eyeglasses, you should have a spare pair made and leave them in your suitcase. It is especially important to have spare glasses if you need them for driving.

If you take prescription medications, you will, of course, pack these. Consider obtaining an extra prescription from your physician. Store it in a different place from the medicine, so that if you become separated from the luggage containing the medicine, you will be able to get the prescription filled.

Most major hotel/motel chains provide some supplies in your room.

Figure 8-5 Professionals who travel frequently learn to pack just what they need—not too much nor too little. (Courtesy of Lands' End.)

These may include soap, shampoo, a shower cap, hair conditioner, a sewing kit, and a shoe polishing cloth. Because you can never be certain that any or all of these items will be provided, you may want to pack your own supplies just to be on the safe side.

SAFETY IN TRAVEL

Try to protect yourself from harm as you travel by understanding how you are vulnerable and compensating for it. Carry a limited amount of cash, credit cards, and traveler's checks (available at any bank) to protect yourself from theft or loss of travel funds. A man should put his wallet in his front pants pocket, not in his jacket or back pants pocket. Some men prefer to keep extra cash in a money belt, which is a zippered belt that holds tightly folded bills. Likewise, a woman should be certain that her purse is protected, not swinging loosely from her shoulder.

Do not open your hotel/motel door to anyone who is not fully identified, even people who say they are hotel employees. Use the peephole in the door to identify callers. If they are carrying food and you did not order room service, send them away without opening the door. Avoid walking alone on dark streets, and keep your car doors locked at all times.

Women may need to take extra safety precautions. For example, the way a woman dresses may signal her business role or her availability for social life. When a woman carries a briefcase and wears a suit or dress and jacket, her image is that of a person who has only business on her mind. Carrying a briefcase or folder adds to the image. The "look" does not encourage social encounters. When women who are traveling alone must find a place to stop for food after dark, it is safest to stop only at well-lighted restaurants with parking near the entrance.

Never leave your passport, plane tickets, or other important documents in your room. Always carry them with you.

In addition to protecting yourself from crime, you must also take other types of precautions. For example, most hotels in the United States provide floor plans of the hotel with fire exits highlighted. These may be posted in each room or in the hotel corridors. Check these to see where your room is in relation to the fire exits. In addition to checking the floor plan, you may want to actually find the fire exit closest to you room. This will probably not take more than a minute or two and the chances are that you will never need to use the fire exit. It is certainly worthwhile to take this extra precaution.

You should carry with you, in your wallet or purse, the name and telephone number of someone who should be contacted in case of emergency. In case of accident or illness, this information will be helpful to the people caring for you.

TRAVEL COSTS

Business travel expenses are handled in one of two ways: pay cash as you go or use a charge card. Professional people who travel obtain information from their superiors about arrangements for travel expenses before starting the trip. Some businesses give cash advances for estimated travel costs. Others reimburse workers for costs after the trip is completed; this means the employee must have the resources to shoulder the burden initially. In either case, careful records of all receipts must be kept and presented as valid claims for travel. In some instances, direct billing is arranged by companies that supply employees with direct-bill credit cards. This means that all charges against these cards are billed directly to the company. Some workers use their personal credit cards as a convenient way to manage travel costs and the records necessary for reporting costs.

TRAVEL ITINERARY

Before you leave your office for a business trip, prepare specific information about your travel plans, your hotel arrangements, your business responsibilities, and numbers where you may be reached. Include flight numbers, times, and airports (arriving and departing); time and location of scheduled meetings and the names of people with whom you will be meeting; and any other information that you need. Leave a copy of your itinerary with your secretary, your manager, and your family. Of course, you will want to take a copy with you, and you may wish to keep one on file for reports required at a future time. See the sample in Figure 8-6.

Itinerary for Margaret Jackson
January 19–21, 199X

Monday, January 19

3:50 p.m.	Depart Chicago, O'Hare International Airport, American Airlines Flight 62.
5:14 p.m.	Arrive Memphis.
	Accommodations: Memphis Hilton Hotel, 2200 Elvis Presley Boulevard, (901) 555–2394 (reservation guaranteed for late arrival).
8:00 p.m.	Dinner meeting with Arnold Manning, Memphis Belle Restaurant, 119 Elm Street.

Tuesday, January 20

9:00 a.m. to 12 noon	Attend sales conference, Hilton Hotel, Marble Room, 2nd floor.
12 noon to 2:00 p.m.	Sales awards luncheon, Hilton Hotel, Grand Ballroom, main floor.
2:20 p.m. to 5:00 p.m.	Attend sales conference.
7:30 p.m.	Dinner meeting with M. Davis, L. Flynn, N. Norris, Hilton Restaurant.

Wednesday, January 21

9:15 a.m. to 11:30 a.m.	Meeting with Sarah Packard, Wences and Packard Associates, 976 Main Street, (901) 555–9823.
12 noon	Lunch with Samuel Wences and Sarah Packard.
4:30 p.m.	Depart Memphis International Airport, American Airlines Flight 43.
5:54 p.m.	Arrive Chicago, O'Hare International Airport.

Figure 8-6 This is an example of an itinerary you might have for a three-day business trip from Chicago to Memphis.

Some of the following tips may seem to be common sense, but if you have not done much traveling, you may not have considered how to best handle the situations.

◆ When attending professional conferences, participate in all meetings that relate to your professional assignment. The unprofessional person skips meetings and considers travel to be a time for fun and leisure. Such an attitude may affect future travel. Some companies may require a written report of your professional activities after you return to the office.

◆ Maintain professional dress and behavior at meetings. Remember that even though you are not in the office, you are still at work and that you represent your company. You are creating an image that will last throughout your career.

◆ Register in a hotel as "John Brown" or "J. Brown," not "Mr. John Brown." Use your business address on the hotel register, not your home address, when you travel professionally.

◆ You may conduct small meetings in your hotel room, if it is more convenient for a small group to meet in your hotel room than in another part of the hotel. Be sure your room is neat and orderly with the bed made and personal belongings properly stored. This works best if the room has a couch or a small table around which people may sit. Perhaps you can arrange to have some extra chairs brought to the room. If you feel uncomfortable about holding a meeting in your room, you can meet in the hotel lobby or arrange for a small conference room.

◆ Tip appropriately (see the list below). It is as inappropriate to overtip as to undertip. A number of tips should be based on 15% of the bill. (In some parts of the country, a 15% tip or gratuity is included in the total of the check; watch for this.) Figure 8-7 is a handy guide for figuring 15% of amounts up to $50.

Tipping Guide

Worker	Tip
Barber	$1 or $2
Hairdresser	15% of bill
Bellhop	$.50 to $1 per bag, depending on size of bag
Coatroom attendant	$1 per coat
Doorman	$1 for ordering car
Garage attendant	$1 for bringing car to front
Ladies room attendant	$.50 to $1
Nurses	No tip

15% Tip Guide			
Amount	Tip	Amount	Tip
$ 1.00	$ .15	$26.00	$3.90
2.00	.30	27.00	4.05
3.00	.45	28.00	4.20
4.00	.60	29.00	4.35
5.00	.75	30.00	4.50
6.00	.90	31.00	4.65
7.00	1.05	32.00	4.80
8.00	1.20	33.00	4.95
9.00	1.35	34.00	5.10
10.00	1.50	35.00	5.25
11.00	1.65	36.00	5.40
12.00	1.80	37.00	5.55
13.00	1.95	38.00	5.70
14.00	2.10	39.00	5.85
15.00	2.25	40.00	6.00
16.00	2.40	41.00	6.15
17.00	2.55	42.00	6.30
18.00	2.70	43.00	6.45
19.00	2.85	44.00	6.60
20.00	3.00	45.00	6.75
21.00	3.15	46.00	6.90
22.00	3.30	47.00	7.05
23.00	3.45	48.00	7.20
24.00	3.60	49.00	7.35
25.00	3.75	50.00	7.50

Figure 8-7   The appropriate tip is usually 15% of the bill. Use this table to help you figure out what a tip should be.

Owners of establishments	No tip
Pianist in cocktail lounge	$1 or $2 per request
Strolling musician	$1 or $5 for request of a strolling group
Skycaps (porters)	$.50 per bag or $2 for cart of bags
Taxi	15% of fare
Waiter/Waitress	15% of bill
Wine Steward	$3 to $5 per bottle

◆ Introduce yourself when appropriate. When you meet someone whom you have not seen recently, give your name again to help the person remember. Never initiate a guessing game with a statement such as, "I bet you don't remember me!" If you have forgotten the name of a professional acquaintance, be warm and straightforward, saying, "Excuse me, but I have forgotten your name."

◆ Assume responsibility for your spouse's expenses. If it is acceptable for spouses to accompany employees on a trip, the employee should assume all extra costs. In addition, the employee should take care to fulfill all his or her responsibilities, not allowing the spouse to interfere with professional commitments.

◆ Avoid taking souvenirs from hotels, trains, and restaurants unless the items are designated as souvenirs. Taking items such as towels, glasses, and pictures is actually stealing, and the consumer pays for such practices in increased travel costs.

◆ Be a considerate traveler. For example, travelers who carry on so many bags that others do not have their share of overhead space in buses and planes are being inconsiderate. The traveler who uses both armrests in a bus or plane is exhibiting the same kind of rudeness. People who drink too much in public, flirt with or demean workers in service occupations, or allow children to go unattended are also travelers who create a poor image.

Occasionally business people have responsibilities and opportunities that involve traveling in groups. Observe these courtesies when traveling with others:

◆ Remain quiet when the tour guides address the group.

◆ Be prompt for departures.

◆ Be cheerful in rotating seats on tour buses.

◆ Smoke only on smoke breaks.

◆ Avoid being a 'loud" traveler.

◆ Don't congregate in the front of the bus.

◆ Don't talk extensively to the driver while the bus is moving.

◆ Take every opportunity to learn about differences you encounter in new places, among new people, and with new foods.

◆ Do not be critical of areas and people whom you visit.

EATING AWAY FROM HOME

The business person has many occasions to dine away from home. The dinner interview, the business luncheon, conventions, conferences, and entertaining clients offer opportunities for eating in restaurants and public dining areas. The professional person is expected to have superior manners and skills in these situations. You probably already have gracious table manners and skills for handling yourself well in public; however, if you feel a need to develop those skills further, the information below may be helpful to you.

It is important to remember that no amount of knowledge will

TEN TIPS FOR CONVENTION BEHAVIOR

1. Register in a hotel as "John Brown" not "Mr. John Brown."

2. Tip bellboys $.50 or $1 per bag for carrying luggage and opening the room. Tip waiters 15% of the bill. For taxi drivers, a 15% tip is correct.

3. Attend all sessions of the conference where you are representing your company.

4. Introduce yourself to a person whom you wish to meet if no friend is present to make introductions. When you have forgotten a name, be warm and straightforward; say, "Please excuse me, but I can't recall your name." When meeting acquaintances whom you have not seen recently, say your name to help them remember.

5. Polite (and honest) people do not take hotel ashtrays, towels, silver, etc.

6. In a crowded elevator, whoever is closest to the door exits first. A man does not remove his hat in an elevator. Always wait for everyone on the elevator to exit before entering.

7. At a restaurant, wait at the entrance for seating by a headwaiter. The group hostess takes the seat pulled out by the headwaiter. It is permissible to ask for a different table if you prefer another, but do not insist if none is available.

8. In a large group, each individual gives his or her own order to the waiter. When the meal is a business one involving a man and a woman, a gracious woman should say to the waiter, "May we have separate checks, please?"

9. Be generally considerate of others; avoid loud behavior that calls attention to yourself.

10. Selected table manners while eating out include:
    a. Olives, cherries, or onions served in cocktails may be eaten.
    b. When an uncut loaf of bread is placed on the table, the person taking the host role slices it and serves it to others.
    c. Paper wrappers should be crumpled tightly and either tucked under the rim of your plate or placed on the edge of the saucer or butter plate.
    d. The usual way to call a waiter is to catch his eye and raise your hand as if to say "Attention." If he does not see you, you may quietly call, "Waiter." If he is too far away to hear you, say to a nearby waiter, "Will you please send our waiter."
    e. Women may put on lipstick at the table, but other grooming should be done in the ladies' room. *Never* leave the restaurant using a toothpick!

FOCUS ON: GIVE ME A BREAK!

"It's that time of year again—time for the Office Products Association Convention."

The speaker is Alex Sung, the Director of Conventions and Meetings for Delat Office Supplies in Seattle. "I love my job, but it's very demanding! This year, the convention will be in Chicago. I've never traveled so extensively before. In this job, I get to see some really exciting places."

Alex is surprised by the nonstop nature of his duties. "I have to arrive a couple of days before the convention begins to make sure that our hospitality suite is ready for the meetings with our clients," he says. "I must see that the suite is stocked with food and drink at all times during the convention. It's also my job to make sure that the booth in the convention hall is stocked with brochures and samples."

His typical day begins early. "I check in with the catering staff the day before the convention to make sure that everything is in order for the reception," Alex says. "It's my job to select the seminars that would be beneficial for our staff to attend."

Alex works specific hours in the booth, usually during lunch hours and at other times when the sales staff is needed elsewhere. "I'm constantly chatting with clients and would-be clients. Because I am the one who sends out invitations, it is important that I remember names and faces. I must choose which clients to invite to breakfast or coffee. It's constant pressure! I really have to think on my feet, and I love it!"

After attending the keynote speech and taking notes for those not able to attend, Alex rushes to the reception to see that the arrangements have been made to his specifications. He checks to make sure that the hosts know where they are to be, and that they arrive on time.

"My professional image is on the line every minute," Alex explains. "I'm always on!"

Alex laughs, obviously enjoying himself. "I don't even have privacy in the elevator. Yesterday, going to my room on the 24th floor, I ran into some convention-goers who read my name tag and began asking me questions! It's a tough job, but I love it!"

provide you with good table manners unless you are willing to practice the skills and discipline yourself to use good manners at every meal. The people who rationalize that they can eat in any manner they choose everyday, changing only when they are in a professional situation, will find that the pressure of the professional situation will cause them to forget to observe correct table manners. They will unconsciously revert to their normal patterns of behavior, exhibiting unattractive manners in important professional situations.

RESTAURANT ETIQUETTE

Maybe your first opportunity to eat in a restaurant in a professional role will be at a lunch or dinner interview. Review these table manners to be sure that you create a positive image.

◆ As you enter the restaurant, wait for a host or maitre d' to seat you. Follow the maitre d' to the table. Women should precede men after the maitre d'. The person following directly behind the maitre d' takes the first chair indicated and others sit around the table as indicated by the leader of the group.

◆ Stand behind your chair until all diners have arrived at the table. Take your seat from the left side of the chair.

◆ Sit with erect posture; do not rest your elbows on the table. When eating, bring the fork to the mouth, *not* the mouth to the fork.

◆ If the waiter offers cocktails, exercise caution in ordering one. Most business people do not drink alcoholic beverages at noon. If others at your table order a cocktail and you want one too, a good choice is white wine. If you choose to avoid alcoholic beverages, sparkling water, tea, or coffee may be ordered. Order whatever you prefer without feeling that you should order alcohol.

◆ When the waiter comes for your order, be ready to give yours clearly and with confidence. Feel free to ask the waiter questions about anything on the menu. For example, if you do not understand a term used, you can ask, "Will you please describe an Alfredo sauce for me?" Or you might ask, "How is this shrimp dish prepared?" If you are still uncomfortable with the selections, ask what the special of the day is; usually it is a moderately priced dish that many people enjoy (often the waiter will describe it when he passes out the menus). When asked about choice of salad dressings and preparation of meat, reply as readily as possible. Avoid being lengthy in ordering, and avoid changing your order. You will not want your indecisiveness in ordering to create the impression that you cannot make decisions.

◆ Wait until all at your table have been served before beginning to eat.

◆ Silverware at the table is used in order, beginning from the outside and working toward the plate. For example, the spoon on the outside, right, may be a long one used for iced tea since the first thing a diner will do if tea is served is sweeten the tea. Similarly, the outermost fork on the left side is one for salad because salad is the first food course served (see Figure 8-8).

◆ After sweetening tea or coffee, remove the spoon and place it on the saucer, coaster, or plate.

◆ After a piece of silverware has been used, do not place it back on the table.

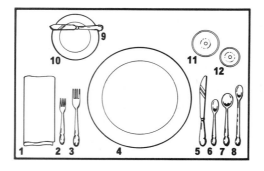

1 Napkin   2 Salad Fork   3 Dinner Fork
4 Plate   5 Knife   6 Teaspoon   7 Soup Spoon
8 Iced Tea Spoon   9 Butter Knife
10 Bread and Butter Plate   11 Water Goblet
12 Wine Glass

(a)

(b)

Figure 8-8   (a) This is a standard place setting for dinner. (b) You can feel confident at a formal dinner if you remember the basic rules of restaurant etiquette. (Courtesy of Great Performances Caterers and David Lindner Photography.)

LUNCH MENU

APPETIZERS

    Smoked Salmon
    Grilled Scallops with Plum Sauce
    Poached Shrimp with Fennel Salad
    Sauteed Crab Patties

SOUPS

    Soup of the Day
    Lobster Bisque
    Boston Clam Chowder
    Onion Soup, Oven-baked

SALADS

    Spinach Salad with Bacon Dressing
    Seafood Salad Vinaigrette
    Green Salad, Supreme
    Caesar Salad

PASTAS

    Flat Egg Noodles with Red Sauce
    Angel Hair Pasta with Mushrooms
    Ravioli with Bleu Cheese
    Noodles with Shrimp and White Sauce

ENTREES

    Broiled Lamb Chops with Mint Sauce
    Sauteed Veal with Vegetable Boat
    Grilled T-Bone Steaks with New Potatoes
    Grilled White Fish with Broiled Tomato

DESSERTS

    Selection from the Dessert Tray
    Fruit Ices
    Vanilla Ice Cream with Fudge Topping

BEVERAGES

    Coffee, Decaffeinated coffee, Tea

Figure 8-9 If some words on a menu are unfamiliar to you, do not feel uncomfortable about asking the waiter or waitress to explain what they mean.

◆ Avoid "bridging silverware," that is, do not prop it half on the plate and half on the table; rather place a used piece of silverware completely on the plate.

◆ Cut only one or two bites of meat at a time.

◆ Take only as much food on a spoon or fork as can be taken off at one time; for example, ice cream.

◆ To determine if a food should be eaten with your fingers, use these criteria: If it will soil the fingers, it is a fork food; if it will not soil the fingers, it is a finger food. Examples of finger foods are uniced cake, bread, pickles, and crisp slices of bacon. In the South, in general, crisp fried chicken, deep fried shrimp, and barbecued spareribs are finger foods; however, these foods are meant to be served only at informal meals.

MENU TERMS

A la carte	Each dish priced individually
Au gratin (oh grah tin)	Topped with cheese or bread crumbs
Au jus (oh zhoo)	Served in natural juices
Bernaise (bare nays)	Sauce made of butter and eggs
Bechamel (bay sha mell)	White sauce
Bisque (bisk)	Cream soup
Canape (can ah pay)	Tiny open-faced sandwich
Chablis (sha blee)	Dry white wine
Chowder	Fish soup
Coq au vin (coke oh van)	Chicken stewed in wine
Demitasse (demee tass)	Strong coffee in small cups
Escargot (es car go)	Snails in garlic and butter
Feta (fay tah)	Cheese made from goat's milk
Florentine (floor en teen)	Containing spinach
Gazpacho (gass pah cho)	Cold soup made of raw vegetables
Guacamole (gwa cah mo lay)	Avocado dip
Lyonnaise (lee oh nez)	Containing onions
Mousse (moose)	A soft, creamy food, often a chocolate dessert
Nicoise (nee swahz)	Containing tomato
Papillote (pappy yote)	Wrapped in paper for cooking
Parfait (par fay)	A dessert of layered ice cream
Pasta	Macaroni or noodle products
Pate de foie gras (pat ay duh fwah grah)	Goose liver spread
Roquefort (roke fert)	A blue-veined cheese
Scampi (scampee)	Usually shrimp cooked in garlic
Sorbet (sor bay)	Sherbet

Souffle (soo flay)	A light, fluffy egg dish
Sweetbreads	Thymus gland of calves
Table d'hote (tah bleh dote)	Complete meal served at a fixed price
Taco (tah co)	Crisp tortilla stuffed with a mixture
Tortilla (tor ti ya)	Thin pancake made from corn meal
Vichyssoise (vee she swahz)	Cold puree of leek and potato soup with cream
Vin blanc (van blank)	White wine
Vin rouge (van rouge)	Red wine
Vinaigrette (vee nay gret)	Dressing made of oil and vinegar

EATING SPECIAL FOODS

Escargot (snails)	Hold each escargot with the holder provided, remove the meat with an oyster fork.
Artichokes	Pull off a leaf at a time; dip the full end of the leaf into the accompanying sauce and eat the pulp out by pulling the leaf through front teeth. Cut artichoke center with knife or fork and eat in bite sizes.
Cold bread	Break bread into pieces for eating. Butter one piece at a time.
Hot bread	Butter an entire piece. When butter has melted, break into pieces for eating.
Corn on the cob	Hold in hand, take a few bites at a time; avoid overbuttering.
Salad	Eat with a fork but feel free to cut large pieces into bite sizes with your dinner knife.
Soups	Dip spoon away from you. Tip the bowl away if you wish to get the last bite. Place used spoon on soup plate. For clear soup served in a bowl with handles, you may drink the soup.
Olives	Eat with your fingers. Remove the stone from your mouth with your fingers.
Oysters on the half shell	Eat with oyster fork; dip in sauce and take a whole oyster in one bite.
Peas	Use bread as a pusher; if none is available use dinner knife—never fingers!
Spaghetti	Spear with fork, then twirl around the fork and cut against the back of a spoon.

French fried shrimp	Hold by the tail, dip in sauce and eat as a finger food.
Pizza	Cut into wedges and eat as finger food.
Southern fried chicken	Eat as finger food; use your napkin frequently.
Barbecued spare ribs	Eat as finger food; use your napkin frequently.
Hot beverages	Try a spoonful for temperature if you desire, then drink when cool enough; never blow on food.
Ice cream	Begin eating immediately when it is served to you; avoid putting more on a spoon than you can remove with one bite.

◆ Signal your waiter with a slightly raised hand. Address waiters, whether male or female, as "waiter." If you cannot catch the eye of your waiter, and if he or she is too far away to hear you call, you may ask a passing waiter to ask yours to come to your table. If your waiter wears a name tag, you may call her or him by name.

◆ Place your knife and fork across the center of your plate to indicate that you have finished eating. Avoid pushing the plate away from you.

◆ Crumple paper products such as wrappers from crackers and foil from potatoes and place them on the table behind your plate.

◆ Toothpicks are meant to be used in private; *never* exit a restaurant with a toothpick in your mouth.

◆ Complaints about food that tastes spoiled or is incorrectly prepared should be made quietly to the waiter, without attracting the attention of other diners.

◆ When served a piece of hot bread, you may butter the entire piece (as in a hot biscuit); however, when the butter has melted, break the bread in half to eat it.

◆ Avoid asking for catsup for use with fine meats—prime rib, filet mignon, etc.

◆ When you are finished eating, place your napkin on the table to the left of your plate.

◆ At the end of a meal, a woman may apply lipstick, but looking in a mirror and dabbing at her face for any length of time is in bad taste. It is better to save freshening up for the ladies' room.

◆ When a group enters a restaurant and sees people whom they know at another table, they should nod and say "Hello" but continue to their own table. To stop for a visit may block the pathway and disturb other diners.

MAKING RESERVATIONS

Before going out to eat, call ahead to ask if reservations are required. You may also ask if jackets and ties are required for men. In addition, if you are unsure whether the cost is within your budget, ask about prices. For example, you may ask, "What is the price range of your entrees?"

KNOWING ABOUT WINES

Wine is often served with meals. Choose according to your own tastes; however, a rule of thumb is this: Choose white wine for appetizers or as an accompaniment to fish or poultry; rose wine with delicate meats such as veal and lamb; and red wine as an accompaniment to red meats—beef, game, and Italian dishes that use red sauces.

Chianti, Bordeaux, and Burgundy are examples of red wines. White wines include Chablis, Rhine, and Chardonnay.

When in doubt about the quality of wine at a restaurant, you may safely order the house wine. The house wine is usually a good quality, moderately priced wine. Wine may be ordered by the glass, by the carafe, or by the bottle. Buying by the glass or carafe is usually more economical than buying by the bottle.

At very expensive restaurants, when a bottle of wine is ordered, the waiter will bring it to the table to be tested. This is merely a ritual. All you need to do is take a taste and tell the waiter it is fine. Only wine that is spoiled should be rejected.

POSITIVE BEHAVIOR IN PUBLIC PLACES

Pedestrian courtesies are important in public places. They distinguish a business person as a generally caring individual. As a business person approaches a doorway, he or she may exhibit courtesy by opening the door for others in the group. A man should not feel that he always has to hold the door for a female colleague. However, one may show deference to others by opening the door for them, regardless of their age or sex. Therefore, you will certainly want to open doors for your superiors and for your clients as a sign of respect.

Elevator courtesy involves waiting until riders exit before entering. People riding in an elevator should face the front of the car. When an elevator stops at a floor, the person nearest the door exits first. It is a mistake for a man who is exiting to step backward to allow ladies to move out first, because in stepping backward he may step on someone or cause unnecessary crowding. When you enter an elevator and only one person is on it, you may nod or say "Good Morning." Men are not expected to remove hats in an elevator; no one should smoke on an elevator.

As a couple or a group approaches a heavy revolving door, the person with the lightest load, or the person with the most strength, should step into the door first, pushing it forward so that others may step into it with ease.

DRIVER COURTESY

Driver courtesy is important for creating a positive image and also for the safety of riders and other motorists. The safe and courteous driver follows all travel rules and avoids expressing emotions when driving.

When riding in a car pool, courtesy suggests that the first rider in sits in the front seat if the car has four doors. However, if the car has only two doors, the first rider sits in the back seat, as does the second rider, leaving the front seat for the third rider.

PUBLIC APPEARANCES

The well-mannered person in public shows consideration for others. For example, a professional person does not chew gum at work, in restaurants, at theater performances, at interviews, or in places of worship. Similarly, courteous people only smoke in designated areas; they do not smoke in other people's cars without permission. If you are a smoker and are considering smoking in someone's home or office, look around you. If there are ashtrays, it is all right to smoke; if there are no ashtrays, avoid smoking until you are outside.

If a man wears a hat, he should remember to remove it when he is in an office, a home, a church, or other place of formal activity. Men remove their hats as a sign of respect during public prayers, the pledge of allegiance to the flag, and the national anthem. A woman's hat is considered to be more a part of her outfit than an item of outerwear and so may be left on when men must remove theirs.

General consideration of others includes not playing radios loudly in public places; use earphones. Arguments with spouses, excessive disciplining of children, and strong displays of affection between couples should take place only in private.

As a professional person, you will have opportunities to attend concerts and other events in a formal theater. A positive image is created by arriving on time, leaving your seat only at intermissions, and not talking during a performance.

1. Explain how using the services of a travel agent makes travel easier.
2. Name three sources of information about a city that you would like to visit.
3. Name three ways you get from the airport to your hotel.
4. Give ten guidelines for eating graciously in a restaurant.
5. Describe three safety measures a person who is traveling should use.
6. What are the characteristics of a desirable travel wardrobe?
7. Describe two ways that finances are handled for travel.
8. Write five general guidelines for travelers.
9. Explain how a professional person may create a positive image in public places.

ACTIVITIES

1. Consider that you have been asked to attend a 5-day conference in New York City in July. Describe the wardrobe you will take.
2. Role play making reservations to eat in a fine restaurant.
3. Identify a city you would like to visit and obtain as much information as possible about it. Summarize your findings in a report and include your sources.
4. Write an itinerary for a 5-day trip you might make if you were a salesperson for an agricultural supply firm. Use the format suggested in this chapter.
5. Research the cost that a salesperson from Dallas, Texas, would incur at a 3-day convention held at a major hotel in your city. Include round-trip airfare, hotel, meals, and entertainment. Summarize your findings in a report.
6. Secure a menu (or a photocopy) from an expensive restaurant in your city. Plan a full meal for yourself. Find the meanings of unfamiliar terms.

CHAPTER 9
CORPORATE ETIQUETTE

CHAPTER GOAL:

To give you confidence for participating in social events associated with your professional role.

CHAPTER OBJECTIVES:

After studying this chapter, you should be able to:

1. Present a positive image when participating in business-related social events.
2. Write invitations and replies correctly.
3. Assume the roles of both host and guest.
4. Plan and implement business-related social events.
5. Respond appropriately to colleagues who are experiencing major life events: marriage, divorce, childbirth, retirement, death in the family.

Have you ever found yourself at a social event where you felt uncomfortable? If you have, you know that you want to avoid experiencing that feeling again. It was especially troublesome if you felt you had a professional obligation to attend the event.

As a professional person you may have opportunities to plan and attend many business-related social events. Office parties, company receptions, retirement banquets, and business luncheons may be a significant part of your professional life.

Figure 9-1   Social events are often an important part of business. (Courtesy of Restaurant Associates.)

To fill this role with confidence, you will need guidelines of business etiquette. This chapter also provides information for planning and hosting business-related events.

ATTENDING SOCIAL EVENTS

Even as a guest at a company-related social event, your professional image must be maintained. You may find yourself a guest at luncheons, receptions, dinners, and office parties. Here are guidelines that will bolster your confidence in attending them.

RESPONDING TO INVITATIONS

When you receive an invitation to an event, respond in the same manner as the invitation was issued. That is, if it was a written, formal invitation, reply with a formally written note. On the other hand, if it was a telephone invitation, give your reply by telephone, and so on.

The phrase RSVP means please reply. Failing to reply is a serious social error, because the person who is hosting the function will plan for food, drink, and other extras based on how many people have said they will attend. See a sample written reply in Figure 9-2. Be definite about whether or not you can attend the function, and do not change your

> Dear Mrs. Jones,
>
> My sister and I will be happy to join you and your family for your picnic, July 4, at 6 p.m. We look forward to celebrating the holiday with you.
>
> Sincerely,
> Anna Hernandez

Figure 9-2 When you send a handwritten reply to an informal invitation, it should look something like this.

mind after you have given a reply. If you have a real emergency that prevents you from attending call the host immediately and explain your problem.

BEING A GRACIOUS GUEST

Never take an uninvited guest to any social event, whether personal or business-related, without checking with the host first. If you have an unexpected visitor whom you cannot leave behind, call your host and explain the situation. The host may then decide whether to excuse you or invite you to bring your guest.

Arrive promptly for the event. Being too early is as incorrect as being late. If you have an emergency that prevents your timely arrival, call and explain, urging the hostess to begin without you.

It is equally important to leave on time. When the function is over, thank your host, and leave without long delays. When considering how long to stay, determine whether the event is a "come and go" function or a "come and stay" party. When an invitation carries two time periods, as 2 to 4 p.m. or 7:30 to 9:00 p.m., you know that you may come at any time between the stated hours and leave as you like—staying from 30 minutes to an hour. If, on the other hand, the invitation states only one time, as 7 p.m., you will know that you are expected to arrive at the stated hour and stay throughout the event.

The well-mannered guest participates in the planned activities. For example, if you are invited to a beach party, plan to swim; if you accept an invitation for touch football, plan to play. If some physical problem prevents you from participating, discuss it with the host beforehand. It is especially important for you to mingle with as many of the guests as possible when you attend a social function. To isolate yourself with one or two friends is not in the party spirit. What would the party be like if everyone else did the same thing?

Polite guests take care of the host's property. For example, they do not set glasses or cups on tables without coasters or napkins under them. They do not walk onto carpeting with muddy feet; they do not drop cigarette ashes on the floor; and they do not waste food or drink. They do not leave spills or messes for others to clean up, and they dispose of trash properly. If they do use the telephone for long distance calls they use their credit cards.

BEING A GUEST OF HONOR

A person is a "guest of honor" when someone plans an event just for the special person—a reception to celebrate an award or a lunch to celebrate a promotion, for example. If you are honored in this special way, there are additional guidelines for you.

The guest of honor arrives at the event before the other guests to be present to greet everyone on arrival. The guest of honor also leaves first (unless the event is a "come and go" party). As the guest of honor, you should try to visit with all guests. After the event, write a special letter of thanks to the host.

BEING A HOUSE GUEST

If you are invited to stay overnight or for a weekend at someone's house who is not a member of your family, you are considered a "house guest." There are special courtesies for this role. In general, adopt the schedule of the family: eat when they eat, go to your room when they go to bed, and so on. Take care of the property: clean the tub after baths, pick up papers after reading, return glasses to the sink after drinking. Participate in whatever activities are planned for the family and for you. Take both casual and more formal clothing to be sure you will be dressed appropriately for whatever is planned. After the visit write a thank you letter expressing your appreciation.

PLANNING SOCIAL EVENTS

You may occasionally be required to plan business-related social events. You may be asked to arrange a business luncheon, an office party, or a reception to honor a person or celebrate an event. Here is some information that can help you carry out this responsibility.

DEVELOPING THE PLAN

Arrange to meet with the manager who gave you the assignment. Ask questions, and make careful notes on the wishes of the management for the event. For example ask: who is to be included; what are their proper titles; and what is the budget for the expenses involved? Get a clear picture of the timelines, responsibilities, and resources you have to accomplish the project. Determine whether the tone of the event should be formal or informal.

Often others in your organization will be asked to help you with a project. When that is the case, call a meeting of the group to make decisions and assign responsibilities. Create a timetable so that each duty will be accomplished when it needs to be. Keep a record of your decisions and progress and keep the manager who assigned you the responsibility informed in writing. Send copies of the report you send to the manager to each person who is responsible for some part of the function.

Plans for social events include these features:

◆ *When* (date and time) the event will occur
◆ *Where* the event will be held
◆ *Who* will be invited
◆ *What invitations* will be issued
◆ *What food* will be served
◆ *What activities* will occur
◆ *Who* is responsible for what
◆ *What resources*, including funds, are available

Figure 9-3 is a planning form that can be used to help you keep track of all aspects of the event you are planning.

ISSUING INVITATIONS

Invitations for business-related events are either formal or informal. Informal invitations may be issued by word of mouth, in person or by telephone, by handwritten note, by preprinted fill-in cards, or by specially printed cards. For a casual event such as the Christmas office party, invitations may take the form of a memo or a notice on a bulletin board. See the example of an informal invitation in Figure 9-4 (a).

Formal invitations are engraved, printed, or handwritten in a carefully worded format. A formal invitation has these characteristics:

◆ It is professionally produced on white or off-white stationery with dark ink or on stationery with the company logo.
◆ No abbreviations are used with the exception of titles and the term RSVP.

```
PLANNING FORM

EVENT _____

DATE _____ LOCATION _____

Duty _____ Assigned to _____ Tele. No. _____
Duty _____ Assigned to _____ Tele. No. _____
Duty _____ Assigned to _____ Tele. No. _____

GUESTS (attach list)

INVITATION FORM:


MENU:


PLANNED ACTIVITIES:


BUDGET:


SPECIAL REQUIREMENTS:
1. Equipment Needed: _____
2. Parking: _____
3. Facilities for Handicapped: _____
4. Guests' Special Diet Requirements: _____
```

Figure 9-3 Prepare a form like this to help you keep track of what you need to do if you are in charge of planning a business-related social event.

◆ Full names are used, even if a person always uses a nickname.

◆ Wording of the invitation is in the third person; that is, "ABC, INC. invites you . . . ," not "we invite you . . . ."

See an example of a formal invitation in Figure 9-4 (b). Invitations to banquets, celebration dinners, and receptions are usually formal ones. When you are asked to design an invitation for an event, refer to the accompanying illustrations to create one you need. Have your design approved by the manager who assigned you the planning responsibility. You will also need to discuss it thoroughly with the typesetter and

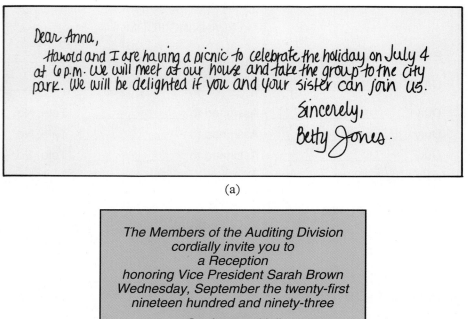

Dear Anna,

Harold and I are having a picnic to celebrate the holiday on July 4 at 6 p.m. We will meet at our house and take the group to the city park. We will be delighted if you and your sister can join us.

Sincerely,

Betty Jones.

(a)

The Members of the Auditing Division
cordially invite you to
a Reception
honoring Vice President Sarah Brown
Wednesday, September the twenty-first
nineteen hundred and ninety-three

Conference Hall

2400 First Street

Dallas, Texas

(b)

Figure 9-4   (a) An informal invitation. (b) A formal invitation.

printer who will complete the project. Be sure that the printer understands the delivery date you require and your budget restrictions.

ARRANGING FOR FOOD

Often, a professional caterer supplies the food for large social events. After you have an idea of what you would like to be served, talk with a caterer to determine how much you will need and what the charges will be. Sometimes professional caterers can offer menu suggestions. You may want to take their advice into consideration before you make a final decision. Unless your company has traditionally used one caterer, you may be expected to get a cost proposal (bid) from more than one so that you can compare services and prices. Your planning committee and/or your manager will choose the caterer who seems to be capable of providing the most at the lowest cost. If possible, check a caterer's references to make sure the caterer has a good reputation.

Figure 9-5 The menu can vary from a light afternoon snack to a complete dinner. (Courtesy of Restaurant Associates.)

There are many good food choices for social events. The examples shown below will help you make choices if you are responsible for specific events. As you decide on a menu, consider that some guests may have dietary restrictions. A dinner menu will be satisfactory to more people if you offer a choice of two entrees. One offering should probably be chicken because many people´ no longer eat red meat. Avoid messy foods, such as crab (which must be cracked), corn on the cob, or barbecued ribs.

SAMPLE MENUS

Formal reception for large group
Coffee
Punch
Petit fours
Assortment of hot and cold hors d'oeuvres
Nuts
Mints
(Alcoholic beverages may also be included)

Less formal reception for large group
Coffee
Punch
Assorted cookies
Finger sandwiches
Nuts
Chips and dips
(Alcoholic beverages may also be included)

Coffee
Coffee
Tea
Miniature sweet rolls
Cheese cubes
Ham-stuffed biscuits
Fruit platter
Pastries

Refreshments for a morning meeting
Coffee
Tea
Fruit
Assorted pastries

Refreshments for an afternoon meeting
Iced soft drinks
Iced tea
Cookies

Fruit
Coffee

Light breakfast (stand-up)
Juice
Rolls
Pastries
Coffee
Tea

Breakfast (seated)
Eggs
Sausages
Pastries or coffee cake
Fruit cup
Coffee
Tea

Luncheon
Cup of soup
Seafood salad
Crackers
Dish of ice cream
Iced tea
Coffee

Dinner
Shrimp cocktail
Tossed green salad
Veal in sauce
New potatoes
Steamed vegetable medley
Rolls
Cheese cake
Water
Coffee
Wine

Cocktail party or Christmas party
Open bar with both alcoholic and nonalcoholic drinks
Cheese balls
Chips
Crab dip
White bread sticks
Fruit tray
Vegetables for dip
Stuffed mushrooms

Cheeses
Olives
Nuts

Notice that menus are light because people do not want to overeat at professional events. It is important to have an adequate supply of food.

DECIDING ON BEVERAGES

Review company policy before you plan beverages for a business-related social event. Determine whether or not your company approves the serving of alcoholic beverages at company functions. In many companies wine is acceptable, but hard liquor is not. These additional guidelines may be helpful as you plan beverages:

◆ If you serve alcoholic beverages, provide nonalcoholic alternatives such as punch or soft drinks. Variety is important to satisfy the taste of all guests.

◆ If punch is served, adults prefer one that is not overwhelmingly sweet. Adding ginger ale gives "bite" to a nonalcoholic punch.

◆ Always serve food when alcoholic beverages are served.

PREPARING PHYSICAL FACILITIES

To find the right facility to hold the event, visit several possible locations and make notes about the suitability of each. Take with you a list of equipment and services you will need. Consider the availability of tables, chairs, microphone, and display tables, and the accessibility of serving areas, rest rooms, coat storage, etc. Is it large enough for the guests to mingle? Is there an area designated for smoking? Is there sufficient, accessible parking? Depending on your guest list, consider whether the site is accessible to the handicapped. Once you have chosen a suitable facility, work with the person in charge of the facility to arrange for the setup you need.

Flowers always add a nice touch to any event. Flowers for the speaker's table and the refreshment table are important. When the budget for an event is limited, green plants may be used, but if at all possible use arrangements of cut flowers to add life, beauty, and a "touch of class." If the event has a theme, such as a special anniversary, you may want to reflect that theme using special decorations or specially designed table favors. Decorations should be tasteful and reflect the company's vision of itself.

Receptions. When a company wants to honor an individual, such as a new president, or celebrate an event, such as the opening of a new division, it may give a reception. A reception may be a "come and go" event where guests come at some time during the stated hours, greet the hosts and guest of honor (if there is one), enjoy refreshments, visit with other guests, and then leave.

The host(s) and the guest of honor stand at the entrance and greet the guests. Each guest gives his or her name and greets people in this receiving line.

A table of refreshments is the focal point at a reception. Flowers and an attractive arrangement of food along with appropriate serving pieces make the table inviting. Assistant hosts (may be company employees) or hired waiters serve the food and make guests feel welcome at the refreshment table.

Office Parties. Holidays and other times of celebration (a new sales record, a move to a new building) may be occasions for parties at the office. Sometimes, especially at Christmas, management hosts the party, and at other times, the staff may sponsor the party. A committee is usually charged with planning food and drink and arranging details such as invitations, decorations, service, and activities. Office parties are usually held near the end of the work day or after office hours. Appropriate dress for the party is what everyone has worn to work that day. Office parties do not generally include the rowdy behavior depicted on television. Even at an office party you will want to present a positive professional image.

Business Lunches. Occasionally people meet for a social event at a restaurant. In that case, the person in charge of the event serves as host. The host arranges with the restaurant to have a room or area reserved. In addition, the host makes arrangements for food, planning for guests to order from the menu, or arranging in advance for a special menu. Arriving early at the restaurant, the host greets guests as they arrive, introduces those who do not know each other, and directs the seating. If the host assumes the host position at the head of the table, he or she asks any special guest who may be present to sit to the right of the host's place.

HOSTING THE SOCIAL EVENT

Although someone from management may assume the role of host at the actual event, frequently the staff member who planned the event is

Figure 9-6 Food should be presented in an attractive display. (Courtesy of Restaurant Associates.)

the host. Certain courtesies and responsibilities assumed by the host make an event successful:

- Plan the event thoroughly and with consideration for the tastes and preferences of the company and the guests.
- Issue appropriate, timely invitations.
- Be at the door to greet all guests; shake hands with each one.
- Direct the guests to the refreshment table; circulate in the room and introduce strangers.
- Make the first toast of the evening.
- In general, be responsible for the comfort and enjoyment of the guests; see that no one is left out, and be sensitive to the guests' needs and to problem situations.
- Do not ask a guest to perform—to sing or play piano, for example—without asking him or her privately first.
- Never urge guests to drink alcoholic beverages; offer options.
- Be at the door to bid guests goodbye.

Offering a toast to a person is a special way to show honor. It is generally the responsibility of the host to offer the first toast of the evening. After that, anyone who wishes to do so may offer a toast.

A toast is a brief comment about a person and his or her accomplishments or attributes. It may or may not be humorous. It is followed by all guests raising their glasses in honor of the person receiving the toast. To propose a toast follow these steps:

1. Rise, and holding a beverage glass, say, "I want to propose a toast to . . . ."

2. As all guests raise their glasses, continue with the toast. For example, if the event is to honor a person who is retiring, you might say something like this. "Harry Brown has led this company for many years, and during his leadership it has tripled in size. More importantly, Harry has helped many of us as beginning professionals to become successful. We offer him our sincere thanks and best wishes. To Harry!"

3. All people (except Harry) take a drink. Although it is true that traditionally the toast is given with an alcoholic beverage, usually champagne or wine, any beverage may be used—coffee, tea, milk, even water. Raise your cup or glass when a toast is proposed. To fail to participate in a toast is an insult to the honored guest.

4. Never include an unkind joke or make an uncomplimentary remark in the toast. After a person has received a toast, the guest of honor may wish to offer a toast . . . and so the toasting continues as long as

Figure 9-7 The host or hostess makes the first toast at business receptions. (Courtesy of Restaurant Associates.)

someone wants to offer words of appreciation or respect. When you are the recipient of a toast, remain seated and do not sip your drink. After the toast, you may rise and offer a toast or simply smile and say, "Thank you."

SHARING LIFE'S MAJOR EVENTS

Since we spend so many hours of our lives with coworkers, we cannot help but share the joys and sorrows of our personal lives with them. Here are some suggestions to help you respond to certain events in the lives of those around you.

MARRIAGE

Whether you are being married or whether you have colleagues who are getting married, special considerations can increase the joy of the event.

FOCUS ON: CELEBRATING IN STYLE

Coffees, cocktail parties, teas, and open houses are popular forms of business entertainment. They fit our needs for flexible timing because they are "come and go" events. Invitations ask guests to come between stated hours, as from 2 to 4. Guests go at anytime between the stated hours and stay 20 minutes or more, depending on the event. Never remain for the entire time. Greet the host on arrival, but it is not necessary to say anything when leaving.

Coffees are usually the least formal of all forms of "come and go" events. A coffee implies a morning function; its formality may vary from a small group having coffee to an elegant party. Foods appropriate for coffees are not too rich or too sweet. Popular menus include nut breads, fruit platters, miniature biscuits, cheese platters, doughnut holes. A choice of beverages is offered, usually coffee and tea, or perhaps coffee and a cold drink such as punch or juice.

The *cocktail* party is popular. Usually held late in the day, it lends itself to a mixture of people. It occurs during the afterwork, predinner hour, generally from 5 to 6, or 5 to 7. Always leave before the dinner hour.

A *tea* is an afternoon function. The tea differs from the coffee in that it is slightly more formal. Also sweet, richer foods may be served. Appropriate foods include finger sandwiches, fancy cookies, tiny cakes, and mints.

An *open house* is an informal method of entertaining a large group on any occasion. Perhaps friends are invited during a holiday season, or to celebrate an accomplishment, or simply to get together. Guests at open houses expect more food than at other types of "come and go" events.

Your Marriage. You may want to tell your immediate superior and your coworkers when you become engaged and when you set your wedding date. During the time of the engagement, it will be easy to let wedding plans consume your time and thoughts. As a professional person, guard against letting such personal considerations interfere with your work. Perhaps these guidelines can help you at this important time in your personal and professional life.

◆ Avoid discussing the details of your wedding plans at work unless you are asked. Others are not nearly as interested in them as you are. Dwelling on the plans at work can seriously limit your productivity. It may help to make a personal rule to discuss your plans only during coffee breaks or lunch hours.

Figure 9-8 When an employee gets married, coworkers often give the person a party at the office. (Courtesy of Restaurant Associates.)

◆ Avoid working on wedding plans during work hours. Even if you are temporarily without an assignment, it may be distracting to other workers to hear you making personal plans over the phone.

◆ If you feel close enough to your coworkers to invite them as a group to your wedding, you may post a wedding invitation on the bulletin board. If you wish to invite individuals to the wedding and reception, send personal invitations. If you send an individual invitation to your manager, be sure to include his or her spouse's name on the invitation.

Marriage of Colleagues. When a colleague marries, you may want to send a wedding gift. Choose one within your means and one that is appropriate for the level of your friendship. In many offices, colleagues collect money for a group gift. If you do not know the person who is getting married well but would still like to participate, this is the best way to do so.

When the person returns from the wedding trip, be gracious in welcoming him or her back with pleasant comments about the wedding and good wishes for the future.

If you are close friends, you may wish to give a party for the bride or groom. Often coworkers will have a wedding shower for the bride-to-be or a bachelor party for the groom-to-be. You may invite both business and social friends if the event is away from the office.

Marriage of Clients. If your company has an important client who marries, a wedding gift from the company may be in order. If so, the cost of such a gift is assumed by the company.

BIRTHS

When a colleague has a baby, coworkers usually recognize the event in some way. You may send flowers to the parents, or you may send a small gift for the baby. You may want to contribute to a group gift. If you do not feel that you are close enough to warrant this expense, send a note of congratulations.

Occasionally the whole staff may want to give a baby shower for an expectant mother. Showers are happy events usually appreciated by parents-to-be and enjoyed by guests; however, if it can be arranged, the shower should take place away from the office unless the company clearly approves. In any case, the shower should be planned for after office hours. The arrival of an adopted baby is treated in the same happy way as the birth of a baby.

If you are having a baby, follow these guidelines for handling this change in your personal and professional life:

- Examine your company's maternity or paternity leave policy early enough to plan effectively for personal and professional responsibilities.
- Investigate child care options and plan ahead to provide quality care that will allow you to work without worry if you plan to return to work.
- When the baby arrives, send an announcement, which may be posted on the bulletin board in your division.
- Write a thank you note to each individual who gives you a gift and a group thank you for a group gift.
- After you return to work, avoid monopolizing the conversation with child care issues or the accomplishments of your baby.
- Avoid using excessive time calling to check on your baby. After choosing competent child care, trust the caregiver to manage your child while you are at work.
- If you have a spouse, discuss ways you may share the emergency requirements of parenting so that you may manage effectively the dual role of parent and professional person.

DIVORCE

If you divorce, protect your professional life by behaving in ways that do not limit your productivity. Here are some guidelines for maintaining your professional demeanor if you are involved in a divorce.

Figure 9-9 A baby shower for a coworker can be a happy event for both parents-to-be. (Photo by Teresa Luterbach.)

◆ At work avoid discussions of the traumas that led to the divorce. Reserve such conversation for your private time.

◆ When you have made a decision to divorce, arrange a conference with your immediate superior and briefly explain your situation. Assure her or him that the change in your personal life will not affect your professional life.

◆ When it is convenient, briefly tell your immediate coworkers that your situation has changed.

◆ Find a person to confide in away from work. Such a support person is critical to your emotional well-being.

◆ Avoid using office time to call counselors, lawyers, spouse, etc.

When a colleague divorces, be aware of the difficult situation the person is experiencing. However, do not pry into the details of the divorce. If you are a personal friend, continue your friendship. Never cut a person off from friendships. Resist the temptation to gossip about the situation. If a coworker tries to engage you in a gossipy conversation, answer in such a way as to change the subject. (Reread the section on handling gossip in Chapter 6.)

When a colleague dies, people at the workplace may fill important roles. Your appropriate response to the death will be determined by your relationship to the person and by your company responsibilities.

When death occurs, a company representative may, according to local custom and company policy, go to the home of the deceased to assist where needed—perhaps to handle telephone inquiries, care for small children, act as a liaison for the family, or serve as a host in the home.

The manager and coworkers should be promptly notified of the death and of the final arrangements. The division secretary needs to know how to respond to requests for information. An obituary may be written for the company newsletter. Most professional organizations encourage and make it possible for workers who were close to the deceased to attend the funeral or memorial services. When the deceased is a member of the executive management team, the office may be closed during the funeral services.

The way you acknowledge the death will depend on how close you were to the deceased and on your resources. There are several options. Neighbors and close friends often take food to the home and call on the family. Close friends send flowers and attend the services. Coworkers who are close to the person may do the same things. People who are not so close may call on the family at the funeral home during the visitation hours. They may send flowers or make a memorial contribution. You may choose one or more of these ways to show sympathy, or perhaps you will choose only to send a letter of condolence. Some people cannot handle the experiences of funerals and visitations. For those people, indirect expressions of support alone are best.

The letter of condolence is especially appropriate when someone with whom you work has lost a family member. See the sample letter of condolence in the chapter on personal communication.

When you attend a funeral or memorial service, wear appropriate clothes. Men usually wear dark business suits with white shirts and conservative ties; women wear dark suits or dresses.

If someone in your family dies, you will want to notify your superior immediately and make arrangements to be away from work. Most companies have stated policies regulating the length of absences in such cases. Usually a short paid leave is provided for the death of a close relative.

You may find it helpful to return to work as soon as possible. Some people find that their work is effective therapy for the sorrow they feel over the loss of someone they love. Send notes of sincere thanks to all your coworkers and managers who assumed your responsibilities while you were away and who offered gestures of sympathy.

GIFT GIVING

Gift giving is frequently a part of the professional world. When should you give a gift? How much should you spend? Should you give a gift to your manager? The following guidelines may prove helpful:

◆ Be aware of the company's policy on the giving and receiving of gifts from people who do business with the organization. Never give a gift that could in any way be construed as a bribe. For example, do not give a gift to a person with whom you are negotiating a business agreement.

◆ Never give gifts of cash unless there are special circumstances such as a medical emergency in a colleague's family.

◆ Consider these reasons for giving gifts: to encourage, to thank, to congratulate, to bear good wishes, to cheer, and to celebrate.

◆ Avoid starting gift collections. Some people feel pressured to give when they do not really want to contribute to the gift. If there is a collection in your office and you do not wish to participate, tactfully decline. It is enough to say, "No, I'm sorry."

◆ When in doubt about what will be an appropriate gift, consider a plant or cut flowers.

◆ Generally employees do not give gifts to their manager; if they do, the gift should be modest.

◆ Do remember all those who have the title of secretary in your division on Secretary's Day. A flower, a card, or a small gift as a token of appreciation is appropriate.

◆ Serve with pride on any company committee organized to select gifts to be given by the company to retirees.

◆ Always write a sincere note of thanks when you receive a gift.

Following are some suggestions for gifts you can consider giving on the occasions noted:

GIFT SUGGESTIONS

For Secretary's Day	A rose in a bud vase or a bouquet of cut flowers Candy Something related to a hobby
For retirement	Tools for a hobby Items for a planned vacation Art object representing the business or industry
For a new baby	A flower arrangement Silver baby spoon Small stuffed animal

Figure 9-10 Appropriate gifts for various business occasions. (Courtesy of Ovations.)

For a hospitalized colleague	Cut flowers Green plant Book Tapes with greetings from colleagues
For clients	Foods from the local area, such as pecans from Texas Baskets of fresh fruit Wine
For a colleague who is going to a new job	Desk accessories such as calendar, date book, or paper-weight Something to decorate a new office Something related to the individual's hobby

1. Explain how a person generally knows the correct way to reply to an invitation.
2. List five guidelines for the polite guest.
3. What is a "come and go" event?
4. Explain the difference between a formal and an informal invitation.
5. List five duties of a host for a company-sponsored reception.
6. List three ways you may show respect when someone in a colleague's family dies.
7. Describe appropriate dress for men and women who attend funerals.
8. Outline three guidelines for corporate gift giving.
9. Discuss how to coordinate your professional role with the birth of your baby.
10. How might you honor an employee on Secretary's Day?

ACTIVITIES

1. Write an invitation to a party in your home to celebrate St. Patrick's Day (March 17).
2. Write a reply to the following invitation:

   Dear Gene,
   Please join the auditing team for lunch on Friday in celebration of our completing the project. We will eat at noon in the building cafeteria.

   Sincerely,

   Joe Smith (signed)
3. Plan appropriate gifts for the following:
   a. Bob Lawson, who is retiring after 25 years as a division manager
   b. Sue Radowski, a coworker who is having a baby
   c. Jean Winn, a colleague in another department who has had serious surgery
   d. Major clients of your accounting firm at Christmas
4. Practice proposing toasts to honorees at a retirement banquet.

UNIT 3

MOVING IN, MOVING UP: PROMOTION AND GROWTH

CHAPTER 10

PRODUCTIVITY
AND
PROMOTABILITY

CHAPTER GOAL:

To assist you in being a productive and promotable professional.

CHAPTER OBJECTIVES:

After studying this chapter, you should be able to:

1. Understand the importance of being a productive worker.
2. Outline ways to be productive.
3. Define prerequisites for promotion.
4. Use strategies for gaining promotions.
5. Describe the skills that are critical to productivity and promotability.

From your first day on the job, you begin to establish yourself within the organization as a productive or a nonproductive worker. At the same time you begin to lay the groundwork for becoming promotable or nonpromotable.

What makes the difference? Much research has been conducted to answer that question. Although evidence supports various theories on productivity and promotability, here we will review only the information that you may need as you begin a career with success as your personal goal.

PRODUCTIVITY

A productive worker yields results that can be in the form of either goods or services. For example, the farmer who grows carrots is producing goods, the plumber who repairs faucets produces services. Likewise, the company that makes oil well rigs produces goods, and the company that provides home health care produces services.

Productivity also refers to the rate, or amount, of goods and services produced. For example, the worker who sells ten insurance policies per week is more productive than the one who sells five per week. The nurse who is able to give inoculations to a dozen babies in an afternoon is more productive than the one who gives only eight during the same time period.

WHY BE PRODUCTIVE?

You may ask, "Why is being productive all that important to me?" Productivity is an important concept in today's business world and to any worker whose goal is success. Being productive is important for these reasons:

◆ *You earn more money.* Often salary is tied directly to the number of units, or amount of work, you produce. This is especially true of careers in sales or telemarketing. For other workers, productivity is taken into account indirectly when an employee is considered for salary increases.

◆ *You get personal satisfaction.* Seeing the results of your work is personally satisfying. For example, as you mow a lawn, you feel satisfaction with each new strip the mower cuts as it moves across the yard. As a secretary, you can get personal satisfaction from each clean, neat letter or report completed.

◆ *Your self-esteem increases.* The two major components of high self-esteem are satisfying work and loving relationships. The first of those—satisfying work—is likely to be both a result of and a motivation for your being productive where you are employed. (If you like the work, you are more likely to be productive, and being productive causes you to be more satisfied with your work.)

HOW TO BE PRODUCTIVE

If you want to be a productive worker, you can begin early in your career by developing work habits and attitudes that contribute to productivity. Here are some important ones:

◆ *Use time wisely.* Start to work on time; do not overstay coffee and lunch breaks; and work until the work day officially ends. Avoid unnecessary absenteeism.

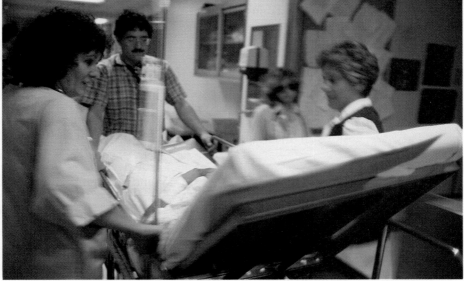

Figure 10-1 The most productive medical workers in a busy hospital emergency room are the ones who have excellent skills and can care for many patients in a short period of time. (Courtesy of New York University Medical Center.)

FOCUS ON: "STICK-TO-IT-TIVENESS"

Interview as many successful people as you can find. Ask them for the secret of their success. Chances are, you will learn that the major quality each of them has is *persistence*.

Many successful people say that they are no more intelligent than the average person, that they have no more important family background than the average person, that they are no more knowledgeable than the average person, but they have set a goal for themselves and they do not allow anything to keep them from pursuing that goal. They do not stop in their efforts. *They are persistent*!

How do these persistent people act? Here are some clues to their behavior:

- They keep their goal in mind at all times.
- They view problems as challenges that have solutions.
- They are positive in their approach to life.
- They are willing to try new ideas.
- They are willing to take risks.
- They work hard; they do not waste time.
- They seek new resources for reaching goals.
- They seldom say: "It can't be done." "We've tried it before." "It's not worth the effort." "I don't have time." "He can't do anything."
- They believe this: "If you can conceive it, you can accomplish it."
- They impress others. Because productivity is highly valued in business, the worker who is productive is noticed and rewarded.
- They increase their chances for promotion. Often promotion is tied to productivity.
- They contribute to the productivity, and thus the economic well-being of their group, their company, and of the entire country. In recent years, productivity in our country has declined, causing economic problems for individuals, families, business, industry, and government. When any person becomes more productive, the economic well-being of the entire country is improved.

- *Commit yourself to high standards of work.* Use the knowledge and skills you bring to the job to do well what you have been hired to do. Take pride in work well done.
- *Improve your skills.* Take advantage of opportunities to learn more about your work. This may mean reading more about your job or attending seminars or classes to improve your technical knowledge. For example, Harriet Brown found that she could double the number of reports she produced by taking an advanced, short course (just two nights) on the use of MicroSoft Word.

- *Manage yourself and your personal resources* so that you can be your most productive. This means keeping well physically and emotionally and being physically rested and ready for work. It means organizing your family responsibilities and your social life so that they do not interfere with your work. For example, Lane McCormack, who is distressed about the possibility of losing his girlfriend, is allowing his feelings to affect his work. Juan Hernandez, who experienced the same emotional distress, managed to overcome his feelings and focus on his work. Juan is, therefore, a more productive worker than Lane. This self-management also means managing your time well. See Chapter 6 to review time management techniques.

- *Stick to your job.* This work habit allows workers to keep their minds and their time committed to a task until it is finished. For example, Erin Upchurch, who is an assistant manager in clothing retail, says that on days when she plans to make a window display, she makes herself finish the display before she goes on coffee break. She does not take telephone calls or confer with coworkers until the task is finished.

- *Be a team player.* In today's complex business world, few people work totally in isolation. The productivity of one person is linked to that of others. For example, Mack Sanchez cannot finish his workload report until Herman Long has completed the time card summaries. Being cooperative and helpful to others is not only a key to company productivity but to yours as well.

- *Be creative and open-minded.* Productivity is often related to problem-solving. The person who shows initiative, is creative, and is open-minded can solve problems more quickly than a person without those qualities. For example, the worker who sits waiting for a technician to repair a machine before continuing to sew tote bags in an assembly line may needlessly lower her own and the division's productivity; instead she might ask for permission to work on another machine that is not being used while her machine is under repair. She will be appreciated not just for her productivity but for her willing attitude and resourcefulness.

PROMOTABILITY

Being promotable means that you possess personal and professional qualities that cause management to consider moving you to a higher position in which you will have more responsibility and usually more pay. In some cases, you may request a promotion; in others, the manager will make the recommendation without your asking.

WHY MANAGEMENT PROMOTES

Management promotes workers for various reasons—to apply the skills of workers in the best way, to meet the need of getting a specific job done, to reward workers for outstanding performance, and to motivate workers.

You are likely to have several reasons for wanting a promotion. You will undoubtedly want the extra status and salary that promotions usually bring; you will want to be recognized and rewarded for your efforts; and you will want the personal and professional satisfaction that comes from being promoted.

HOW TO BE CONSIDERED FOR PROMOTION

The promotable worker must take certain steps that put him or her on the path to being promoted. Following are several steps you can take:

◆ *Set a promotion goal.*

◆ *Learn what the requirements are to be promoted* to the job you want. Then decide when you think you will be able to meet the requirements. Write the date on a piece of paper and put the paper where you can see it every day.

◆ *Plan strategies* for reaching your goal. For example, you may need additional skills to be promoted to the next level. If you do, plan to take a course or attend a seminar that will provide the skills training. Some companies have formal goal-setting as a means of evaluating employees for annual raises or promotions; that is, each employee is expected to submit written goals for the year, and then he or she is measured against them at evaluation time.

◆ *Meet the company's requirements for promotion.* Many companies have length of service, skill, and productivity requirements for promotions. For example, you may not be promotable during the first year of employment, or you may not be promotable until you achieve a certain level of productivity.

◆ *Exceed requirements for promotion.* Do more than the minimum required of you. Whether it is working longer hours, products created, or a cooperative attitude demonstrated—go beyond the requirements if you expect to be promoted. Often several workers meet minimum requirements, but because a limited number of positions are open, only a few workers will be promoted at any one time. If you have *more* than the minimum requirements, you are more likely to get the promotion than if you have only minimal ones.

Figure 10-2 You can sharpen and increase your skills by taking courses at night or on weekends. Increased skills will put you on the path to a promotion. (Courtesy of Johnson & Wales University.)

HOW TO ASK FOR A PROMOTION

Once you feel that you either meet or exceed your company's requirements for promotion, you must determine how you will go about achieving your goal. Some companies schedule periodic reviews, either annually or semiannually. This is the ideal time to discuss a promotion with your manager. If the manager does not raise the issue during the review, be prepared to raise the issue yourself. If your company does not schedule regular reviews, make an appointment to meet with your manager. Some companies prefer that requests for promotion be in writing.

You must be well prepared to make a strong case for yourself. While you have been working toward meeting the requirements for promotion, you should have kept careful, detailed records of your accomplishments. When you are ready to ask for the promotion state clearly in writing what your skills and accomplishments are. Consider the quality of your work, your relationship with your manager and coworkers, and your overall work record. List reasons why you think you deserve a promotion. Also list the contributions you believe you will make to the company if you are promoted to a higher level. See the list below for examples of objective reasons that one worker gave for requesting a promotion.

WHY ONE WORKER FEELS SHE DESERVES A PROMOTION

1. I have met the length of service requirements (1 year) for promotability.
2. My productivity records show that I have exceeded the standard requirements by 25% (I made ten sales a month when the standard is eight).
3. I attended a sales improvement seminar conducted on four weekends and received a certificate of completion.
4. I served on the company's United Way Fund Drive Committee and represented the company in the Community Walk-a-thon.
5. I am willing to set goals for further improvement and productivity.

If you are granted an interview or when you have your periodic review, take with you the materials you prepared. Present your case in a straightforward, nonemotional manner. Avoid getting defensive if the supervisor makes critical or negative remarks. Continue to present your case in a positive manner, using the evidence you have assembled as proof that you have a valid request. After you have presented your case and listened to the supervisor's response, thank him or her, and return to work.

Wait patiently for a formal response to your request, knowing that in many organizations supervisors must get permission from other officials to grant your request. Continue to work well while you wait. If your request is denied, ask for reasons in a tactful, objective manner. You may ask your supervisor to tell you what you must do to become promotable. You may also ask when you may be considered again. Once you have this information, you will have several options. You may decide to continue working at your present level; you may double your efforts to meet company requirements as outlined by your supervisor; or you may seek work elsewhere.

WHEN YOU ARE PROMOTED

You will feel wonderful when you receive the news that you have been promoted. You will probably want to tell your family and friends immediately and celebrate the good news. Most importantly, you will want to start your new level of responsibility in an appropriate way. You should immediately set goals that will ensure your success in the new job. To do that, remember these suggestions from others who have been promoted:

◆ *Be modest.* Avoid bragging about your success. Others will respond more comfortably if you let *them* say how great you are rather than your telling them about your special qualities and abilities.

Figure 10-3 One way to feel confident about asking your manager for a promotion is to be well prepared for the meeting. (Photo by Paul E. Meyers.)

- *Learn all you can about the new job.* Begin your new position determined to learn quickly about the new tasks, your new coworkers' skills and responsibilities, standard policies and procedures, and the goals of the division.

- *Initiate change carefully.* Assuming that you are in a position to institute changes, remember that people are slow to accept change, but they are willing to change if they see the need for change and if they can participate in the planning for change.

- *Respect all workers.* Be fair; show respect for your peers, as well as for people who may work under your direction.

- *Be a role model.* Set an example for the people you supervise. When you come to work on time and stay until the work is done, they will be more willing to give an extra measure of effort. When you set high standards, they will follow with the same effort, and when you follow company policy and rules, they will understand the importance of doing so as well.

- *Share with others.* This means you must delegate responsibility—you cannot do everything yourself. Both you and the company will be more productive if you learn to delegate work to others. Share credit with others to develop good relations among the staff. Likewise, take responsibility for what goes wrong in your division.

◆ *Learn about the roles of those in middle and upper levels of management.* Review the section in Chapter 6 on relating to superiors and coworkers.

QUALITIES NEEDED FOR PRODUCTIVITIY AND PROMOTION

Throughout this book, you have read about qualities that people who are successful in their work and professional lives exhibit. For example, you know that these skills are important for productivity and promotion:

◆ Knowledge and skills related to a specific job

◆ Communication skills

◆ Interpersonal skills

◆ Personal commitment skills

Add to these two other aspects or working life that are important: critical thinking skills and being positive and open-minded about others.

CRITICAL THINKING SKILLS

Nearly everyone can improve the ability to analyze situations and make decisions if they make a conscientious effort. Critical thinking uses certain ways of analyzing information to make timely, workable, and creative decisions. For example, the person who wishes to make the best decision will need to develop qualities such as open-mindedness, flexibility, patience, and curiosity.

TEN MENTAL ATTITUDES NEEDED FOR CRITICAL THINKING

1. Open-mindedness
2. Flexibility
3. Honesty
4. Curiosity
5. Persistence
6. Willingness to listen to others' views
7. Objectivity
8. Lack of bias
9. Ingenuity
10. Patience

The critical thinker will follow these steps when making a decision:

1. *Identify the problem.* When we are unhappy with a decision, we sometimes discover that we rushed to solve the problem before we had it

clearly identified. For example, James quit his job because he was unhappy, thinking that he disliked the work. In reality, it was his inability to relate satisfactorily to his supervisor that made him unhappy. He actually liked doing the work. If he had clearly identified the problem before acting, perhaps he could have solved his problem without leaving the company.

2. *Consider as many alternative solutions as possible.* Failure to consider all the alternatives may be the most frequent cause of dissatisfaction among decision-makers. The qualities of open-mindedness and curiosity aid in the search for all alternatives. For example, Mary thinks she must quit school because she does not have tuition money; however, if she were a critical thinker, she would realize that she has options. She might borrow the tuition from a financial institution, from friends, or from family; she could apply for a scholarship; she might apply for a federal loan; or she might get a part-time job. Perhaps she could arrange to pay the tuition fees in installment payments. (You may think of other possibilities.)

3. *Evaluate each alternative.* Consider the outcome of each one. The careful decision-maker completes this step with the use of pencil and paper to review all the possible consequences. It may help to ask friends or family members to help you do the evaluation, because they may think of alternatives that you would not.

4. *Choose the best alternative and act on it.* After the action is completed, evaluate your decision to help yourself in future decision-making. For example, ask these questions about a decision:

   ◆ What will others think about my decision?
   ◆ How will this decision affect others?
   ◆ Would I make the same decision again?
   ◆ What have I learned from this decision-making?
   ◆ What would happen if everybody made this decision?

To practice using critical thinking skills, review the practice exercise in Figure 10-4. Prepare a form like the one shown and answer all the questions.

OPEN-MINDEDNESS AND A POSITIVE ATTITUDE

You know by now that the key to positive human relationships is communication. (Review communication skills discussed in Chapters 2 and 7 in this book.) In addition to skills in communication, open-mindedness and positive attitudes toward others produce good relations. Negative attitudes, such as stereotyping, sexism, and prejudice destroy good relationships.

```
┌─────────────────────────────────────────────────────────────────┐
│                  Critical Thinking Practice Exercise              │
│                                                                   │
│   1. DESCRIBE A PROBLEM YOU HAVE:                                 │
│                                                                   │
│                                                                   │
│   2. LIST THOSE THINGS RELATED TO THE PROBLEM THAT ARE            │
│      IMPORTANT TO YOU (VALUES):                                   │
│                                                                   │
│                                                                   │
│   3. WRITE YOUR GOAL(S) THAT RELATE TO THIS PROBLEM:              │
│                                                                   │
│                                                                   │
│   4. LIST POSSIBLE SOLUTIONS TO THIS PROBLEM:                     │
│                                                                   │
│                                                                   │
│   5. CONSIDER THE CONSEQUENCES OF EACH POSSIBLE                   │
│      SOLUTION (Place a "+" or a "−" beside each option for each   │
│      positive or negative thought you have about the solution.)   │
│                                                                   │
│                                                                   │
│   6. CHOOSE THE BEST SOLUTION                                     │
│                                                                   │
│                                                                   │
│   7. EVALUATE YOUR DECISION BY ASKING THESE QUESTIONS:            │
│      a. What would happen if everyone chose this solution?        │
│      b. What do others (friends, family, teachers, older people,  │
│         experts in the area) think about this solution?           │
│      c. Would I choose this solution if the problem arose again?  │
└─────────────────────────────────────────────────────────────────┘
```

Figure 10-4 Prepare a form like this for yourself and then respond to all the questions.

Discrimination. People may exhibit discrimination toward individuals or groups. Discrimination in business is often directed at women, handicapped people, and various ethnic groups. Discrimination results in one person being treated differently from others; that is, out of three job candidates with outstanding credentials, one may be eliminated from consideration just because he or she is in a wheelchair. Fear and ignorance are the basis of discrimination.

Discrimination in the workplace includes using different job qualifications for hiring, using different criteria for promotions, maintaining different salary levels, and using different job classification systems. Hiring and recognition systems that do not provide equal freedom and opportunity for all people are harmful to all of society. In such cases, people are denied the chance to achieve their greatest potential. The truly professional worker does not participate in discriminatory behavior against any individual or group.

In the United States, discrimination in the workplace is illegal. Laws have been enacted to prevent discrimination because of race, creed, religion, sex, or color. Where discrimination does occur, workers may report the activity, and management is obligated to eliminate it. However, the greatest deterrent to such behavior is a high standard of fairness on the part of all workers.

Stereotyping. Stereotyping is assuming that all people in a group behave in a certain way. For example, it is stereotyping to say, "All women like flattery," or "All elderly people are senile." Stereotyping is unfair and unpleasant; it can also inhibit productivity.

Closely related to stereotyping is sexism, which is behavior that suggests that people are somehow less qualified for a task because of their sex. Sexist attitudes are most often directed against women in the workplace, although men may also be the subject of sexist treatment. For example, if a company considers only women for its customer service positions because women can be employed for less money, that is sexist on two grounds—it prevents men from being hired, and it suggests that women are worth less money than men. Another example of sexism is found when management chooses to promote a less qualified man instead of a woman. Such a decision is based on an assumption that men are the "bread-winners" for their families and need more money. Sexist attitudes limit the achievement of both individuals and companies.

Prejudice. Prejudice exists when someone has negative feelings toward someone else based on assumptions that are not necessarily true. Prejudice may also exist against groups. For example, you may have negative feelings about a particular man because of his appearance. You may decide that he must be uninteresting, so you are against his working with you on a special project. This attitude, like discrimination and stereotyping, is counterproductive.

The following list summarizes important skills.

CRITICAL BEHAVIOR FOR GOOD HUMAN RELATIONS

1. Be sensitive to others.
2. Listen with care to what coworkers say to you.
3. View each coworker as a whole person with many needs.
4. Respond to people as individuals.
5. Treat people fairly.
6. Recognize people for work well done.
7. Be friendly to coworkers (use their names, show an interest in them as human beings).
8. Be tactful in your speech.
9. Do not be argumentative.
10. Be positive.
11. Admit your errors.
12. Do your own work well and on time.
13. Be a good communicator.
14. Avoid discriminatory behavior.

REVIEW QUESTIONS

1. Define the term productivity.
2. Explain why productivity is important to a worker, to a company, and to the country.
3. List three reasons for a company to promote a worker.
4. Give five qualities that are needed for a worker to be considered promotable.
5. Explain how to successfully apply for a promotion.
6. Write five guidelines for behavior after a person has been promoted.
7. Outline the steps in the critical thinking decision-making process.
8. Write five questions you may ask to evaluate a decision.
9. List three mental attitudes that are important to critical thinking.
10. Explain the concept of discrimination. Why is it harmful in the workplace?

ACTIVITIES

1. Visit a public library and read an article on productivity from a current business or news magazine. Write a one-page report summarizing the article.

2. Interview at least two successful workers and report how they manage their lives to be productive workers.

3. Interview a worker with many years of experience and find out how he or she was able to get promotions through the years. Give an oral report to the class.

4. With the aid of a friend, role play a scene in which you ask your employer for a promotion.

5. Identify a recent decision you made and apply the five recommended evaluation questions to your decision. Was your decision a satisfactory one to you? Discuss why or why not.

CHAPTER 11

ETHICS IN YOUR PROFESSIONAL LIFE

CHAPTER GOAL:

To explore the development and importance of personal and business ethics.

CHAPTER OBJECTIVES:

After studying this chapter, you should be able to:

1. Define ethics.
2. Understand the function of ethics.
3. Understand the concern for ethics in the professional world.
4. Consider ethical dilemmas that confront professional people.
5. Determine what is important to you.
6. Determine a set of values.
7. Establish a code of ethics.
8. Discuss ways personal and business ethics interrelate.
9. Define and maintain personal ethical standards.
10. Develop practical professional ethics.

A Wall Street financier pleads guilty to trading on inside information . . . a White House employee resigns after charges of using improper influence . . . a TV minister is sued for using church funds for personal gain . . . a presidential candidate withdraws after newspaper reports of marital infidelity . . . a large corporation is charged with selling products that are harmful to children . . . .

What is the underlying cause of all these scandals? Many people believe that these and similar problems result from a lack of a code of ethics to guide individuals and organizations in their activities. In other words, the problems occurred when individuals abandoned an existing code of ethics in favor of personal or corporate gain.

What is a code of ethics? How does it influence the professional worker? In this chapter we examine ethical behavior, giving particular consideration to its role in the world of work.

ETHICS

Ethics is the study of right and wrong action. Ethics are also a set of principles that guide behavior. Ethics are at issue when a company does not pay illegal aliens fairly or when one worker takes credit for another's idea.

THE PURPOSE OF ETHICS

Ethics concerns major questions. What is right or wrong? How should we treat others? A code of ethics is the collection of rules or guidelines that direct behavior. The purpose of a code of ethics is to guide conduct. A code of ethics for a professional group or for a business establishes ideals for decision-making and for behavior.

You know that society has laws to guide our actions. Then you may ask, "What is the need for ethics?" or "What is the difference between laws and ethics?" You can distinguish between laws and ethics by considering laws as *required* behavior and ethics as *ideal* behavior. A law establishes minimal requirements of personal behavior, but ethics goes beyond the minimum. For example, the law requires that you do not steal a person's food; but ethics challenges you to give food to a person who is starving.

The study of ethics today seeks answers to difficult questions such as these:

◆ What are the rights of a surrogate parent?

◆ Do embryos have rights?

◆ Is it acceptable to take a gift from a customer?

◆ Should a university conduct research that may be used to produce military weapons?

◆ May a teacher use student research in writing a professional paper?

◆ How much profit may a business make on a product?

◆ May a worker use company resources to meet family needs?

ETHICAL CODES IN HISTORY

When selected ethical principles are grouped together they are called an ethical code. You may understand better what an ethical code is if you consider some codes that are well-known. For example, the Ten Commandments form perhaps the best-known code of ethics in the Western world. This code was first used thousands of years ago by the Hebrew people, and it continues to be the basis for behavior for many people in the world today. The world's major religions all have beliefs that form the basis of ethical codes for their followers. Medical doctors take an oath based on a code made by Hippocrates in ancient times. This code provides a guide for their ethical behavior as physicians.

VALUED ETHICAL PRINCIPLES

What ethical principles are important to you? When that question is asked to a variety of people, a range of answers is given. However, two principles inevitably appear among the answers given by any group: honesty and concern for others. Among the most commonly valued principles are these:

- Respect for life
- Honesty
- Fairness
- Equality
- Freedom

In the business world, honesty, responsibility, fairness, and loyalty are highly valued ethical principles. After completing this chapter, you may want to add to these lists other principles of behavior that are important to you.

SOURCES OF CODES OF ETHICS

Codes of ethics for individuals vary somewhat from those of business organizations, yet there are many similarities. This chapter examines the source of codes of ethics for individuals, for professional groups, and for businesses.

For the Individual. An individual's code of ethics is developed from his or her experiences, family, religion, and education. When people begin to consider their behavior in terms of its effects on themselves and others, they begin to consciously develop an ethical code. Education on the value of citizenship, tolerance, kindness, rights, and responsibilities contributes to the further development of a personal code. Family and culture (including religion) are the strongest forces in the formation of an individual code of ethics.

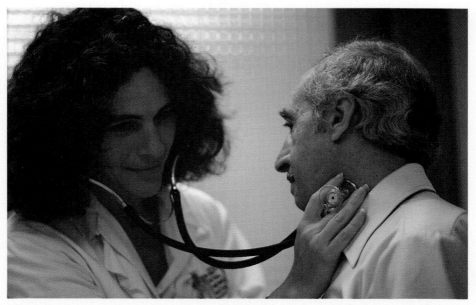

Figure 11-1 Doctors, like all professionals, must perform their work in an ethical manner. (Courtesy of New York University Medical Center.)

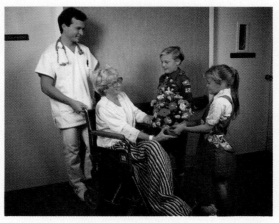

Figure 11-2 You begin to form ethical values as a child. (From Hegner and Caldwell, *Nursing Assistant*, 6th edition, Delmar Publishers Inc.)

For a Profession. The ethics of a specific profession is the code that guides the actions of its members. The purpose of the code is to ensure high standards of behavior and competence; it exists to strengthen members and promote the welfare of the group. Professional codes are developed by committees made up of members of the profession. See Figure 11-3 for an example of a code of ethics for a professional group.

Code of Ethics and Standard Practices
for Texas Educators

Adopted by the Teachers' Professional Practices Commission   **Revised March 30, 1988**

The Texas educator should strive to create an atmosphere that will nurture to fulfillment the potential of each student.

The educator is responsible for standard practices and ethical conduct toward students, professional colleagues, parents, and the community.

The Code is intended to govern the profession, and interpretations of the Code shall be determined by the Professional Practices Commission.

The educator who conducts his affairs with conscientious concern will exemplify the highest standards of professional commitment.

PRINCIPLE I

PROFESSIONAL ETHICAL CONDUCT

The Texas educator should endeavor to maintain the dignity of the profession by respecting and obeying the law, demonstrating personal integrity, and exemplifying honesty.

STANDARDS

1. The educator shall not intentionally misrepresent official policies of the school district or educational organization and shall clearly distinguish those views from his personal attitudes and opinions.
2. The educator shall honestly account for all funds committed to his charge and shall conduct his financial business with integrity.
3. The educator shall not use institutional or professional privileges for personal or partisan advantage.
4. The educator shall accept no gratuities, gifts, or favors that impair or appear to impair professional judgment.
5. The educator shall not offer any favor, service, or thing of value to obtain special advantage.
6. The educator shall not falsify records, or direct or coerce others to do so.

PRINCIPLE II

PROFESSIONAL PRACTICES AND PERFORMANCE

The Texas educator, after qualifying in a manner established by law or regulation, shall assume responsibilities for professional teaching practices and professional performance and shall continually strive to demonstrate competence.

STANDARDS

1. The educator shall apply for, accept, offer, or assign a position or a responsibility on the basis of professional qualifications and shall adhere to the terms of a contract or appointment.
2. The educator shall possess mental health, physical stamina, and social prudence necessary to perform the duties of his professional assignment.
3. The educator shall organize instruction that seeks to accomplish objectives related to learning.
4. The educator shall continue professional growth.
5. The educator shall comply with written local school board policies, Texas Education Agency regulations, and applicable state and federal laws.

PRINCIPLE III

ETHICAL CONDUCT TOWARD PROFESSIONAL COLLEAGUES

The Texas educator, in exemplifying ethical relations with colleagues, shall accord just and equitable treatment to all members of the profession.

STANDARDS

1. The educator shall not reveal confidential information concerning colleagues unless disclosure serves professional purposes or is required by law.
2. The educator shall not willfully make false statements about a colleague or the school system.
3. The educator shall adhere to written local school board policies and legal statutes regarding dismissal, evaluation, and employment processes.
4. The educator shall not interfere with a colleague's exercise of political and citizenship rights and responsibilities.
5. The educator shall not discriminate against, coerce, or harass a colleague on the basis of race, color, creed, national origin, age, sex, handicap, or marital status.
6. The educator shall not intentionally deny or impede a colleague in the exercise or enjoyment of any professional right or privilege.
7. The educator shall not use coercive means or promise special treatment in order to influence professional decisions or colleagues.
8. The educator shall have the academic freedom to teach as a professional privilege, and no educator shall interfere with such privilege except as required by state and/or federal laws.

PRINCIPLE IV

ETHICAL CONDUCT TOWARD STUDENTS

The Texas educator, in accepting a position of public trust, should measure success by the progress of each student toward realization of his potential as an effective citizen.

STANDARDS

1. The educator shall deal considerately and justly with each student and shall seek to resolve problems including discipline according to law and school board policy.
2. The educator shall not intentionally expose the student to disparagement.
3. The educator shall not reveal confidential information concerning students unless disclosure serves professional purposes or is required by law.
4. The educator shall make reasonable effort to protect the student from conditions detrimental to the following: learning, physical health, mental health, or safety.
5. The educator shall endeavor to present facts without distortion.
6. The educator shall not unfairly exclude a student from participation in a program, deny benefits to a student, or grant an advantage to a student on the basis of race, color, sex, handicap, national origin, or marital status.
7. The educator shall not unreasonably restrain the student from independent action in the pursuit of learning or deny the student access to varying points of view.

PRINCIPLE V

ETHICAL CONDUCT TOWARD PARENTS AND COMMUNITY

The Texas educator, in fulfilling citizenship responsibilities in the community, should cooperate with parents and others to improve the public schools of the community.

STANDARDS

1. The educator shall make reasonable effort to communicate to parents information which should be revealed in the interest of the student.
2. The educator shall endeavor to understand community cultures and relate the home environment of students to the school.
3. The educator shall manifest a positive role in school public relations.

Figure 11-3 This is a code of ethics for teachers in Texas. (Courtesy of Texas Education Association.)

FOCUS ON:
LIE DETECTOR AND HONESTY TESTS

If you apply for a job in which money, merchandise, or drugs are handled, you may have to take an "honesty test." One type is a polygraph (lie detector) test. A polygraph is an electronic machine that is connected to the body of a subject. The person is asked a series of questions, while the machine records electronic impulses on a graph. If the person tells a lie, the device supposedly detects slight changes in the body's chemistry.

Many experts in the field question the accuracy of polygraph tests. As a result, Congress passed a law in 1988 to restrict the use of such tests. Before that, about two million polygraph tests were administered each year to employees and job applicants.

The law, which went into effect in December 1988, prohibits the use of polygraph tests for screening job applicants. An exception is for those seeking jobs in government, as security guards, or who will be handling narcotics. The new law also curtails the use of polygraphs for workers already on the job. Managers can't ask employees to take the test unless there is a "reasonable suspicion" that they have committed a crime. Even then the test is voluntary. An employee can't be fired for refusing to take it. The law will probably eliminate the use of most polygraph tests.

To avoid the problems and cost of polygraph tests, some companies use written honesty tests. Even before polygraphs were restricted, more written tests were probably administered each year than polygraphs. Honest tests consist of multiple choice and yes-no items. For example:

- Have you ever stolen anything from an employer?   yes   no
- Have you ever cheated in school?   yes   no
- Have you ever lied to a teacher or boss?   yes   no

The test is interpreted by comparing an applicant's answers to those of persons already judged to be honest. This type of test is as controversial as a polygraph test. Whether they help to screen out the most honest job applicant is open to debate. But unless laws are passed restricting their use, millions of job applicants will probably be required to take them.

Reprinted with permission from Larry Bailey, *Working Skills for a New Age*, copyright 1990 by Delmar Publishers Inc., page 403. All rights reserved.

For Business and Industry. Some authorities on business ethics say that in general, what is ethically good for the individual is also good for the business organization. However, business ethics do differ in some ways from an individual's ethics.

When a company recognizes that ethical issues are daily concerns for management and employees, it will probably develop a written code and provide it to all workers. In this way, workers do not have to labor over each ethical decision; they know what the company's stand is on customer returns, irate callers, unfulfilled contracts, and other issues. Employee compliance establishes the value of a code of ethics in a business organization.

A company's code should provide guidelines for actions in response to a variety of situations that normally arise in the business. For example, if a corporation decides that honesty is an important ethical principle, it may have statements such as the following in its written code of ethics:

"All product labels will carry directions for optimum use."

"All service agreements will be straightforward, without hidden meanings."

"Contract agreements will be honored for all workers."

Some large businesses have ethics compliance committees charged with clarifying and distributing company codes and with reinforcing the codes in various ways. That same committee may review violations and suggest changes.

Some business organizations employ a professional person to work with their organizations to develop a practical code of ethics. Such a professional person is called an "ethician" or an "ethicist." These people help a company evaluate goal-setting, performance measurements, and incentives. They also look at social responsibilities and at the ways in which employees are treated. Reports suggest that as many as 75% of the top 1,200 companies in the United States have written ethical codes.

PERSONAL CODE OF ETHICS

Your family and the culture around you provide the strongest influences on your moral beliefs and conduct. Once you become an adult, you will find that you develop your own ethical principles that incorporate what you have acquired from your family and other influences with your own experiences.

To create your own code of ethics, you must first identify what is important to you (what you place a high value on), or what motivates you. You must also establish your own set of values. Values are those qualities and principles that are important to you. When you weigh your

Dear Customer:

We have been making and selling women's clothing for some years, going back to the start of our apparel catalog. It seemed natural for us because of our concentration and expertise in the area of cotton, wool, and cashmere... particularly cotton knits. And our experience made it easy to bring quality to women's apparel of the same kind as men's wear.

Yet in the last several years, we have expanded the horizon of our women's offering. We have invested in experienced women's buyers who have focused on classic styling and the coordination of classic clothing items that go together most attractively... so that you, our customer, can identify with these styles.

We have concentrated on important core basics for your wardrobe, whether that wardrobe be for your working days during the week, or whether it includes those things you want to put together, in a more casual manner, for the weekend.

We have done this at our usual, honest prices with never an allowance for designer markups as practiced elsewhere. But the cutting edge in the Lands' End proposition is found in the inherent quality of the merchandise. It is our belief that in the long run you will want to return to Lands' End because of this quality, even though it will be the basic styling and appearance that may draw you into your first purchase. Like always, your experience with our products counts more than words, but nevertheless our senior writer, responsible for these pages, did come up with a series of words that does seem to describe what we are trying to do, i.e. "Lands' End women's wear, not just better basics, but better basic values."

The testimonials on our cover indicate that our customers tend to feel the same about our value concept. Please write if you have any questions concerning our women's offerings.

Sincerely,

Dick Anderson

Dick Anderson, President, CEO

Figure 11-4 The code of ethics for the retail clothing company, Lands' End, allows employees to know how to behave and customers to know what quality and service they can expect. (Reprinted courtesy of Lands' End Catalog.)

values against your wants, you determine if your own code of ethics will dictate how you will act. For example, you want money but you value honesty. Is money so important that you would rob a bank? Probably not, but would you cheat on your expense account?

WHAT IS IMPORTANT TO YOU?

Numerous elements in all aspects of our lives are important to us. The following is a list of items that many people value. Examine the list carefully and select at least 10 items that are most important to you. Then, of those you selected, rate each in order of importance with 1 being the highest ranking.

Work	Love	Independence
Wealth	Marriage	Individuality
Power	Family	Education
Recognition	Friendship	Freedom
Possessions	Children	Security
Rank and status	Relationships	Acceptance
Achievement	Affection	Formality
Authority	Beauty	Informality
Respect	Health	Cooperation
Competition	Tradition	Involvement
Efficiency	Faith	Energy
Religion		

Consider also your professional life. What is most important to you in a job? High salary? Challenging work? Security? Following are the results of a survey that shows in order of importance what motivates a group of workers.

Do you agree with the results shown in this list? Prepare a list of your own. Include any of the items on the list and include others as well. For example, an ideal manager, an opportunity to help others, work you like doing, work that does not require overtime.

You have now determined what is most important to you in your personal and professional life.

YOUR ETHICAL CODE

You should now identify those principles of behavior that you feel most strongly about. For example, you often see in the news people demonstrating for or against something that may relate to the environment. The people demonstrating have strong feelings about something they believe to be wrong or immoral. The demonstration is an outward sign of their ethical principles. Examine the following list of commonly held principles. You may add others to the list if you wish. Then rank each

WHAT MOTIVATES PEOPLE

Survey of 383 employees ranking 15 job-related motivational factors in order of importance.

Challenging work (96.9%)
My opinion matters when decisions are made (96%)
Recognition for job well done (90.9%)
Pay clearly tied to my performance (88.7%)
Working for a company I can be proud of (87.2%)
Good, fair performance measures (85%)
Autonomy on the job (82.3%)
A competitive salary (80.9%)
Clear performance goals (77.6%)
Opportunity to learn on the job (76.4%)
Clear career opportunities (74.4%)
Harmonious relationships with co-workers (70.7%)
Job security (58.8%)
Generous benefit program (54.1%)
Special incentives, such as merchandise and travel (8.8%)

(Source: American Productivity & Quality Center)

Figure 11-5 Survey of factors that motivate people. (Courtesy of American Productivity and Quality Care.)

of the principles in order of importance to you with 1 being the highest ranking.

Honesty	Respect for human life
Integrity	Kindness
Loyalty	Tolerance
Fairness	Concern for the environment
Concern for others	Concern for all life

You have identified the things that are most important to you in your personal and professional life. You have also identified the principles you cherish most. Now examine each of the lists you have prepared and weigh the first two against the third. Do you see any potential conflicts? You should now be able to begin to develop your own code of ethics.

USING YOUR ETHICAL CODE AS A RESOURCE

As a professional you may encounter major or minor ethical dilemmas in relation to your clients, company, or coworkers. Your personal code of ethics will help guide you through these problems.

Figure 11-6 These demonstrators are showing their values by taking a stand on an environmental issue. (Courtesy of Save the Dolphins Project, Earth Island Institute.)

When you encounter an ethical problem at work, asking the right questions is critical to solving the problem:

1. What is the business issue?
2. What is the ethical issue related to the business decision?
3. What would be the result of various responses?
4. What action will I take?

MAKING ETHICAL DECISIONS

Your answer to the last question, what action will I take, may be difficult. Two approaches are generally used by people facing an ethical dilemma. You may choose to use one or both approaches. Neither of them is incorrect; they are simply chosen by personal preference. One is to make your decision based on a set of rules, or principles, that you believe are important. The other is to analyze the situation and base your decision on what you believe to be the appropriate action for the particular situation.

As you observe others making ethical decisions, you will find that there are different levels of ethical maturity just as there are different levels of physical maturity. Notice how the bases for decisions vary with maturity.

Level 1 Decisions based on personal desires
Level 2 Decisions based on a set of rules
Level 3 Decisions based on consideration for others as well as for yourself
Level 4 Decisions based on a global perspective

As you consider an ethical dilemma, you may find these guidelines helpful in resolving the problem. Make these determinations:

1. Is it legal?
2. Does it reflect my moral beliefs?
3. How will it affect others?
4. Am I using objective thinking?
5. What sort of person would make this decision?
6. Does it reflect my ethical code?

Use the communication skills you have studied to help you reach a course of action. Listen well. Speak clearly, and disagree tactfully. These are essential in solving difficult problems. Understand and be concerned with the common good (that of your company and of coworkers). Think carefully about each of the statements or questions in Figure 11-7. Do your answers reflect your own professional ethics?

As you encounter new situations, such as a new job, you will be confronted with challenges and faced with such questions as "How do I remain true to my personal code of ethics and be responsive to the

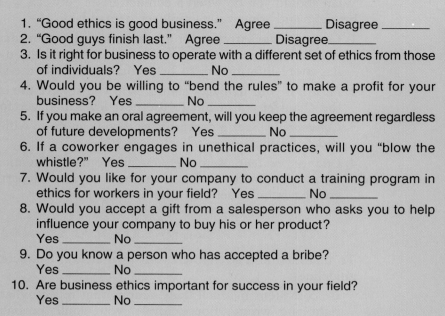

YOUR PROFESSIONAL ETHICS

1. "Good ethics is good business."   Agree _____ Disagree _____
2. "Good guys finish last."   Agree _____ Disagree_____
3. Is it right for business to operate with a different set of ethics from those of individuals?   Yes _____ No _____
4. Would you be willing to "bend the rules" to make a profit for your business?   Yes _____ No _____
5. If you make an oral agreement, will you keep the agreement regardless of future developments?   Yes _____ No _____
6. If a coworker engages in unethical practices, will you "blow the whistle?"   Yes _____ No _____
7. Would you like for your company to conduct a training program in ethics for workers in your field?   Yes _____ No _____
8. Would you accept a gift from a salesperson who asks you to help influence your company to buy his or her product?
   Yes _____ No _____
9. Do you know a person who has accepted a bribe?
   Yes _____ No _____
10. Are business ethics important for success in your field?
   Yes _____ No _____

Figure 11-7   Prepare a form like this and respond to the statements or questions.

demands of my employer? What compromises can I make and still retain my personal integrity?"

Answers to these questions will vary from person to person, but with each decision, you will build your ethical character and your skill as a decision-maker. Here are some attitudes that discourage ethical behavior:

Conformity	"Everybody does it."
Dependence	"Take a pill if you feel depressed or guilty."
Selfishness	"I am only concerned with myself."
Apathy toward others	"I have no idea how she will be affected by the situation."
Limited morals	"I'm not concerned with theories of right or wrong."

These responses are only rationalizations. They are easy answers to difficult questions, but they are not the right answers for responsible professionals.

BUSINESS VERSUS PROFESSIONAL ETHICS

What should you do when a conflict arises between what you believe to be right and what your employer demands?

1. *Communicate.* Arrange for a conference with your manager. Talk with him or her about your concerns. Ask for clarification. Ask if he or she has more information to help you understand the situation.

2. *Persist.* If your manager cannot help you resolve the conflict, move up the chain of command to the next level manager for help.

3. *Compromise.* Seek a compromise if you can do so within your personal code of ethics.

4. *Change positions.* Remove yourself from the situation if you cannot resolve it; that is, seek a transfer to another department, or, if the conflict is quite serious, find another job.

MAINTAINING PERSONAL ETHICAL STANDARDS

To maintain and strengthen your own ethical character, practice these guidelines:

◆ Be consistent in small daily actions that reflect what you believe are right and wrong. For example, you would probably not consider taking a desk or a computer from your company, but you may consider taking home a calculator for your personal use. Small violations of your ethical code build up until you reach a point that you no longer know where to draw the line. This ultimately weakens your character and your moral resolve.

◆ Resist following the suggestions of coworkers to do something unethical, to cheat the company in some small way. Become known as a person with strong ethical character.

◆ When you are mistaken, admit your mistake. When you are strong enough to take responsibility for your own actions, you build a positive ethical and professional image.

◆ Develop skills in responding to people who ask you to act in inappropriate ways. For example, try these responses:

"I'm sorry I can't do that because it violates company policy."
"I would like to help you, but it doesn't feel right to me."
"I just wouldn't be comfortable doing that."
"I don't see the issue that way."
"As I understand the situation, that would not be fair."

As you can see, it is best to avoid belittling the other person for making the suggestion. Emphasize the difference in the way you feel about the action rather than the way you feel about the person. You will have a more positive influence on that other person by calmly stating your position rather than attacking his or her ideas.

ACTING ON YOUR PRINCIPLES

To gain experience in dealing with ethical dilemmas, consider the cases that follow. Read each one, analyzing it thoroughly. Then answer the questions in Figure 11-8 for each case. You can prepare a form like the one in Figure 11-8 for yourself and make enough copies for each case. You can also simply write your answers to correspond to the numbered questions. You may wish to review the information on critical thinking skills found in Chapter 10 before you proceed.

1. Joyce has worked as a mail clerk for several years in the XYZ Company. Recently, she has noticed that her manager is removing envelopes containing cash from the mail. What should Joyce do?

2. Martin and Elena are celebrating Martin's new job with dinner at a nice restaurant. Their entrees cost about $12 apiece. They each had two drinks ($8 total), plus an elegant dessert costing $3.95, which they shared. When the check arrives, the total is $21.65, which is obviously too low. Because checks are paid at the cashier, they could pay the $21.65 and leave. What should they do?

3. Enrique has a small business that produces and markets chocolates. The demand for the candy has tripled in the past year and it is now possible for Enrique to make a 400% profit on his candies. Enrique wonders if it is ethical for him to make such an enormous profit. What should he do?

4. Reports issued regularly by ABC Accounting Firm have been found to be inaccurate. The reports, with serious errors, have greatly damaged the company's image. Management has investigated and attributed the errors to workers in the word processing department. However, Helena Grimes knows that the errors originated in her auditing division. If she admits the truth, both she and her colleagues will be in serious trouble and may even lose their jobs. What should Helena do?

5. Lee has worked for the GEP Company only one year. Previously he worked for the HIJ Company, which patented a new design for footwear. His new manager has promised him a big raise in salary if he will reveal the secrets of the HIJ design. What should he do?

6. Cathy had a conference with a teacher about her daughter, who is in the third grade. The conference concerned the child's grades and conduct. Cathy wanted the teacher to show her the grades of other students in the class so that she might make a comparison of her own child's work and that of other students. What should the teacher do?

ANALYZE AN ETHICAL DILEMMA

A description of the dilemma: _____

_____

_____

_____

1. What is the ethical issue? _____

_____

_____

2. What are three possible solutions?

Alternative A _____

_____

Alternative B _____

_____

Alternative C _____

_____

3. What would be the result of:

Alternative A _____

_____

Alternative B _____

_____

Alternative C _____

_____

4. What action should be taken? _____

_____

_____

_____

Figure 11-8 Filling out this form will help you analyze an ethical dilemma.

7. Craig and his partner, Jim wrote an insurance policy on a mobile home for $10,000. Their commission was only $100. Yet Craig and Jim had to appraise the property and take photos to send to the home office. They traveled approximately 50 miles to find the mobile home, but after searching for over an hour, they could not locate it. Jim had another appointment later in the day and had to get back to the office. He suggested that they take a picture of any mobile home in the area and send it to the company. What should Craig do?

8. Beth, who is a chef, was hired to train food service workers in a local hotel. She developed a videotape to use in the training. She used her own time and resources to make the tape. It was a very good training tool, and it worked well with the hotel staff. The owner of the hotel took the training video without Beth's permission, had several copies made, and began marketing the video to other hotels. Beth feels that the hotel owner was wrong to take credit for and profit from her work. What should Beth do?

9. While on a business trip, LuAnn stops at a fast food restaurant for lunch. As she slides into a booth, she notices a money clip nearly hidden in the crack of the booth. It contains $75. It would be easy to just slip the money into her purse and leave the restaurant. What should she do?

As you can see, we face ethical dilemmas every day, especially when we enter the work world where many of our decisions affect many people. That's why it is important to have codes of ethics that provide for the well-being of others as well as ourselves. The ideal is for decisions to be right and to be good business as well.

REVIEW QUESTIONS

1. Write a definition of ethics.
2. What is the major function of a code of ethics?
3. How are codes of ethics developed by individuals? By professional groups? By businesses?
4. How may your personal code of ethics benefit you as a professional person?
5. Describe three ways to respond to coworkers who ask you to act in ways that you believe are unethical.
6. Write three questions you may ask yourself when you confront an ethical dilemma.

7. What ethical principle do you think is the most important one for a manager to practice?

ACTIVITIES

1. Interview a person in business management to learn what ethical principles are important to her or his business. Give an oral report.
2. Write a paragraph describing an ethical dilemma you have faced recently. Apply the questions recommended in this chapter to analyze the dilemma. Summarize the process and your decision.
3. Visit your library and read an article in a current business journal or newsmagazine about ethics in business. Write a one-page report.
4. Over the course of a week, collect newspaper or magazine articles that illustrate conflict over ethics. This may involve human interest articles about someone who is taking a stand personally or professionally or may include stories about a breach of promise or other unethical activities by business. Depending on how much access you have to newspapers, you may clip the articles, photocopy them, or write summaries.

CHAPTER GOAL:

To emphasize the relationship between health and job performance and to provide information needed to maintain wellness.

CHAPTER OBJECTIVES:

After studying this chapter, you should be able to:

1. Describe signs of wellness.
2. Relate diet to good health.
3. Plan and implement a personal exercise program to maintain optimum physical condition.
4. Use various methods to control stress.
5. Analyze health risks.
6. Practice habits that minimize health risks.
7. Understand the relationship of emotional health to physical health.
8. Obtain necessary health care.

R ecall a day when you were excited about your plans *for the day* and felt "on top of the world." Why did you feel so great that day? Probably because you felt healthy, energetic, and stimulated by the prospect of the day's events. Wouldn't it be wonderful to feel that way every day? Many factors contribute to feelings of well-being, but basic to them all is good health. In this chapter we review information and practices that promote wellness.

WELLNESS

Wellness is simply good health. In addition, there is a feeling of well-being along with an absence of sickness. Maintaining wellness is a self-help process that means you take responsibility for your body and its condition. When you are committed to the goal of wellness, you conscientiously study to learn what practices are healthful, and you make it your goal to develop habits of eating, exercising, and relaxing that produce physical, emotional, and social health.

SIGNS OF WELLNESS

Who are the healthiest people you know? How do they look? How do they act? Good health shows in appearance, in resistance to disease, in daily energy, and in attitudes. Prominent signs of good health, or wellness, are:

- Appropriate body weight
- Good posture
- Energy
- Clear eyes, skin, hair
- Resistance to disease
- Cavity-free teeth and healthy gums
- Good muscle tone
- Ability to sleep well
- Ability to adapt to change
- Positive attitude
- Ability to manage normal stress

MAINTAINING WELLNESS

Your daily living habits, or your life-style, are the key to health. The most important considerations for health are diet, exercise, daily routines, management of stress, and wise response to health risks. You can manage all these factors in your life if you have information about each of them and if you are willing to discipline yourself for healthful living.

FOOD FOR WELLNESS

You know that food is essential for health; unfortunately, food can also contribute to poor health. Therefore, it is important to know how to select what you eat so that you can feel well, look attractive, and have energy for your activities (see Figure 12-1).

What are your food needs? What special efforts should you make to be well-nourished? *Nutrition* is how food is used by the body. The study of nutrition has provided some basic information that can help us choose foods that will result in health and well-being.

NUTRITION BASICS

Food is composed of nutrients (the elements in food that furnish nourishment), which are essential for life and health. Over 40 nutrients have been identified, and they may be grouped into six categories: proteins, fats, carbohydrates, vitamins, minerals, and water. Table 12-1 shows major nutrients with their functions and sources.

CALORIES

A *calorie* is a measurement of the amount of energy that your body gets from the foods you eat. Calories are generally referred to in terms of how many calories a certain food contains; for example, you may say that a Diet Coke has only one calorie. Calories are also viewed in terms of how many are used to accomplish a particular activity; for example, playing tennis for a certain amount of time uses a certain number of calories.

By comparing the number of calories in the food you eat with the number of calories you use during your daily activities, you can determine whether you gain, lose, or stay at the same weight. When a person consumes foods containing more calories than the body uses, the body converts the extra calories to body fat. So, you can see that achieving and maintaining your ideal weight is related to the number of calories in the foods you eat. The following list provides information on the number of calories in some common foods.

CALORIES IN COMMON FOODS

FRUITS AND VEGETABLES

Apple, 1 medium	80
Applesauce, 1 cup	230
Banana	100
Orange juice, 1 cup	110
Green beans, 1 cup	30
Corn, whole kernel, $1/2$ cup	65
Potato, 1 medium, baked	145
Potato chips, 20	230

Potatoes, French fried, 20	270
Potato salad, $^1/_2$ cup	125

MILK AND MILK PRODUCTS

Whole milk, 1 cup	150
Lowfat milk (2%), 1 cup	120
Cheddar cheese, 1 oz.	110
Cottage cheese, lowfat, 1 cup	200
Ice cream, 1 cup	270
Butter, 1 tablespoon	100

MEATS AND MEAT SUBSTITUTES

Broiled hamburger patty, 3 oz.	270
Steak, 3 oz.	330
Bacon, 2 slices	90
Chicken breast, fried, $^1/_2$	160
Chicken leg, fried	90
Chicken quarter, broiled	120
Fishsticks, 1	50
Egg, hard cooked, 1	80
Macaroni and cheese, 1 cup	480

GRAIN FOODS

Biscuit	90
Muffin	120
Angel food cake, 1 piece	100
Chocolate cake, iced, 1 piece	230
Oatmeal, 1 cup	130
Spaghetti, 1 cup	190
Rice, 1 cup	230

MISCELLANEOUS

Popcorn, 1 cup	25
Cola	100
Mayonnaise, 1 tablespoon	100
Sugar, 1 tablespoon	45

As you determine how much food you need to support your lifestyle, you will also need to know how many calories you use in various types of physical activities. Notice in Table 12-2 how many calories are used in various kinds of activities. For example, when you bicycle for an hour, you use 360 or more calories. Obviously, the more energy you use (by going faster or uphill), the more calories you can use without weight gain, which means that you can eat more.

TABLE 12-1: DIETARY GUIDELINES FOR AMERICANS

GUIDELINE	EXPLANATION	EXAMPLES
1. Eat a variety of foods.	◆ Most foods contains several nutrients, but no single food can give you all the nutrients you need. The greater the variety, the less likely you are to develop either a deficiency or an excess of any single nutrient. ◆ Eating a variety of foods reduces the likelihood of being exposed to excessive.	◆ Select foods each day from each of the four food groups: Milk-Cheese, Fruit-Vegetable, Meat-Poultry-Fish-Beans, Bread-Cereal.
2. Maintain healthy weight.	◆ If you are overweight, your chances of developing certain disorders are increased. These include high blood pressure, increased level of blood fats and cholesterol, and diabetes. These disorders, in turn, increase your risk of heart attacks and strokes. ◆ If you are much underweight, you will have little strength and tire easily.	◆ Choose healthy food and eat in moderation, neither too much nor too little. ◆ Avoid limited nutrition-giving foods. ◆ Exercise regularly.
3. Choose a diet low in fat, saturated fat, and cholesterol.	◆ High blood cholesterol levels increase the risk of heart attacks. In some people, high blood cholesterol levels are related to high intake of fats, particularly saturated	◆ Eat lean meats, fish, poultry, and dried beans and peas for protein. ◆ Eat eggs in moderation. ◆ Limit your intake of butter, cream, shortening, and hydrogenated margarine,

	fats, and cholesterol in the diet.	sauces, and sandwich spreads. ◆ Trim fat off meats. ◆ Avoid fried foods.
4. Choose a diet with plenty of vegetables, fruits, and grain products.	◆ Complex carbohydrates-starches provide more nutrients per calorie than simple carbohydrates-sugars. ◆ Certain complex carbohydrates provide fiber. High-fiber foods help reduce the symptoms of chronic constipation, diverticulosis, and some types of "irritable bowel."	◆ Eat at least five fruits and vegetables each day. ◆ Select foods high in fiber and starch.
5. Use sugars only in moderation.	◆ Eating too much sugar, especially sticky sweets and sugared soft drinks, increases the likelihood you will get cavities in your teeth. ◆ Too much sugar may cause hyperactivity.	◆ Use less of all sugars-white sugar, brown sugar, honey, and syrups. ◆ Eat less sweet foods.
6. Use salt and sodium only in moderation.	◆ A little sodium is essential for health, but most Americans consume far more than they need. Excess sodium intake may increase the likelihood of developing high blood pressure.	◆ Reduce the amount of salt used. ◆ Limit your intake of salty foods, such as potato chips, and pickled foods.
7. If you drink alcoholic beverages, do so in moderation.	◆ Excessive consumption leads to uncontrolled behavior and various health risks.	◆ Limit consumption.

Adapted from Duyff & Others, *Family Health* p. 12, Peoria: Glencoe Inc.

Figure 12-1 It is important to eat the right foods. (Courtesy of National Dairy Council.)

TABLE 12-2: ACTIVITIES AND CALORIES EXPENDED

ACTIVITY	CALORIES EXPENDED PER HOUR[1]	
	MAN[2]	WOMAN[2]
Sitting quietly	100	80
Standing quietly	120	95
Light activity:	300	240
Cleaning house		
Office work		
Playing baseball		
Playing golf		
Moderate activity:	460	370
Walking briskly (3.5 mph)		
Gardening		
Cycling (5.5 mph)		
Dancing		
Playing basketball		
Strenuous activity:	730	580
Jogging (9 min./mile)		
Playing football		
Swimming		
Very strenuous activity:	920	740
Running (7 min./mile)		
Racquetball		
Skiing		

[1]May vary depending on environmental conditions.
[2]Healthy man, 175 lbs; healthy woman, 140 lbs

Source: U.S. Department of Agriculture Home and Garden Bulletin No. 232

In general, inactive women and older adults should consume about 1,600 calories a day. Children, teenage girls, active women, and inactive men can consume 2,200 calories a day. Teenage boys, active men, and very active women can consume 2,800 calories a day. Everyone's body chemistry and life-style are different, so you will have to experiment to find out how many calories a day are right for you.

DIETARY GUIDELINES

All foods can be divided into five groups:

1. Grains

2. Fruits and vegetables

3. Milk

4. Fish, poultry, meat, eggs, beans, and nuts

5. Foods that provide few nutrients or excessive sugars or fats

If you want to eat a well-balanced diet, you should eat foods from the basic four groups each day. Various theories exist concerning which foods we should eat and in what quantities. Table 12-3 provides recommendations from the U.S. Department of Agriculture for amounts of food an average person needs to maintain health. (Note that fruits and vegetables have been separated into two groups.)

Notice that breads, cereals, and other grain products represent our greatest needs; every day we need from 6 to 11 servings. These may be obtained from bread, rolls, biscuits, muffins, crackers, oatmeal, rice, pasta, or ready-to-eat cereal.

Vegetables make up the second group with second largest number of servings: the average person needs 3 to 5 servings daily. Cooked vegetables and salads are the most common way to obtain these foods.

Fruits form the next group. You need 2 to 4 servings daily. These can include fruit juice, apples, bananas, grapefruit, berries, and cooked fruit.

Meat, poultry, fish, and alternates are also needed. The average person needs 2 to 3 servings daily for a total daily intake of 5 to 7 ounces of cooked lean meat. One egg or $1/2$ cup of cooked beans or 2 tablespoons of peanut butter represent alternatives to meat, fish, and poultry in the diet.

Finally, milk and milk products are needed. Two to 3 servings daily are recommended with a serving being 8 ounces of milk or $1 1/2$ ounce natural cheese.

Within each of the four food groups are some foods that we can eat anytime, some that we should eat only sometimes, and some that we should eat rarely (see Table 12-4). So although we should eat 6 to 11 servings from the grain group each day, we should avoid certain foods within that group.

In addition to selecting the correct foods from the food groups, there are other guidelines for eating to maintain your health. These guidelines are the Dietary Goals for the United States, provided by the Senate Select Commission on Nutrition and Human Needs. Here are the recommendations:

TABLE 12-3 USDA RECOMMENDATIONS

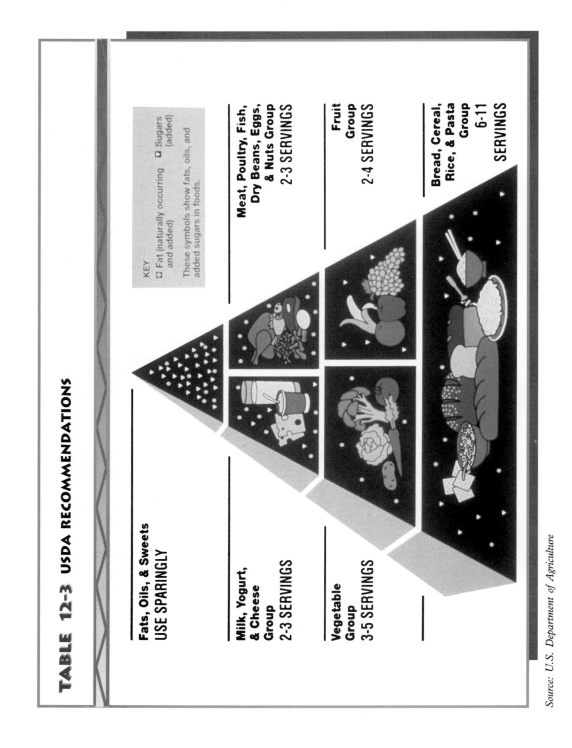

Fats, Oils, & Sweets
USE SPARINGLY

KEY
◻ Fat (naturally occurring   ◻ Sugars
and added)   (added)

These symbols show fats, oils, and
added sugars in foods.

Milk, Yogurt,
& Cheese
Group
2-3 SERVINGS

Meat, Poultry, Fish,
Dry Beans, Eggs,
& Nuts Group
2-3 SERVINGS

Vegetable
Group
3-5 SERVINGS

Fruit
Group
2-4 SERVINGS

Bread, Cereal,
Rice, & Pasta
Group
6-11
SERVINGS

Source: U.S. Department of Agriculture

TABLE 12-4 HOW OFTEN WE SHOULD EAT CERTAIN FOODS

ANYTIME	SOMETIMES	SELDOM
GRAIN GROUP		
Whole-grain breads and cereals	Muffins	Croissants
Brown rice, bulgur	Waffles, pancakes	Doughnuts
Pasta	Heavily sweetened cereals	Danish pastries
Bagels, rolls	Granola cereals	Bread stuffing from mix
FRUIT & VEGETABLE GROUP		
All fruits and vegetables (except those at right)	Avocado, guacamole	Coconut
Applesauce, unsweetened	Dried and canned fruit	Pickles
Potatoes, white or sweet	Fruit juice	Scalloped or au gratin potatoes
	Canned vegetables with salt	
	French fries, fried in vegetable oil	
MILK GROUP		
Dry-curd cottage cheese	2% low-fat or regular cottage cheese	Soft and hard whole-milk cheeses
Skim milk	Reduced-fat or part-skim cheeses	Processed cheeses
1% low-fat milk products	2% low-fat milk, low-fat yogurt	Whole milk, whole-milk yogurt
Nonfat yogurt	Ice milk, frozen nonfat or low-fat yogurt	Ice cream
FISH, POULTRY, MEAT, EGGS, BEANS & NUTS GROUP		
FISH		
All fin fish	Fried fish	
Salmon, canned	Tuna, oil-pack	
Tuna, water-pack	Shrimp	
Shellfish, except shrimp		
POULTRY		
Chicken breast (without skin)	Chicken breast (with skin)	Fried chicken thigh or wing
Turkey breast, drumstick, thigh	Chicken drumstick, thigh	Chicken hot dog
Ground turkey (without skin)	Fried chicken, except thigh or wing	
	Ground turkey (with skin)	

RED MEATS

Pork tenderloin	Bottom round, sirloin steak	Chuck blade, rib roast
Beef eye round and top round	Lean ham	Extra-lean or lean ground beef
	Pork or lamb loin chop	Pork or lamb rib chop, bacon
	Leg of lamb, veal sirloin	
	Veal loin or rib chop	Bologna, salami, hot dog
		Any untrimmed red meat

EGGS

Egg white   Whole egg or yolk

BEANS, PEAS & NUTS

Beans, peas, lentils   Tofu, peanut butter, nuts

1. Eat a variety of foods.
2. Maintain healthy weight.
3. Choose a diet low in fat, saturated fat, and cholesterol.
4. Choose a diet with plenty of vegetables, fruits, and grains.
5. Use salt and sodium only in moderation.
6. Use sugars only in moderation.
7. If you drink alcoholic beverages, do so in moderation.

Table 12-5 provides a full explanation for why and how we should follow these guidelines. When you analyze these recommendations, you can see that as a nation we need to consume less fat, sugar, salt, and alcohol. At the same time, we need to choose foods that provide variety and emphasize complex carbohydrates and high fiber goods.

These recommendations for types and amounts of foods needed, paired with the national dietary guidelines, provide excellent advice for eating to be healthy and stay healthy.

EXERCISE FOR WELLNESS

Physical activity throughout life is a key ingredient for wellness. People who exercise regularly report that they feel better and have more energy than they do when they are not exercising regularly. In addition, their bodies are in better shape when they exercise. Exercise improves circulation throughout the body and builds up muscles, including the heart muscle.

BENEFITS OF EXERCISE

Health professionals have identified these benefits of regular physical exercise:

- Improved physiological functioning
- Improved ability to control weight
- Improved appetite
- Improved appearance
- Strengthened heart muscle
- More positive attitude
- Increased ability to relax
- Reduced risk of heart disease
- Reduced stress
- Increased energy levels

PLANNING AN EXERCISE PROGRAM

What kind of exercise is right for you? How often should you exercise and how long at one time? Where can you exercise safely and comfortably? These are questions to consider if you are considering beginning an exercise program.

Experts recommend that you exercise regularly and strenuously at least three times a week for 20 to 30 minutes at a time. Choose an aerobic exercise (exercise that is designed to increase oxygen intake) such as: walking, running, swimming, dancing, bicycling, yoga, weight lifting, or calisthenics.

Remember to allow time for warm-up and cool-down before and after you exercise. Ten minutes of warm-up exercises, such as stretching, will help to reduce possible injuries from exercise. Ten minutes of cool-down exercises gradually brings your heart down to its normal rate at the end of the exercise period. When you begin an exercise program, you may want to exercise for only 10 minutes. Gradually increase your exercise time to 30 minutes as your endurance develops.

Aerobic exercise raises the heartbeat. If you are a young adult, your resting heart rate is about 75 beats per minute. As you begin an aerobic exercise program, aim for an exercise level that will raise your heartbeat to 140 beats per minute.

You can determine your resting heart rate by placing the first two fingers of your hand on your neck below the jaw. Count the beats for 15 seconds, then multiply by 4 to find the rate per minute. After 10 minutes of exercise, check again. If your heart beat is too fast, slow down. It is not wise to exercise to the point of feeling weak or out of breath.

Follow these guidelines for your personal exercise program:

1. Have a medical checkup before beginning an exercise program, especially if you have or suspect a health problem.

(a)

(b)

Figure 12-2 Make exercise a regular part of your life. (a) Courtesy of Bally's Health and Tennis Corporation; (b) U.S. Army photo.

2. Set reasonable goals.

3. Select a program that you will enjoy and that will meet your needs in terms of level of difficulty, variety of exercises, and coordination with the rest of your schedule. It may be an aerobics class taught by a certified instructor in the local gym or other organization in your community. Here you may also benefit from companionship and the enthusiasm of the instructor. Audio and video tapes are available for home use. Regularly scheduled aerobic programs appear on television. These also have enthusiastic instructors and enable you to work exercise into your schedule. Of course, other types of aerobics such as walking, running, and bicycling can be easily adjusted to your schedule and have their own special appeal.

4. Begin gradually.

5. Expect some soreness when you begin.

6. Discipline yourself to exercise regularly. Enrolling in a class helps. If you are exercising at home, set a regular time on given days and stick to it.

7. Practice warm-up and cool-down.

8. Select a safe place for exercising. Some people find malls and exercise clubs to be the safest places for them. Others find safety in their own neighborhood parks or just walking or running close to home. Some workers have facilities for exercise available at their workplace.

9. Wear comfortable clothing and shoes.

MANAGING STRESS

The stress of everyday living makes physical and emotional demands on you. Both your body and your mind respond to those demands, so that you are under strain, pressure, or tension. Some stress is good; it motivates people to action. Most individuals perform at their best when there is a moderate level of stress or motivation. On the other hand, when the stress is so high that a person is tense or anxious, he or she does not perform well.

Stress levels vary from individual to individual. What is stressful to one person may not be stressful to another. Also, some people have learned to manage stress better than others.

The causes of stress are called *stressors*. These may be large or small. For example, missing the bus to class is a stressor, as is breaking up with the important person in your romantic life. The small stressors are generally handled easily unless many of them are concentrated in a short time period. Larger stressors may demand conscientious stress management if you are to maintain wellness and continue to be productive. Events such as death, divorce, critical illness, loss of job, arrest, and loss of income are the most stressful events you may encounter.

STRESS AND YOUR BODY

When you experience a stressful event or situation, your body responds both physically and emotionally. Examples of reactions to stress may be sweaty palms before you make an oral presentation in class or a stomachache when you are anxious about telling your manager of a mistake you made.

Your body's normal reactions to stress are increased breathing and heart rate, slowed digestion, and tense muscles. You may perspire, which is the body's way of cooling you down. Usually these conditions disappear when the stress is removed.

When the body experiences severe stress for a long period of time, health problems may result. People who are under stress are more accident prone and may overeat. In addition, unrelieved stress can lead to high blood pressure, ulcers, heart attacks, abdominal pains, diarrhea, severe headaches, and insomnia.

Stress is closely related to mental health. The mentally healthy person controls stress more effectively than a person with poor mental health. The experience of long-term stress, coupled with poor or ineffective responses, can lead to mental illness.

RESPONDING TO STRESS

When you experience stress, you may respond in one of four ways:

1. You may avoid the conditions that cause stress.
2. You may endure the stress.
3. You may change the way you look at the situation.
4. You may change the conditions that produced the stress.

You will probably use all these methods at various times in your life. To become a person who responds to stress in healthy ways, you will need skill in applying all these methods.

Avoiding Stress. Some people stay home from work when they anticipate a problem, or they take vacation days. These practices may work occasionally, but as a general rule, they are nonproductive, because they delay rather than eliminate the need to face the problem. You may be able to avoid stressful situations, however, through productive life management techniques. Here are some ways you can conduct your own life to avoid harmful stress:

(a)

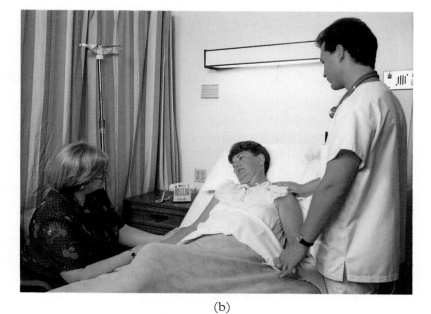

(b)

Figure 12-3 (a) Normal kinds of stress, such as waiting in line for a job interview, can usually be handled with ease. (Photo by Paul E. Meyers.) (b) Unusual stress, such as coping with the critical illness of a loved one, can be very difficult emotionally. (From Hegner and Caldwell, *Nursing Assistant*, 6th edition, Delmar Publishers Inc.)

◆ *Have personal goals.* Prioritize them and break them into manageable objectives. It is stressful not to know what you want from life or in what direction you should go. Even if you are uncertain about the overall direction of your life, try to set some realistic short-term goals so that you can feel good about your efforts. Complete the work required for one goal before beginning another. Avoid trying to do too many things at one time.

◆ *Be organized in your personal life.* Establish some routines—a regular time for work, for TV, for seeing friends, for eating, for running errands, and for sleep. Organize your possessions; for example, keep keys in one special place so you will always know where they are. Don't go overboard if a friend calls during TV time and wants to do something spontaneous, do it. Being organized does not rule out spur-of-the-moment fun.

◆ *Say "no" to some demands* that exceed the time you feel you can give to others and still fulfill your own responsibilities.

◆ *Learn to delegate.* Share tasks with coworkers and family members.

◆ *Improve communication skills.* Use tact and the appropriate vocabulary to explain your position, and listen creatively to concerns and ideas of others in your life.

◆ *Work efficiently.* Finding the most effective method of performing at-work and at-home tasks will relieve frustrations.

◆ *Maintain a healthy body.* Good health repels and/or responds well to stressors.

◆ *Keep a positivie attitude.* Mental outlook is an important factor in determining whether your reaction to stress will be major or minor.

◆ *Expect change in your life.* It is a normal part of living.

◆ *Reward yourself* for work well done and for tasks completed.

◆ *Avoid being a perfectionist.* Do not make unreasonable demands on yourself and others. No one is perfect; therefore, if you are only satisfied with perfection, you will often experience stress.

◆ *Develop a spiritual life.* For some, the spiritual life means organized religion; for others, it may be developing the spiritual self through other activities. Inner strength is a shield against outside stressors.

◆ *Develop supporting relationships.* Cultivate a family relationship or a friendship that allows you to talk in confidence to someone about private matters. (For your professional well-being, this should be someone away from your workplace.)

Enduring Stress. When you cannot avoid stress, you must endure it. Endurance is called *coping with stress.* Some of the ways of enduring stress are similar to the ways just listed for avoiding a stressful life-style.

Enduring stress is easier if you are in good physical condition. Support people and support groups can also help you endure stress. Having a friend or family member to talk to when you are feeling the results of stress is extremely important. If you are married, your spouse probably fills this role. If you are single, find a friend or relative with whom you feel comfortable sharing your thoughts.

Spiritual life gives strength for endurance. You may choose to develop your spiritual life through a religious group or some other group. You may also use books, magazines, and tapes.

Emotional release may make endurance possible. Stressors often cause feelings of irritation, hurt, or anger. Having strong emotional feelings is normal, and accepting them is important. But it is equally important to respond to strong emotional feelings in appropriate ways. For example, when you feel irritated or hurt, you may need to communicate your feelings to the person who caused those feelings. Talk to the person, using good communication skills.

When you feel angry, find acceptable release. Many people find physical activity helpful, such as exercise or involvement in a hobby. Walking, jogging, punching a bag, playing the piano, or some similar activity will release angry tension.

Altering Your Viewpoints. Another way to respond to stress is to change the way you view the circumstances. When you have complete understanding of the total situation, you may have a different response. Talking with others is a major way to get more information for better understanding.

Sometimes, we simply need to develop an accepting attitude. To say, "This is life," or "This, too, will pass," is a way of altering our view of circumstances and relieving stress.

Changing Circumstances. Sometimes you may relieve stress by changing circumstances. Changing your body's condition and changing relationships are ways to change circumstances.

To change your body's condition, learn to relax it. You can learn many relaxation exercises. Relaxation tips are available in books and on audiotapes and videotapes. There are also hand-held devices for relaxing muscles. If you practice these techniques before you desperately need them, they will be easy to use when you need to relieve the pressure of extreme stress. Your body will give you clues such as these when you need to relax:

◆ Headache

◆ Stomachache

◆ Muscle tightness

◆ Dry throat

◆ Tense feeling

◆ Tightness in chest

◆ Eye twitch

Here are some very simple techniques you can use to relax your mind and body:

◆ *Take a work break.* Change your body position. Work in another location. Get something to drink. Think about something unrelated to work for a few minutes. Visit with someone.

◆ *Go outdoors,* breathe some fresh air, and look at objects in the distance. Go "window shopping."

◆ *Take a short nap* (obviously, this may not be possible except at break time).

◆ *Take a hot bath.* Do it right after work, and you are ready for a great evening!

◆ *Exercise* with stretch routines for a few minutes.

◆ *Do a breathing routine.* Begin by breathing in deeply, holding your breath, and breathing out. In the first series, mentally count to 2 in each phase; in the next series, mentally count to 3, and so on, until you are counting to 8 with each phase in the series. Next, reverse this count until you are back to a count of 2. For example, while inhaling, slowly count "1, 2," then hold your breath and mentally count "1, 2," next exhale while slowly counting "1, 2."

◆ *Conduct a body-relaxing visualization.* Find a place where you will feel uninhibited (a private place) and sit comfortably in a chair with your feet on the floor. Place your hands in your lap, and close your eyes. Slowly repeat these phrases to yourself and feel your body relax.

"My feet are relaxed; my lower legs are relaxed; my knees are relaxed; my thighs are relaxed; my hips are relaxed; my abdomen is relaxed; my waist is relaxed; my chest is relaxed; my shoulders are relaxed; my arms are relaxed; my hands are relaxed; my neck is relaxed; my head is relaxed; my eyes are relaxed; I am relaxed all over."

Slowly open your eyes, stretch, and return to work. Similarly, while sitting in your office, close your eyes and think of the most beautiful spot you can remember. Concentrate on that view until the feeling of stress is relieved. You may want to visualize the beauty of a park; hearing a bird sing; or feeling a cool breeze. Linger there for several minutes.

Another way to change circumstances is to change relationships, assuming that relationships are causing stress. Your relationships may be improved through improvement of communication. Review the

(a)

(b)

Figure 12-4   (a) Relaxing is a way to relieve stress. (Courtesy of McCann-Erickson Inc.; photo by Gerry Trafficanda.) (b) Strenuous physical activity is another way to relieve stress. (Photo by Kenneth A. Deitcher, M.D.)

sections in this text on communication and on relating to people in your work environment to find other ways to relieve stress.

HEALTH RISKS

Living a healthy life-style is accomplished not only through good nutrition, exercise, and stress management, it is also necessary to avoid harmful habits. The most harmful health habits are called health risks. Harmful diets, use of tobacco, substance abuse, excessive drinking, and unsafe sex are among health risks that cause great harm.

HARMFUL DIETS

Good health is based on eating a balanced diet in amounts needed for body maintenance and normal growth. Unfortunately, in this country many people eat more food than their bodies need. Nutrients from the excess food are stored in the body as fat.

A certain amount of body fat is desirable. However, excessive fat causes a variety of health problems—heart disease, high blood pressure, diabetes, cancer, and liver disease. In addition to disease, many people also want to avoid excess fat to have a pleasing appearance.

Normal weight for an individual is determined by age, height, and body structure. The information in Table 12-6 shows recommended weights for adults.

Losing weight can be accomplished safely by adjusting your diet to lose one pound per week until you reach your desired weight. You can lose one pound per week by maintaining your normal activity, while at the same time reducing your caloric intake by 500 calories per day. Since 3,500 calories equal one pound of weight, a reduction of 500 calories per day for 7 days will result in the one-pound loss. Table 12-7 suggests how a person might adjust a normal eating pattern to reduce the caloric intake.

Many diets are advertised as resulting in sure weight loss. Although this may be true, all diets are not healthy. Harmful diets include low-carbohydrate/high-protein diets, liquid diets, one-food diets, and fasting. These fad diets, as well as the use of diet pills, may result in a variety of problems—even death—because they seriously interfere with the body's own chemical processes.

Instead of choosing one of these harmful diets, continue to eat a balanced diet while reducing calories and participating in regular exercise. If you want to lose more than 10 pounds, see your physician for a checkup and for advice on the best weight loss method for you. The most effective diet is one that results in changed eating patterns so that weight is not regained. Fad diets often have the opposite result—that is,

TABLE 12-6 SUGGESTED WEIGHTS FOR ADULTS

HEIGHT[1]	WEIGHT IN POUNDS[2]	
	19 TO 34 YEARS	35 YEARS AND OVER
5'0"	97–128[3]	108–138
5'1"	101–132	111–143
5'2"	104–137	115–148
5'3"	107–141	119–152
5'4"	111–146	122–157
5'5"	114–150	126–162
5'6"	118–155	130–167
5'7"	121–160	134–172
5'8"	125–164	138–178
5'9"	129–169	142–183
5'10"	132–174	146–188
5'11"	136–179	151–194
6'0"	140–184	155–199
6'1"	144–189	159–205
6'2"	148–195	164–210
6'3"	152–200	168–216
6'4"	156–205	173–222
6'5"	160–211	177–228
6'6"	164–216	182–234

[1] Without shoes.
[2] Without clothes.
[3] The higher weights in the ranges generally apply to men, who tend to have more muscle and bone; the lower weights more often apply to women, who have less muscle and bone.

U.S. Department of Agriculture Home and Garden Bulletin No. 232

although they may cause rapid weight loss, the weight is soon regained when the person returns to old eating habits.

When you are considering a specific diet, raise these questions:

◆ Does the diet plan make unrealistic weight loss claims? (Healthy weight loss or gain should be no more than 3 pounds per week.)

◆ Does the related advertisement depend on alleged personal testimonials? Advertisements for healthy diets should contain scientific facts such as those you have learned in this chapter.

TABLE 12-7: ALTERING MENUS TO REDUCE CALORIES

USUAL BREAKFAST		REDUCED CALORIE BREAKFAST	
Orange juice	100	Orange juice	100
Scrambled egg	110	Oatmeal w/milk	175
Fried Bacon (2 strips)	90	Milk, skim	90
Toast (2 slices) w/butter	280	1 slice light bread toasted w/1 tsp margarine	100

USUAL LUNCH		REDUCED CALORIE LUNCH	
Hamburger	305	Chicken, broiled 3 oz.	115
French fries w/catsup	310	Apple	80
Coke	100	Mixed greens (diet dressing)	50
		Diet coke	1

USUAL DINNER		REDUCED CALORIE DINNER	
Chicken strips	220	Chicken strips	220
Mashed potatoes	225	Mashed potatoes	225
1 Roll w/butter	200	Raw carrots	40
Tea		1 Roll w/margarine	100
		Tea	

USUAL SNACKS		REDUCED CALORIE SNACKS	
Coke	100	Iced Tea (unsweetened)	0
Buttered popcorn	200	Plain popcorn	50
		Apple	80

Totals	2140		1526

These reductions (with normal exercise) will allow the eater to loose slightly more than 1 pound per week.

◆ Is the diet endorsed by people with training in health, nutrition, or medicine?

SMOKING AND TOBACCO USE

Most medical experts agree that smoking is harmful to health. Cigarette smoking is believed to be responsible for the majority of all cases of lung cancer. Additionally, lung diseases such as emphysema are aggravated by smoking and kill about 16,000 people in this country every year. Smoking also contributes to heart disease and high blood pressure. Pregnant women who smoke may have problem pregnancies and babies with low birth weight.

If you are a smoker, consider the health risks you take each time you smoke. Then if you wish to stop smoking, talk with a counselor or a physician about a program designed to help you stop. Many people have effectively dropped the habit. After you quit smoking, you will have an improved sense of taste; you will breathe more deeply; your teeth will be whiter; your breath will be fresher; you will have more physical stamina; and you will have more money to spend for other things you may want.

In addition to cigarettes, pipe and cigar smoking and the use of snuff and chewing tobacco may also contribute to ill health.

SUBSTANCE ABUSE

Misuse of drugs among people in the United States is a major problem today. Using chemical substances for nonmedicinal, nonlegitimate reasons is a dangerous practice. Misusing drugs leads to drug addiction—the condition in which the body requires the drug to function.

Among the commonly abused drugs are stimulants, such as cocaine and amphetamines; depressants, such as tranquilizers and barbiturates; hallucinogens, such as LSD; cannabis, such as marijuana and hashish; and narcotics, such as heroin, morphine, codeine, and opium.

The use of addictive drugs causes multiple problems. First, the habit is very expensive, often leading people to crime to pay for the drugs. Second, use of drugs alters the functioning of the body and mind, making people act differently from the way they would without the drugs. In fact, the initial appeal of the so-called "recreational drugs" is that the user feels that he or she can do or be anything without limits. The results are disastrous.

In addition, people who use drugs often suffer paranoia, which makes them suspicious and distrustful of others. They may misinterpret other people's actions and statements. They often make poor decisions under the influence of the drugs. Drug use causes auto accidents, destroys family relationships, and ruins professional careers. Eventually, drug use causes physical addiction, destruction of major body organs, and risk of death. Using a combination of drugs, or drugs with alcohol, can be immediately fatal.

Help for drug abusers is available in almost every community in the United States. Local clinics are listed in telephone directories, and many agencies work to help people with drug problems. If you think you have

Figure 12-5 Informal counseling sessions, like the one pictured here, in which people share their feelings and experiences, are also a part of drug rehabilitation programs. (Courtesy of Westinghouse Electric Corporation.)

a drug problem, consult your school counselor or contact a minister, a physician, or some other person in a helping profession.

EXCESSIVE ALCOHOL USE

The most misused of all drugs is alcohol. Alcohol acts on the central nervous system and on the body by passing directly from the stomach into the blood stream. The blood carries it immediately to the brain. When blood alcohol levels are approximately .05%, thought, judgment, and restraint may be affected. The drinker feels carefree, and his or her inhibitions disappear. At a level of .10%, the body becomes clumsy, and at .20%, all body motor control and emotional control is affected. At .30% the person is confused and may lapse into a stupor, while at .50% death is nearly certain.

Different people are affected in different ways by alcohol. The effect that alcohol has on a person depends on the size of the person, his or her experience with alcohol, the condition of the body, and on the presence of food in the body. Drinking only one drink per hour will have little effect on many people. On others, just a few sips can cause changes in mood and behavior. For alcoholics, even one sip is too much because they are unable to stop until they are drunk.

Immediate problems for the ordinary drinker are loss of self-control and auto accidents from driving while intoxicated. Heavier drinking habits can result in social, personal, and family problems, because alcohol affects the emotions. Drinkers are less responsible. Some take greater risks; some become violent; others become depressed. In addition, tests show that large doses of alcohol make a person sexually ineffective.

The most deadly problem related to drinking is mixing alcohol with other drugs. When used with alcohol, drugs such as sleeping pills, tranquilizers, pain killers, antihistamines, and sedatives greatly increase the effect both the drugs and the alcohol have on the body.

The long-term effect of drinking is damage to the heart, brain, liver, and other organs. Cirrhosis of the liver occurs eight times as often in alcoholics as nonalcoholics. Gastritis, ulcers, and pancreatitis are other diseases often associated with people who drink heavily for a long period of time. Even serious mental disorders may result from long years of heavy drinking.

If you suspect that you have a drinking problem, ask yourself these questions:

- Do I need a drink to cope with problems?
- Do I get drunk often?
- Do I drink in the morning?
- Do I drink before going to work?
- Do I drink and then drive?
- When I drink, do I act in ways I would not act if I were not drinking?

If you answered yes to any of those questions you may have a drinking problem. The mature person seeks help before a drinking problem becomes a threat to her or his personal and professional life.

Help for people with drinking problems is available throughout the United States. People who feel they may have a problem should seek help immediately from a school counselor, a family physician, a minister, or from groups such as Alcoholics Anonymous. Other help is also available. Most communities have local health clinics for the treatment of any form of drug abuse.

AIDS

Acquired immunodeficiency syndrome (AIDS) is a disease caused by the human immunodeficiency virus (HIV). There is no known cure for the disease once it attacks the body, and it is fatal. Anyone can acquire AIDS if he or she participates in activities known to cause transmission of the disease.

FOCUS ON: DRUG TESTING IN THE WORKPLACE

During the orientation to his new job, Frank was surprised to learn that his employer had a drug testing program. After the first month of employment, all workers at Allied Receiving are subject to random drug testing. The purpose of such test is to identify employees who use illegal (illicit) drugs such as marijuana and cocaine. Not only is the use of such drugs illegal and dangerous, but the drugs have also been linked to accidents, absenteeism, and low productivity. For example, it was found that drugs were a factor in a 1987 train crash that killed 16 passengers and injured 176 others. The engineer had been smoking marijuana.

To identify drug users, employers often require each employee to submit a urine sample for analysis. The analysis can detect traces of cocaine up to two days after the drug was taken. Marijuana has been known to show up in the urine as long as a month after use.

In 1986, the Reagan administration asked all federal agencies to test employees in "sensitive" jobs. Many local governments and private employers followed suit. By 1988, half of the nations' 500 largest corporations had drug testing programs. Testing may be required for job applicants, employed workers, or both. Some employers test workers for "cause"; for instance, if they notice a worker is not performing well. Others test randomly, without announcement and without even suspecting wrongdoing.

Even though drug testing is widely used, the practice remains controversial. Some people claim that the tests are often inaccurate. Others claim that tests violate the Fourth Amendment's prohibition on unreasonable searches. A number of lawsuits have been filed to stop drug testing. It will probably be many years before the courts decide on these issues.

AIDS is acquired in any of the following ways:

1. Through sexual intercourse with a man or a woman. This happens if a person infected with the AIDS virus has the virus in his semen or her vaginal fluids. The virus can enter the body through the vagina, penis, rectum, or mouth.

2. By sharing drug needles and syringes with a person who is infected.

3. By receiving blood transfusions from persons with the AIDS virus. The risk of getting AIDS from a blood transfusion has been greatly reduced through screening of donors and careful testing of blood.

4. By infected mothers passing the virus to a fetus.

There is no evidence that AIDS can be transmitted through everyday contact with people in the workplace, at parties, in swimming pools, etc. Neither will you get AIDS from a mosquito bite or from saliva, sweat, tears, urine, or feces. No one has contracted AIDS from kissing. At this time, research shows that only semen, vaginal secretions, and blood are implicated in the transmission of the HIV virus.

The information provided here on AIDS comes from the Surgeon General of the United States. The information was taken from HHS Publication No. (CDC) HHS-88-8404, from the U.S. Department of Health and Human Services.

To avoid this deadly disease, be careful about a person with whom you become sexually involved. Find out if the person has a sexually transmitted disease. Find out if the person has experimented with drugs and what the person's sex life has been like in terms of number and type of partners. After all, if you know someone well enough to have sexual intercourse, then you should be able to talk with him or her about AIDS. If he or she is unwilling to talk with you about this serious matter, you should not have sex with the person.

Married people who are uninfected, faithful, and do not take drugs are not at high risk for AIDS, although contaminated transfusions account for a small percentage of AIDS cases. If you do decide to have sex outside of marriage, find out if the person you are involved with is at risk. If you think he or she is not, and you decide to become sexually involved, use condoms, which is the best preventive measure against AIDS. Remember, however, that even condoms are not foolproof. They must be used according to directions, and they must be used every time you have sex, from start to finish. Of course, abstinence is the safest of all possible sexual practices.

OBTAINING HEALTH CARE

Do you know where to go or whom to see when you need a doctor? What hospital would you use if you had an accident? These and similar questions need answers *before* you have a health problem.

Shop for health care as you would shop for other services. Identify your needs and then ask reliable people you know about physicians and available health services. Ask your parents, older friends, or teachers to recommend someone. Many large communities have physician referral agencies affiliated with local hospitals. When you move, ask your present doctor to recommend a doctor in the area to which you are moving. Everyone needs a family doctor. A family doctor is a generalist who makes health evaluations and treats common illnesses. These physicians in family practice may refer their patients to specialists when complicated or unique health problems arise. Many people say that having a family doctor gives them a feeling of security because they feel they have someone to visit with any health problem that they have.

When you move to a new location, it is important to identify other health care givers such as a dentist, for regular dental care, a pediatrician if you have children who need special care, and an opthamologist for regular eye care. These health care professionals will be available for recommended annual checkups. They will advise you about which tests are needed to determine that your body is free of health problems. For example, women will want to have regular Pap smears and periodic mammograms.

When you visit a doctor, be prepared to explain your condition. Write down questions that you want answered. During the first visit, evaluate the office, services, and the professional. Choose a physician you can respect and talk with comfortably, who does not talk down to you or try to rush you from the office.

Inquire about the health services provided where you work. Some workplaces provide health clinics, nursing services, health insurance, and other services. Learn about your health benefits before you become ill. Refer to the chapter on Managing Financial Resources (Chapter 13) for information on health insurance.

Keep your medical records up-to-date and in a safe place. Information about previous health problems, reactions to medications, and inoculations are important for proper treatment of new conditions. It is wise to keep a small card in your wallet with vital medical information on it, in case you are involved in an accident and cannot inform the medical team yourself. Some people prefer to wear bracelets or necklaces with critical medical information, such as an allergy to penicillin, or diabetes.

RELATING EMOTIONAL HEALTH TO WELLNESS

Your total feelings of health and well-being are a result of physical, emotional, and social health. *Social health* refers to our relationships with individuals and groups, such as family, work, and communities. Can you recall a time when you felt pains in your stomach at the thought of a frightening experience? Or do you remember getting a headache because of stresses at work? These are examples of the effects of emotional and social health on your physical health.

Specialists continue to learn about the complex field of social and emotional health. Here are guidelines for good health in those areas:

- Learn to express strong emotions in nonviolent ways.

- Take steps to help you feel positive about your appearance and behavior. For example, if you feel so strongly about a physical condition that if affects your personality, investigate a treatment or way to camouflage it.

- Learn the language of love—giving it *and* accepting it. It may be difficult for some people to accept love because they do not feel worthy of love. If you feel that way, explore your feelings. If you feel that you are unloved, think about ways that you can get love into your life. Some people find that a pet is one answer. Others join groups where a common interest can bring people together. You may find the answer in activities especially for singles or in volunteering to work with other people who need more love in their lives too, such as the elderly or the physically challenged.

- Recognize your personal limitations and accept them. Realize that you have unique abilities to do some things but not all things.

- Build your personal strengths. Take classes or join interest groups in which you can use your strengths. You could teach adult classes in the community or teach a skill to children at a community center. It is a great boost to self-esteem to excel at something.

- Balance your life between work and play (relaxation).

- Have someone in your life in whom you can confide.

- Laugh and enjoy humorous elements of life. Plan activities that will get more humor into your life—movies, shows, comedy clubs, more time with light-hearted friends.

- Expect that there will always be some problems in life.

- Develop some hobbies or activities that allow you to be satisfied when you are alone.

- Revise or add to personal or professional goals. Goal-setting is an ongoing process. Goals grow and change as you grow and change.

- Work to make satisfactory choices. Analyze past situations that turned out badly and determine how you can make better choices in the future.

- Enjoy your successes. Celebrate them with friends or by treating yourself. Buy a new party outfit, spend a weekend in the country, or do something else that reinforces how special you are.

(a)

(b)

Figure 12-6 (a) Feeling that you belong to a group and (b) that you are loved is important for good mental health. (a) Courtesy of SIUC University Photocommunications. (b) Courtesy of Sears, Roebuck and Co.

1. Summarize the dietary guidelines for all Americans.
2. List the six categories of nutrients and name two or three sources of each category.
3. Outline questions one may ask to determine if a diet is a wise one or a potentially harmful one.
4. Explain the concepts of warm-up and cool-down in an exercise program.
5. Describe the value of a personal exercise program.
6. Name five common stressors.
7. Describe two good ways to respond to excess stress.
8. Is it accurate to say there is good stress and bad stress? Explain.
9. What health risks have been attributed to cigarette smoking?
10. List ten ways a person may manage his or her life to promote mental and social health.

ACTIVITIES

1. Review the Dietary Guidelines and the Basic Four Food Groups, then plan 3 days of healthy menus for yourself. Prepare and eat these meals, then evaluate your feelings and your experiences with making healthy meals available for yourself.
2. Investigate opportunities for exercise in your neighborhood and get involved in one. Describe your experience to the class.
3. Practice two of the stress reduction exercises found in this chapter. Describe and evaluate in writing their effectiveness at reducing your stress levels.
4. Find three articles in your local newspaper that report on substance abuse in your neighborhood. What are the local problems? What action is being taken? How might you act to reduce abuse in your neighborhood? Put it all in a two-page report.
5. Discuss how you would get professional health care for:
   ◆ An attack of appendicitis
   ◆ A bad toothache
   ◆ Injuries in an auto accident
   ◆ An annual checkup
6. Do a two-page report on the life of a famous person whose downfall is attributed to drugs or alcohol. Your instructor will suggest names.

7. Write a list of the resources available in your community to help people with substance abuse (including alcohol) problems. From the library and telephone book you can get names and numbers of agencies; call them to get more information about their services. They may send you brochures and other materials.

8. Prepare a report on a contemporary nutrition issue. Some possibilities: the role and importance of fiber in the diet; how to lower cholesterol; sugar substitutes. Your instructor will help you think of others.

CHAPTER GOAL:

To examine information needed for personal money management.

CHAPTER OBJECTIVES:

After studying this chapter, you should be able to:

1. Identify personal financial goals.
2. Analyze and use a money management planning process.
3. Compare services of various types of financial institutions.
4. Choose and use banks and credit.
5. Understand insurance as a component in financial security.
6. Explain the effect of savings on money management.
7. Practice money management skills.

Money does more than buy the goods and services we need and want. It influences how we feel about ourselves and other people. It has a great deal to do with our level of living and with our goals. The way we feel about money and the methods we use to manage it are important to our growth and behavior as professionals. If you act responsibly with your own resources, then observers will feel confident that you will be similarly responsible with the resources of an employer.

No one is born with the ability to manage money. The skill is learned and developed with practice. Most of us would like to have more money. Yet, when we make the statement, "I need more money," we are really saying that we need the goods or services that the money will purchase. A better apartment, a newer car, or perhaps a new wardrobe are some of the objects we would purchase with "more money." When you develop money management skills, you will be able to buy more with the money you have.

Effective and personally satisfying money management varies from individual to individual. This chapter can help you develop your own management system. As you can see from Figure 13-1, financial security is more than having a good job. To keep yourself comfortable and secure requires a planned combination of all the resources and demands at your fingertips.

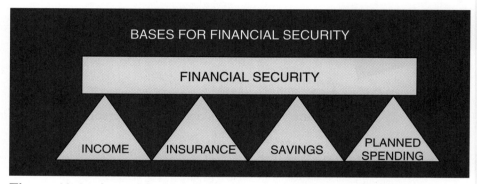

Figure 13-1 A good income is not the only element needed for financial security.

MAKING A BUDGET

A plan for spending helps many people to get more for their money. A money management plan is a set of choices based on your goals and values. For example, consider the demands on your income and what you are willing to do to get more for your money. Do you spend time making your own clothing or repairing your car, thus cutting costs so that you can take a summer vacation? Do you live in a modest neighborhood or share an apartment to save money for education? Would you dip into savings to buy a new suit and accessories because you need them for an interview for a higher paying job? These questions reflect decisions that must be made about purchases based on values. Successful money management begins with an analysis of what is really important to you.

A money management plan, or budget, shows income and expenditures for a certain period of time. A budget may help you to:

◆ Control where your money goes

◆ Work toward short-term and long-term goals

◆ Avoid overspending

◆ Reduce wasteful spending

Budgeting involves four steps:

1. Establishing financial goals

2. Identifying income

3. Recording expenditures

4. Analyzing spending and making plans for the next spending period

ESTABLISHING FINANCIAL GOALS

It is possible to establish financial goals. Consider what is important to you. "What do I want my money to buy?" or "What are my goals for the month? The year?" Reaching short-term goals may be possible during each pay period, whereas long-term goals, such as having enough money to buy a home, may require several years to be reached.

Writing your goals will help you feel a sense of control over your money regardless of the size of your income (see the list below). Few people have an income large enough to meet all their wants. When your goals exceed your income, you must exercise a degree of choice that provides a sense of direction and confidence.

SHORT-TERM FINANCIAL GOALS

This paycheck:	Pay back loan to Sheila—$10
	Buy the textbook for accounting class
	Put $15 in savings
This month:	Pay off charge account
	Get stereo repaired
	Treat Lily to dinner
This year:	Save at least $250 for Christmas
	Donate the equivalent of 2 hours' wages per month to a charity
	Start a savings account for my son

IDENTIFYING YOUR INCOME

Identifying your income is the second step in budgeting. Typically, most income is from wages and salary. When you consider your income, remember that the amount should be based on the amount of money you have after deductions. This amount is sometimes referred to as your *net income* or take-home pay (*gross income* is your salary before deductions). The money deducted from your paycheck is usually for:

◆ Taxes (federal, state and/or local)
◆ Social Security
◆ Health or life insurance
◆ Retirement benefits, or pension

After these regular deductions are made, most salary checks are one fourth to one third less than the gross income; Figure 13-2 is the stub of a paycheck. All deductions are included on the stub.

Other sources of income may be:

◆ Tips, bonuses, commissions
◆ Child support or alimony
◆ Profits from sale of assets
◆ Public assistance
◆ Interest from investments and savings

RECORDING YOUR EXPENDITURES

To keep track of where your money goes, record all your expenditures. At first you may think that keeping track of everything you spend is an impossible task; but once you grow accustomed to it, it will seem routine. With check or credit card purchases, you have built-in records in the form of your monthly bank statement. For cash items, carry a small note pad and jot down the items you buy along with their cost. Some people record their expenditures at the end of each day. Once you see exactly where your money is going, you may find yourself reconsidering some purchases on your way to the cash register.

At the end of a month (or of a specified amount of time) review your purchases. Then classify them into categories similar to those shown in Figure 13-3. As you can see, the expenses are divided into two major categories—fixed and variable.

Fixed expenses are those that are the same amount paid at regular intervals. Rent, car payments, and insurance premiums are good examples of fixed expenses. *Variable expenses* are those paid in varying amounts; some are on irregular schedules; others are one-time payments. Food, clothing, utilities, transportation, and recreation are good examples of

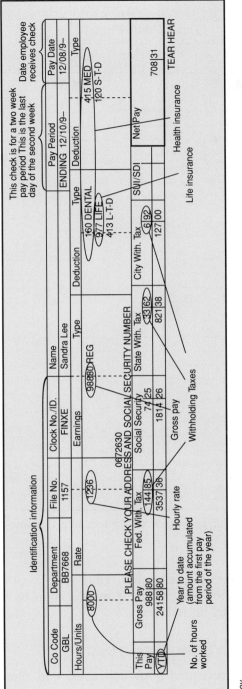

Figure 13-2 This stub from a paycheck shows typical payroll deductions and is the part you keep after you cash the check.

WORKSHEET FOR INCOME AND EXPENSES
Three Month Period

	Mo. 1	Mo. 2	Mo. 3
INCOME:			
Net pay			
Alimony			
Child support			
Interest from savings			
Gifts			
Other			
TOTAL INCOME			
EXPENSES:			
Fixed:			
Rent			
Insurance permiums			
Car payments			
Savings			
Variable:			
Transportation			
Food			
Utilities (gas, electric, water)			
Medical			
Entertainment			
Clothing			
Credit card payment			
Miscellaneous			
TOTAL EXPENSES			
BALANCE			

Figure 13-3 When you get a job, prepare a worksheet like this one to help you budget wisely.

variable expenses. For example, your rent is the same amount every month and cannot be put off. Your decision to buy a VCR you have been wanting can be delayed.

ANALYZING YOUR SPENDING

After you have recorded your expenses, add them and subtract them from your total income. Is there enough income to cover your expenses?

Is there enough money to handle unexpected expenses? You must analyze your expenses in relation to your income and make decisions concerning them. Do you need to cut back? What are your long-range financial goals? You must adjust your budget to ensure that your money is doing what you want it to do, for the present and for the future.

FINANCIAL INSTITUTIONS

Professionals need a variety of money management services. Commercial banks, savings and loan associations, and credit unions are the most common sources of these services. Some often-used services provided by financial institutions include checking accounts, savings accounts, loans, electronic funds transfers, and investment planning.

COMMERCIAL BANKS

Commercial banks provide a full range of services that include all those noted above. In addition to the range of services, the advantage to commercial banks is that all your money and all your banking activities are in one location.

CREDIT UNIONS

Credit unions are cooperatives made up of individuals who have a common bond. For example, a large business such as General Electric has a credit union for all its employees. Credit unions offer services similar to those offered by banks; however, only members can use their services.

SAVING AND LOAN ASSOCIATIONS

Savings and loan associations offer similar services to those of commercial banks and credit unions. However, they have traditionally focused on savings for individuals and on loans for the purchase of land and housing. The interest on savings accounts is frequently higher than the interest offered in a commercial bank.

 The financial services offered by commercial banks, credit unions, and savings and loan associations are similar to one another. Your selection of a type of institution may depend on such things as the convenience of branches or money machines, differences in interest rates, friendliness of personnel, and the institutions' willingness to make loans.

CHECKING ACCOUNTS

Checking accounts are needed by people who do not like to carry a large amount of cash. Unless you are very disciplined about spending, the more cash you have with you, the more likely you are to make sudden, unnecessary purchases. Furthermore, cash is easily lost and may be stolen. To avoid these problems, carry little cash and keep the rest of your money in a checking account. Although you may pay a small fee for the account, it has these advantages:

◆ Provides a safe place for your money.

◆ Gives you an easy method for paying bills and withdrawing cash.

◆ Provides a record of your receipts and payments.

◆ Helps you establish a credit rating. When you apply to make a purchase on credit, it helps if you list bank accounts.

◆ May earn interest.

TYPES OF CHECKING ACCOUNTS

You may select either a *demand account* or a transaction account. The *demand account* allows the customer to write checks on the account with only a small service fee charged. The account does not accrue interest. The *transaction account* combines the checking service with a savings feature that does accrue interest.

Automatic transfer service (ATS) accounts allow for payment deduction. For example, you might want your bank to make a car payment from your account each month. MMDA (money market deposits accounts) and Super NOWS are other accounts which pay slightly higher interest rates; these usually have restricted checking.

WRITING AND ENDORSING CHECKS

You will write checks to pay bills, such as your rent or mortgage payments, and you will write checks to pay for goods that you purchase in a store. The guidelines below serve two purposes: to ensure that the check you write is complete and to ensure that no one can alter the amount or the name of the person or company the check is written to.

1. If there is not a preprinted number on the check, enter the check number in the upper-left corner.

2. Enter the date; spell out the month.

3. Enter the payee's name (the name of the person or company to whom you are writing the check) in full. Do not use titles, such as Mrs. or Dr. Draw a line from the end of the payee's name to the dollar sign.

FOCUS ON:
CHECKING IT OUT

Since checking accounts can vary in the services and features offered, you must shop for a checking account just as you would for clothes or other purchases so that you will get the most for your money. To make an informed decision about a checking account, you will need the following information:

Service charge. The service charge is, in a sense, the price of the checking account, or the amount that you pay to the financial institution for handling your account.

Check writing fee, if any. Some financial institutions charge for processing each check that is written. The amount will vary.

Minimum balance requirements. In some cases, if you keep a minimum amount in your account, you will not have to pay a service charge and/or a check writing fee.

Amount of interest paid. Some checking accounts pay interest; others do not. Of those that do, the interest rates will vary.

Cost of checks. When you open a checking account, you are usually not charged for your first supply of checks. When you use all the checks and must order more, you are charged for the number of new checks you order. The amount you are charged will vary.

Amount of detail in monthly statement. Each month you will receive a summary of all transactions relating to your checking account. This summary is called a statement. Some statements provide more specific information than others.

Availability of automatic drafts or electronic transfer of funds. Many financial institutions provide a service that automatically pays regular bills for customers. For example, you may ask your bank to pay your utility bills each month. You arrange to have the bills sent directly to the bank and the bills are paid by the bank from your account. Electronic transfers are transfers of money from one bank to another by computers communicating with each other.

Penalty for overdraft. If you write a check for more money than you have in your account, the check is called an overdraft, or a bounced check. Financial institutions charge you when this happens.

Automatic coverage of overdraft. Some financial institutions will cover the amount of an overdraft. This is a special service, which is included in your monthly service charge.

With this information, you can choose the financial institution and the account that will best meet your needs.

4. Enter the amount of the check in numbers. Always write the numbers as close to the dollar sign as possible. Cents are written as a fraction.

5. Enter the amount of the check in words, starting at the far left of the line. The dollar amount is followed by the word "and"; the cents are written as a fraction. Draw a line from the end of the amount to the word "dollars."

6. Write your signature as it is on file at the bank.

Some checks have a line in the bottom left corner. This is generally used for your account number if you are paying a bill or a brief note indicating what the check is for, such as "Oct. rent, Apt. 2-B."

In addition to writing checks, you will also be receiving checks from time to time—your paycheck, for example. All checks must be endorsed in order for them to be cashed or deposited. There are three common types of endorsements:

1. A *blank endorsement* is only the signature of the payee. Once a check has been endorsed in this manner, it is the equivalent of cash and should be handled carefully.

2. A *full endorsement* is used when the payee wishes to give the check to someone else. With this kind of endorsement, only the person named in the endorsement can cash the check.

3. The safest kind of endorsement is the *restrictive endorsement*. This specifically states how the check is to be used.

If you have either a checking or savings account at the bank at which you are cashing the check, you should always write your account number on the check, below your signature.

USING CREDIT

Credit is a powerful tool for the money manager. Credit allows a person to "buy now and pay later." Almost everyone uses credit in one form or another. For example, every time you turn on the lights or use water in your apartment, you are using credit. In those examples, you are using *service credit*. The utility companies allow you to use their services and in turn they bill you for the services you have used.

Consumer credit is credit used by individuals and families for goods and services. It is based on trust in the individual's ability to repay a debt and on his or her willingness to repay the debt. Credit works because most people are honest and responsible; they do pay their debts as they have promised.

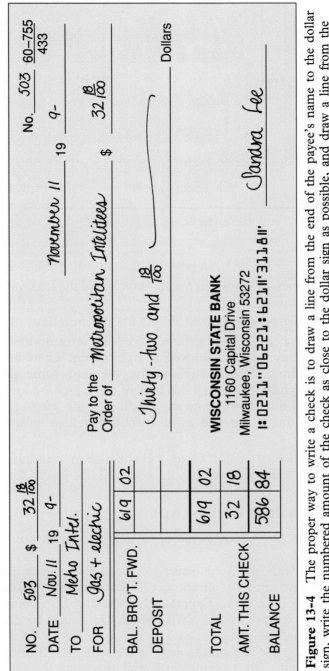

Figure 13-4 The proper way to write a check is to draw a line from the end of the payee's name to the dollar sign, write the numbered amount of the check as close to the dollar sign as possible, and draw a line from the last letter of the written amount on the next line to the letter *d* in the word dollars. This makes it difficult for additions or alterations to be made on the check.

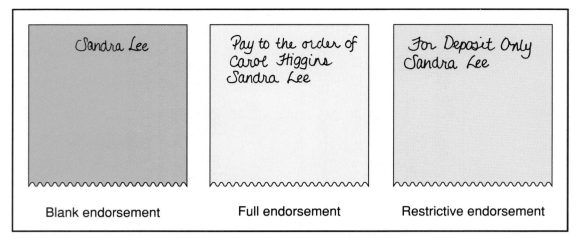

Sandra Lee	Pay to the order of Carol Higgins Sandra Lee	For Deposit Only Sandra Lee
Blank endorsement	Full endorsement	Restrictive endorsement

Figure 13-5 Three ways to endorse a check.

TYPES OF CREDIT

Various types of consumer and service credit are available. Common forms are these:

1. *Residential mortgage credit.* Used for the purchase of housing.

2. *Installment credit.* Used primarily for long-term nonresidential purposes such as buying a car, television, or clothing. There are different kinds of installment credit, such as the "90 days same as cash" method. The purchaser may pay the cost of the purchase any time within 90 days and not have to pay any credit charges. However, after 90 days, the amount is handled as an installment loan with monthly finance charges.

3. *Noninstallment credit.* Used for short-term purchases such as your monthly electric service.

CREDIT AND DEBIT CARDS

The most widely used forms of installment credit are credit cards and debit cards.

Credit cards are used instead of cash for making purchases. There are different kinds of credit cards: bank cards (MasterCard, VISA), travel cards (American Express, Diner's Club), gasoline cards (Mobil), and retail or store credit cards, which are issued by department stores or store chains.

Many people use credit cards for convenience. They make purchases, pay for them with a credit card, and then pay the entire bill at once. Other consumers make large purchases, such as furniture, using a credit card and pay only a portion of the bill each month. In the first example, there is usually no extra charge; however, for the person who pays in installments interest is charged. Most large department stores, for example, issue credit cards for what is called "revolving" credit. The customer may make purchases and, for a stated amount of interest, pay a fraction of the total amount (usually between 10% and 20%) per month. The amount is nearly always changing or "revolving" because though payments are being made, other items are often charged during a month.

The principle advantage of credit cards is convenience. The principle disadvantages are the temptation to overuse them and the additional cost their use requires.

Debit cards allow the user to pay for purchases by direct electronic transfer of funds. A familiar way of using the debit card is to make deposits and withdrawals of cash from an automated teller (see Figure 13-6). When you withdraw cash, the amount you requested is electronically withdrawn from your checking account. You may shop at a grocery store or department store that is equipped to handle debit cards as a substitute for handwritten checks.

Whatever form of credit you use, it is important to keep receipts and to check them closely against the monthly statement. Computers do make mistakes, and so do the people who operate them; you could be billed for something you did not buy.

ADVANTAGES OF CREDIT

Credit offers advantages that can improve your life-style.

1. A loan can make it possible for you to buy a car or a home which you would not otherwise be able to afford.
2. Credit allows you to have something and use it while you are paying for it. For example, you may borrow money to buy a washing machine and use it while you are paying for it.
3. Credit makes buying goods and services convenient. Often it is inconvenient—even dangerous—to carry large sums of money. When credit is available, you may buy without carrying cash. Credit in the form of a credit card is especially helpful to the professional who is traveling on business.
4. Credit helps people meet emergencies. Credit can offer temporary solutions for unexpected financial difficulties, such as when your car breaks down on a long trip.

DISADVANTAGES OF CREDIT

Credit is a useful tool for the money manager. However, it can become a problem if it is misused. Lack of self-discipline may contribute to

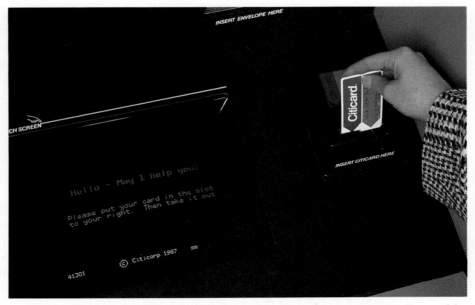

Figure 13-6 Automated teller machines allow customers to handle a wide variety of financial transactions—even when their banks are closed. (Photo courtesy of Diebold and InterBold, a partnership of Diebold Incorporated and IBM Corporation)

mismanagement of credit, and some disadvantages are built into the credit concept. Among the disadvantages are these:

1. **Credit involves cost.** Financial organizations and businesses charge interest on money that they lend or on goods that they sell on credit. For example, if you were to borrow $500 to pay your tuition, the cost of using the bank's money (cost of credit) would be $33.16, if you were charged a 12% rate of interest. As a consumer you must decide if making a credit purchase is worth the cost of the item (or service) *plus the cost of the credit.* Interest rates vary. For example, rates of interest charged on bank credit cards range from 16% to 20%.

2. **Using credit commits a portion of your future income** to pay for present or past purchases. Thus, you reduce the choices you will be able to make in the future. Credit payments become either a fixed or variable expense in your budget until the debt is paid. If you neglect to meet the payments, the lender may repossess the item you purchased and/or seriously damage your credit rating (chance of getting credit in the future), and you will have nothing to show for the payments that you already made (no refund).

3. **Credit makes overspending easy.** Many people are tempted by "buy now and pay later" opportunities. Advertisers are skilled at convincing

people to buy goods and services immediately regardless of their ability to pay. For example, you may frequently see ads that carry a slogan such as "Buy now—your first payment will not be due for 3 months!" It is all too easy to buy more than you can afford and get into serious financial trouble.

While credit offers a convenient way to purchase, there is one basic fact to remember: *Credit is only a temporary substitute for cash.* Although you may use credit to defer a payment until your cash flow is better, if your cash flow is always poor, using credit is not a good option for acquiring goods. You may need to evaluate some other factors in your life, such as cutting expenses or increasing your income.

AVOID CREDIT ABUSE

◆ Use credit when you need the use of a product or service while you are paying for it, or when your expenditures temporarily exceed your income, or when you want to take advantage of a bargain before you have the money to pay cash for it, or when credit is a convenience you can afford.

◆ Keep a record of your charges. Know approximately how much you owe each of your creditors.

◆ Don't use credit for impulse purchases.

◆ Avoid paying only the minimum amount due each month. Pay all you owe, or as much as you can, on each due date to avoid excessive interest costs.

◆ If you have trouble controlling your use of credit, close your credit account. Then determine which credit cards you really need to carry and leave the others at home so that you will not be tempted to overuse credit.

◆ If you continue to have trouble managing credit, seek the help of the Consumer Credit Bureau. This organization is found in most cities. It is a free, reliable service to help consumers avoid credit abuse.

COST OF CREDIT

If you plan to use credit, always find out ahead of time how much it will cost. Knowing the exact cost can help you compare finance charges and select the best source of credit. The Federal Consumer Protection Act (commonly known as Truth-in-Lending Act) requires that all lenders and retailers provide credit cost information before credit is extended. The Act requires that two kinds of information be given to customers:

1. The dollar amount of finance charges
2. The annual percentage rate of credit

For example, if you need $500 to enroll in a semester of classes, you may go to the credit union and borrow $500 with a plan to repay the money in 12 equal payments during a 1-year period. If the credit union advertises loans at a rate of 1% per month, the contract you sign must state that the dollar cost of credit is $33.16 and that the annual percentage rate is 12%.

The annual percentage rate is the cost of credit in percentage terms (a percent of the loan that remains each month). Lending agencies must calculate this rate in the manner required under the Consumer Protection Act. This figure allows you to compare costs of credit among different lending agencies. The finance charge and annual percentage rate can substantially affect the amount you owe.

UNDERSTANDING INSURANCE

Think of the largest and most serious financial disaster that you might face—a fire in your house or apartment, an accident with your car, or a serious illness that requires your being hospitalized. How would you pay the costs of such calamities? Most of us could not handle such enormous costs from our salaries and our savings. We have great fear of facing such demands; therefore, as a society we have developed a system of protection from the financial demands of illness, accidents, theft, death, and other losses. The system is called insurance. Simply stated, insurance is sharing risks; that is, a group of people pay a certain amount of money (a premium) into a pool of funds. When an individual within the group encounters a serious financial catastrophe, the costs are paid from the common pool.

Most people buy insurance as they mature and acquire greater financial responsibilities. As teens, our greatest need for insurance may be to cover the possible loss of a used car. As we grow older, we may have a family, which may cause us to feel the need to insure our lives so that our families will be protected if we are injured or die. The need for insurance builds as life progresses.

As adults we may consider four major types of insurance: life, health, home, and auto.

LIFE INSURANCE

The primary purpose of life insurance is to protect against the loss of income to a family when a wage earner dies. Basic insurance is known as *term insurance*. With term insurance a person's life is insured for a specific amount of money for a specific period of time. If the person dies during that period of time, his or her family receives the contractual value of the policy. If the person does not die during that period of time, the family receives no money, but they have had the assurance of financial protection during the period covered by the insurance contract (or policy). Relatively speaking, term insurance is low-cost insurance.

In addition to term insurance there are other types of insurance known as *permanent insurance*, which add savings and investment features to the basic insurance policy. These types include whole life insurance, limited-pay life insurance, endowment policies, and universal life insurance. With permanent insurance, the family receives the value of the policy when the insured dies, but there is also cash value in the policy, which the owner may borrow or recover at retirement. These cash value insurance policies are much more expensive than simple term insurance because the owner is saving as well as buying protection against the risk of dying with his or her insurance payments (premiums).

Seek the help of a reputable insurance agent when you are ready to purchase life insurance. And remember to shop for insurance just as you do comparative shopping for all purchases.

Many employers offer life insurance at no cost, or at very low cost, to their employees, with the option to increase the basic coverage at a later date. For many young people, particularly those without children, the company-provided insurance may be sufficient. As family responsibilities increase, people may consider more life insurance.

AUTOMOBILE INSURANCE

When people are involved in auto accidents, the costs of repair to the cars and to the people injured are often too great for most people's budgets. Automobile insurance is the best way to protect yourself from the financial burden of an auto accident. Some states require that a person show proof that he or she has auto insurance to purchase license plates. The extent of coverage varies in several categories.

Property Damage Liability. Property damage liability pays for damages to the property of those people other than the driver responsible for the accident. This does not cover damage to the responsible driver's car. The amount of coverage chosen is indicated by a set of figures such as 100/300/10. These figures mean that the insurance company will pay up to $100,000 for injury of a single person, $300,000 for all injuries, and $10,000 for property damage. Property liability coverage is often a form of insurance *required* by state government.

Bodily Injury Liability. If you are legally liable for an accident in which others are injured or killed, bodily injury liability covers the medical costs.

Collision. Collision coverage pays for the repair cost of the damage to your car caused by a collision with another vehicle or object. Frequently this coverage is required by the financial institution that lends money for the purchase of a car. When the car loan is paid, you may choose to discontinue this kind of insurance.

Medical Insurance. Medical insurance covers medical expenses resulting from an accident.

Comprehensive Insurance. Comprehensive insurance pays for the cost of repairing damage to your auto caused by events other than collision with another car; for example, damages or losses from theft, fire, water, or vandalism.

HEALTH INSURANCE

Everyone needs regular health care; yet, bearing the full cost of today's health care can be financially devastating. Three types of insurance are available to help people manage the costs of health care.

Basic medical insurance covers a percentage of the costs of physicians' services, testing, care as a hospital out-patient, and some limited hospitalization.

Major medical insurance covers a percentage of the costs of hospital and medical care beyond the scope of basic medical insurance, including surgery and recovery costs, comprehensive treatments, and extended hospitalizations. It helps cover the cost of long-term illness.

Figure 13-7 Collision insurance pays for most repair costs for damage done to your car in an accident. (Photo by David W. Tuttle.)

Disability insurance provides regular income to the policyholder when accident or illness forces the individual to be off work for a long period of time.

Many employers provide health insurance at little or no cost to employees. Sometimes an employer offers more than one plan, and the employee may choose the plan that fits his or her needs; this may include extra coverage at additional expense to the employee. Disability insurance may be offered at low cost; it may or may not be subsidized by the company.

The scope of insurance benefits is an area of great change in the workplace. Keep up with changes in benefits as they occur in your company.

RESIDENTIAL INSURANCE

If you rent an apartment or house, or if you own or are planning to buy a home, you will need to consider some form of residential insurance. This kind of insurance covers the loss of household items—furniture and other possessions—as well as the structure itself. In addition to protection from fire, theft, and water damage, homeowners' policies may also provide protection against financial loss if others are injured on your property.

Most mortgage lenders require proof that you have purchased homeowners' insurance before they will lend you money. After the loan is granted, insurance premiums will often be built into your monthly mortgage payment. In some parts of the country, flood, hurricane, or tornado insurance may be available.

SAVING

Effective money management includes regularly setting aside money for savings. Savings are important to individuals and families for these reasons:

◆ To meet emergencies
◆ To make expensive purchases
◆ To provide security
◆ To make investments

Saving is a matter of planning and self-discipline. It is easier for most people when they have a specific savings goal. For example, you may save to buy a stereo or to make a down payment on a car.

People who have been successful at saving some of their money recommend setting aside a specific amount of money at the beginning

Figure 13-8 Parts of the United States are prone to hurricanes, tornadoes, or earthquakes. Special homeowner's insurance is available to cover these natural disasters. (Photo copyright © Cameramann/The Image Works.)

of each pay period. Very few people have savings if they wait to save what is left at the end of a pay period.

Saving is also easier if you have devised a way to discipline yourself to save. Payroll deduction is a method chosen by many workers. With this method, money is deducted from your check each month—the amount determined by you—and placed in a savings account. Many workers say that it is easier to save when they never have the money in hand to spend. The following list suggests effective (versus ineffective) ways to save.

WAYS TO SAVE

Effective	*Ineffective*
Payroll deduction	Putting away cash
At the beginning of each pay period	At the end of each pay period
With a goal in mind	For general purposes
A set amount each month	Whatever amount you have
In an insured financial institution	In a safe place at home

Economists recommend that individuals and families save 10% of their income. In reality, Americans generally save about 5% of their income. (People who are in school may choose to invest in themselves as an alternative to traditional savings plans.)

Basic savings may be kept in savings accounts or credit unions. People are less likely to spend their savings if it is kept in a place where the money is not readily accessible. After a person has increased personal savings beyond 1 or 2 month's take-home pay, the individual may wish to invest some of it in a form of savings that pays a higher interest rate than a regular savings account. One option is to buy a Certificate of Deposit (CD), that is, a specific amount of money (minimums determined by the financial institution) on deposit for a specific amount of time, usually 6 months or longer. In return, the financial institution agrees to pay a specific rate of interest on the money.

MANAGING A FINANCIAL PLAN

Money management, like other skills, becomes easier with practice. Here are some tips for managing your money easily and effectively.

◆ Determine who will be the primary money manager in a household. Most households find that having one person manage the money is most efficient. This does not mean that the other household members do not participate. In fact, it is important that all have a share in the decisions made about the group's financial resources, but having a designated manager just eliminates confusion.

◆ Organize the records. Select a specific place in the home where records (receipts, bills, statements, etc.) may be kept. Here the money manager may also do the required paperwork—write checks, balance the checkbook, evaluate statements, and compose correspondence. This money management center may be a desk, a table, or a kitchen counter that can be used for work and for storage of important family records.

◆ Keep accurate, complete money management records. A number of records are important for personal and family money management as well as for tax purposes. They include canceled checks and bank statements for the past 5 years, medical and dental records, receipts for purchases, copies of insurance policies, bank account records, rent agreements, tax records, and employment contracts. Credit agreements are also important if you use credit.

TAXES

Taxes are payments that citizens and businesses are required to make to city, county, state, and federal governments. Taxes are paid when we purchase goods (sales tax). The state requires registration of cars, which is a form of taxation. In addition, taxes are withheld from salaries each pay period. Employers send the withheld monies to the Internal Revenue Service (IRS) or local tax collection agencies in the employee's name. In addition, homeowners pay property taxes on their houses, and heirs may pay estate taxes on property willed to them.

In addition to paying taxes throughout the year, you must also file tax returns at the end of the year. (The deadline for filing taxes in a given year is' April 15 of the following year.) The returns are filed with the IRS and state and local tax collection agencies.

When filing a tax return, forms must be completed. These can vary in length and complexity, depending on the complexity of your finances and on the amount and kind of deductions you take. A deduction is money you paid out on items that are not taxable. The total or a percentage of the total amount of the deductions is subtracted from your income, so that you pay taxes on a lower income, or lower taxes. These include:

◆ Medical and health expenses (the amount not paid by your health insurance)

◆ State and local taxes

◆ Interest on home mortgages

◆ Gifts to charity

◆ Moving expenses (if moving was job related)

Figure 13-9 It takes concentration to keep receipts, bills, and statements in order. (Photo by Paul E. Meyers.)

◆ Casualty or theft losses not covered by insurance

◆ Job expenses not reimbursed by your company

Different incomes require different amounts of taxes to be paid. The tax returns you file indicate whether you overpaid or underpaid your taxes during the year. If you overpaid, you will be reimbursed for the difference between what you should have paid and what you actually paid. If you underpaid, you will have to pay additional taxes to make up the difference.

Filling out tax forms can be difficult and complicated. You can pay for assistance from an accountant or company that specializes in preparing an individual's taxes. You can also prepare your tax returns yourself. The IRS, state, and local tax agencies have numbers that you can call for assistance and to answer questions.

As a citizen, you should keep informed of taxes and the government's use of tax money.

As an informed professional, you should understand the rules and regulations that relate to tax returns, even if you do not fill them out yourself. Here are some ways to learn more about taxes:

◆ Obtain tax guides from newsstands and book stores to read about current tax laws and responsibilities.

◆ Visit city and county libraries for further information.

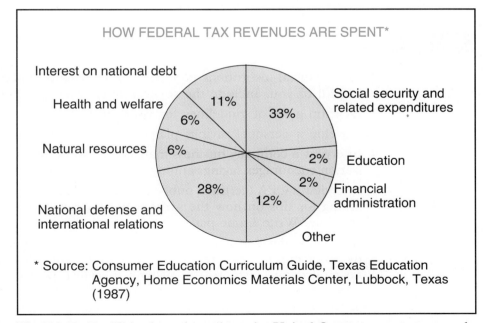

HOW FEDERAL TAX REVENUES ARE SPENT*

Interest on national debt — 11%

Health and welfare — 6%

Natural resources — 6%

National defense and international relations — 28%

Social security and related expenditures — 33%

Education — 2%

Financial administration — 2%

Other — 12%

* Source: Consumer Education Curriculum Guide, Texas Education Agency, Home Economics Materials Center, Lubbock, Texas (1987)

Figure 13-10 This chart shows how the United States government spends tax dollars.

◆ Attend tax seminars to learn from tax experts.

◆ Call the Internal Revenue Tax Service to ask questions for specific information you may need.

REVIEW QUESTIONS

1. Explain the term take-home pay. How does it differ from the amount you consider to be your salary?
2. Identify each of the following expenses as either fixed or variable: entertainment, utilities, clothing, rent.
3. Give three reasons for making a money management plan or budget.
4. Name and describe two types of checking accounts.
5. What is a demand deposit?
6. List three advantages and three disadvantages of credit.
7. Explain the purpose of savings and describe how one may save effectively.
8. Outline the four common types of insurance.
9. Name three different kinds of tax.
10. What elements are required to achieve financial security?

ACTIVITIES

1. List financial institutions in your town or neighborhood that may be helpful to you. Include the services offered at each one.
2. Develop a set of guidelines for your own effective use of credit.
3. Develop a personal savings plan.
4. Interview a company business manager for ways that his or her organization encourages savings among employees. Write a one-page report.
5. Interview a CPA (certified public accountant) or certified tax preparer, asking for tips on how the average person can be more prepared at tax time. Write a one-page report.
6. As a class, develop a scenario in which a fictitious person is injured in an accident that results in a trip to the emergency room, hospitalization, tests, treatment by a specialist, physical therapy, and a long recovery at home (several weeks off work). If possible, have a doctor or other specialist work with you to estimate the cost of the care. Your instructor may suggest a range of benefits that could be provided with insurance protection.

CHAPTER 14
PROFESSIONAL GROWTH

CHAPTER GOAL:

To identify ways you may continue to develop as a professional person.

CHAPTER OBJECTIVES:

After studying this chapter, you should be able to:

1. Identify the characteristics generally attributed to a professional person.
2. Outline activities that promote professional growth.
3. Establish a work record.
4. Use appropriate strategies when changing positions.
5. Manage the dual role of private and professional person.

You know that professional success can be yours. This book focuses on factors that contribute to growth, productivity, and promotability, all of which lead to success. In this final chapter, you will review some of the ways to grow and new insight into how to present yourself in the best possible light to all the people with whom you work.

DEFINING THE PROFESSIONAL

A professional may be defined in various ways. Traditionally, the word "professional" has been used to describe someone in a particular field that requires special training or a long period of formal education. The fields most often associated with the term professional are medicine or law. Professionals defined this way have the following characteristics:

- The field has a unique knowledge base.
- The field requires special training.
- Members perform a service for society.
- Members are self-governing.
- Entrance into the profession is controlled; entrance requirements include tests, certification courses, etc.

Over the years, the word professional has come to refer to any person, working in any field, who has the qualities that were once associated with members of a traditionally recognized profession. The following is a profile of a professional in any field:

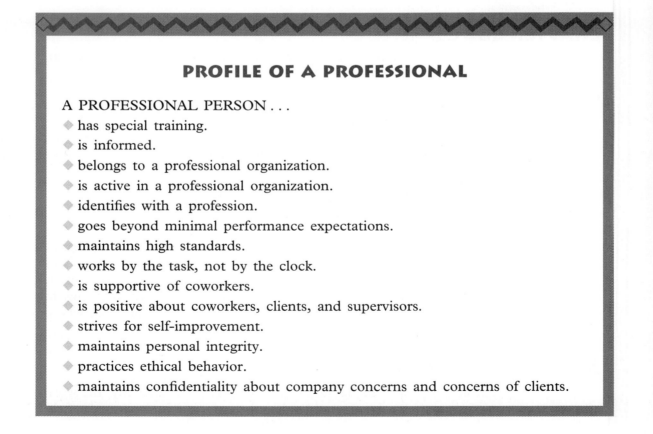

PROFILE OF A PROFESSIONAL

A PROFESSIONAL PERSON . . .

- has special training.
- is informed.
- belongs to a professional organization.
- is active in a professional organization.
- identifies with a profession.
- goes beyond minimal performance expectations.
- maintains high standards.
- works by the task, not by the clock.
- is supportive of coworkers.
- is positive about coworkers, clients, and supervisors.
- strives for self-improvement.
- maintains personal integrity.
- practices ethical behavior.
- maintains confidentiality about company concerns and concerns of clients.

WAYS TO GROW PROFESSIONALLY

As you have learned, getting a job is not the end of anything—not even the end of your search. From the first day on a job you are searching to find your niche, your work role, your strengths and weaknesses, and your future with that company and in that field of work. Continuing your education, learning from your experiences, making the most of opportunities in the community, and working with professional organizations are ways to help you grow professionally.

RATE YOURSELF AS A PROFESSIONAL

	YES	NO
1. Am I enrolled in a course of study that prepares me to enter a career field?		
2. Do I belong to a student professional organization?		
3. Am I actively involved in the professional student organization?		
4. Do I identify myself with a career field?		
5. Do I participate in some form of service activity?		
6. Do I work at self-improvement?		
7. Do I work by tasks, not by the clock?		
8. Do I talk positively about my career field?		
9. Do I strive to improve relationships with others?		
10. Am I seeking job information about work in my career field?		

FORMAL EDUCATION

You may feel the need at various stages of your career to enroll in college or continuing education courses to expand your general education or to increase your work-related skills. You may even want to work toward a specific educational degree. This does not mean that you made incorrect choices about education earlier. It shows that you are capable of reevaluating your life and doing what you feel can improve your life-style. The changing work environment has required that many people retrain. Employees with insight may be able to foresee shifts in the local and national economy and changes in their own company. They are willing to adapt to change.

Investigate resources in your community. You will probably find a variety of educational institutions that offer courses and degrees designed for working people who attend school on a part-time basis. Community colleges, private schools, and colleges or universities are available to almost everyone. They offer weekend courses and evening classes as well as day classes. Many schools have departments or schools of adult and continuing education. Research your company's educational policies. Many organizations encourage employees to take classes; some even pay the costs of tuition, books, and fees for their workers. Most companies fully reimburse workers for work-related courses; some offer partial reimbursement for non-job-related courses. Many companies offer on-site courses in business and self-improvement subjects.

INFORMAL LEARNING EXPERIENCES

Informal learning experiences may be something as simple as reading professional literature. Your company will likely have literature available that relates to the business. You can find literature relating to your profession or the kind of business in which you work in bookstores and libraries. Professional organizations often publish informative newsletters or other literature, which are usually distributed to members.

You may find that attending seminars and short courses (1 or 2 days) related to your work to be helpful. Short courses may be offered by local and area colleges, by professional groups, and even by your own industry. Ask your manager, a personnel administrator, or your company's public relations office for information on short courses.

Observe and talk with experienced workers to find out what has made them successful. You can learn a great deal from coworkers. Making a friend of an older, more experienced worker will help you to learn the business and will give you a valuable information resource.

WORK EXPERIENCES

Many people feel that the best way to learn is through hands-on experience. If you are a conscientious worker and if you are willing to take direction from your manager, you will grow through your own work experiences. As you work, seek feedback from your manager to establish what you do well and in what areas you can improve.

Once you have mastered what you have been assigned, request or volunteer for more and different assignments to broaden your skills and knowledge.

New Technical Courses in the Learning Center

The Learning Centers now offer several new technical courses including the following:

- *LANS, MANS, and WANS (VVDØ541M)* – Local Metropolitan and Wide Area Networks are discussed and explored from the End User perspective. This ten-hour video tape presentation consists of 12 units that can be selectively viewed.

- *WordPerfect (VVDØ368B)* is a basic course for new users, a word processing package to create/edit/save a document. Additional features of WordPerfect include a help facility, capability of merging documents, and use of a SpellChecker. WordPerfect will also create macros, a table of contents and an index providing more than adequate functions.

- *Paradox (VVDØ4Ø3M)* is intended for PC users who want to learn how to use the basic features of the PARADOX database package. Topics include accessing data in a PARADOX data table, creating data tables, entering and editing data in a data table, query information and creating basic reports in a variety of formats.

- *Paradox Advanced Features (VVDØ4Ø4M)* includes the following topics: creating form memos; creating different types of graphs from the table data; creating, editing, and using PARADOX scripts; writing complex scripts using the PARADOX Application Language (PAL) and designing and creating entire PARADOX applications.

For further information on these and other Learning Center offerings, contact your local Learning Center administrator. Please refer to our February newsletter for a complete list of Learning Center contacts.

NOTE: Effective May 4, the Franklin Lakes Learning Center will be closed.

Figure 14-1 Many companies offer courses in self-improvement and business-related subjects. (Courtesy of IBM.)

CHANGING JOBS

Once you are working, you may choose to remain with one company, advancing up the career ladder as opportunities arise. On the other hand, you may decide to move to other companies or organizations to advance. If growing and advancing is important to you, you will need to determine whether staying with one company or moving around has been most successful for others in your field of work. Interview several successful people, some who have stayed with one company and some who moved to other companies to advance.

Many people value the security and stability that staying with one company offers, even though promotions may come slowly. Also, some people find it difficult to leave behind good relationships with coworkers. Others value the immediate increase in salary or the challenge of unfamiliar work that moving to a new company may offer. Some people move because they want improved work schedules, physical surroundings, or locations. Your answers to the following questions may help you decide whether to stay at a job or leave.

Professional Questions:

◆ How does this fit in with my professional and personal priorities?

◆ What skills that I already have can I use in the new position?

◆ What new skills can I develop in the new position?

◆ How will this move relate to my long-term career goals?

◆ Are there clear opportunities for advancement at the new position?

◆ How will the new environment, salary, and benefits compare with my present situation?

Personal Questions:

◆ How will this move affect my family?

◆ Will my career change affect my spouse's career goal?

◆ Is this new position in a convenient and accessible location?

◆ What personal and family sacrifices am I willing to make for my career?

Economic Questions:

◆ How do the salary and benefits differ from those at the job I am leaving? (Be sure to take into account the number of work hours expected at the new job compared with the number of hours you work now.)

◆ What will be the long-term financial benefits?

◆ Will I have to pay for the cost of relocation?

◆ How long will it take to recover the costs of relocating?
◆ Will the other company help with moving costs and details?

Experts in career-building strategies caution people against "job hopping." In other words, it is not wise to move so often that you leave the impression that you are asked to leave or you are not staying long enough to be of any real value to the organization. A company does not benefit from the time spent training you if the training is not applied. Certainly you should stay in all your positions long enough to give a fair measure of service to the company that hired you, and you will want to stay long enough to increase your own knowledge and skills. Finally, when you are ready to move on, make the move in a professional way. See the section on Resigning from a Position for more information on this topic.

CIVIC RESPONSIBILITIES

All communities have organizations that are always in need of volunteers. When you join a civic group you profit in these ways:

◆ You have an opportunity to meet new people with whom you share similar interests.
◆ You have an opportunity to develop leadership skills.
◆ You learn new things and develop new skills.
◆ You profit from working with people who are different from those with whom you usually work.
◆ You broaden your social life.
◆ You find opportunities to help those who may be in real need.

Investigate what is available in your community by reading the daily newspapers, by contacting the Chamber of Commerce, or by telephoning the office of the mayor of your town. The following kinds of organizations are often in need of volunteers:

Chamber of Commerce   Youth clubs
Junior League   Volunteers of America
Jaycees   Women's groups
Men's clubs   Big Brothers/Big Sisters
Church groups   Literary groups
Garden clubs   Environmental groups
Alumni groups

SOCIAL ACTIVITIES

You also grow by participating in activities that are purely social. Sports, games, and visiting with others add balance to your life. Social activities

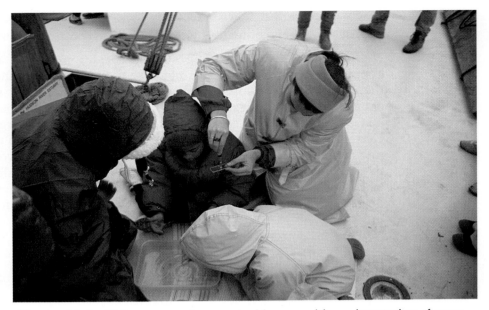

Figure 14-2 Volunteer work can provide you with an interesting change of pace. On board the Clearwater's classroom of the waves, a volunteer staffs the water chemistry teaching station. (Courtesy of Hudson River Sloop Clearwater, Inc.)

are important for relaxation, for stress reduction, and for meeting new people. The "people skills" you develop in social situations carry over to working with others in your professional role. You may also develop leadership skills here, too—most group activities need a leader.

PROFESSIONAL ORGANIZATIONS

Many professions have organizations. For example, office workers can belong to the Office Automation Society, and interior designers may join the American Society of Interior Designers.

Find out what organizations exist in your profession. Membership in a professional organization has these advantages:

◆ Provides prestige and support (encouragement) for its members.

◆ Provides strength from combined efforts, such as influence on legislative action.

◆ Provides access to current information and job openings in the profession.

◆ Provides access to activities that promote professional growth and development, such as seminars, luncheons, and field trips.

Inquire about student membership in organizations in your targeted profession. Many organizations give discounts to students. You can distinguish yourself early as someone who is interested in contributing to the profession.

COMMUNICATING YOUR PROFESSIONAL WORTH

Communicating your professional worth to your managers is critical to career advancement, as is discussed in Chapter 10. Usually employers look at achievement in the following areas when they consider someone for promotion:

- General work skills
- Technical skills
- People skills

GENERAL WORK SKILLS

Behavior or actions that are impressive in general work skills are:

- Promptness to work and promptness in completing tasks
- Working by the task, not by the clock
- Serious commitment to each task
- Willingness to learn
- Positive response to supervision, including criticism
- Care of equipment
- General neatness in work and surroundings
- Problem-solving ability
- Expressing positive attitudes, for example, enthusiasm about projects assigned and the company in general

TECHNICAL SKILLS

Evidence of superior technical skills are:

- Productivity
- Work well-done, complete, and error-free
- High standards
- New ideas and methods presented to solve problems
- Additional assignments requested

PEOPLE SKILLS

Evidence of people skills are important for all aspects of your personal and professional life. Here is a partial list of actions and behaviors that are signs of people skills:

- Cordial relationships with coworkers
- Courtesy and respect shown to management, clients, and coworkers
- Positive attitudes
- Absence of gossip
- Support of coworkers and management
- Maintenance of high ethical standards
- Acceptance of blame when blame is deserved
- Avoidance of cliques
- Consideration of subordinates as respected colleagues

It is important to know how to impress management and present yourself in the best light. It is also important to remember what *not* to do. The following is a list of actions or behavior that hinder advancement opportunities:

- Dressing too casually—without regard for professional appearance
- Expressing a lack of self-control, such as crying or swearing
- Ignoring the chain of command—going over one manager to seek help from the next higher level manager
- Exhibiting a negative attitude—criticizing others, complaining about conditions, failing to seek solutions to problems
- Working as a loner—unwilling to share, failing to work as a team member
- Developing a romantic relationship with a colleague
- Having poor work habits—procrastination, leaving work incomplete, lack of organization
- Misusing company time—late to work, early to leave, abuse of lunch time and coffee breaks, bringing personal activities to work

BUILDING A WORK RECORD

Many types of actions, documented and undocumented, go into building a work record. You may establish a solid record in a variety of ways.

KEEP RECORDS

Keep a record of your significant professional accomplishments, and refer to it when you ask for a promotion, update your resume, complete required work reports, or justify special requests. Some people keep a monthly desk calendar, which becomes a good record of day-to-day responsibilities. Others keep a notebook. Devise a system that is right for you. In addition, take notes at both formal and informal meetings, and keep them on file.

SEEK EVALUATION

Regular reviews, or formal evaluations, are standard procedure in some organizations; in others, you may need to request a review in order to have one. Such reviews will provide you an opportunity to present your accomplishments to your superior. In addition, you can learn from the reviewer how you are perceived and how you may improve your work. Together you can decide on professional goals that will benefit you and your company. Requesting such evaluations when they are not required is a good way to prove your commitment to doing a good job.

CONFER WITH SUPERIORS

On occasion, you may wish to meet informally with your manager to discuss your work. Be sure that you do not do this so frequently that you irritate or bore your boss. Make a list of items you want to discuss, and be brief and direct.

VOLUNTEER FOR NEW ASSIGNMENTS

Ask for challenging assignments. The worker who volunteers for high-visibility tasks builds a good work record rapidly. Before you volunteer, be sure that you are capable of performing the task. Also be sure that the additional assignment does not interfere with your regular work. Volunteering can make you look good only if you are able to do well and if none of your other assignments suffer as a result.

RESIGNING FROM A POSITION

You may choose to leave a position for a variety of reasons—an offer of a better position, displeasure with your present position, or an opportunity to go into business for yourself. You may also want to become a full-time homemaker. Regardless of the reason for resigning from a position, you can maintain a positive relationship with the company by planning your exit carefully.

THE NOTICE OF RESIGNATION

After you have made the decision to resign, talk with your immediate supervisor about your decision, emphasizing that you will be professional in your work and relationships during the remainder of your time on the job. Submit your notice of resignation in the form of a letter to the appropriate manager after you have spoken to him or her in person. An appropriate letter of resignation should include the date on which your resignation will be effective and at least the following three parts:

```
3502 Bettis Street
Georgia, Wisconsin 77988
December 1, 1990

Mr. Hiram Goodroe, Director
Johnson and Bloom Manufacturing
P.O. Drawer 1112
Georgia, Wisconsin 77987

Dear Mr. Goodroe:

I am submitting my resignation, effective December 21, 1990. I recently
accepted a position as office supervisor for the Lascoe Company in Port-
land, Oregon. Although I will miss the challenging work and the fine people
here, I feel I must take advantage of this new professional opportunity.

Management at Johnson and Bloom Manufacturing has provided me with
excellent opportunities to be productive and to grow as a professional. I
particularly appreciate the support you have given me during the two years
we have worked together.

Best wishes for you and the entire staff of Johnson and Bloom.

Sincerely,

Madge Porter

Madge Porter
```

Figure 14-3 A sample letter of resignation.

◆ A statement of regret that you are leaving your position
◆ A reason for leaving diplomatically stated
◆ A compliment to the organization

TIME FOR RESIGNING

It is important to time your resignation appropriately. The correct time
may vary depending on the type of work you have. For example, a
teacher usually submits a notice of resignation one semester in advance.
The minimum advance notice considered acceptable is 2 weeks. When
you have a supervisory or management position, a longer notice is
customary. This gives the company time to find a replacement. If you
are still in your job when your replacement is named, you may be asked
to help train this person.

BEHAVIOR AFTER RESIGNATION

Between the time you submit your resignation and your last day of work, perform your job as you always have. Do not let down or boast to your coworkers about your new position.

After you leave a position, it is not ethical to reveal confidential information or speak against the organization. In addition, workers who complain about their former managers do not create a positive image for themselves.

WHEN NOT TO RESIGN

Job placement experts advise people to keep the jobs they have until they find others, even when they are eager to make a change. Most people have more success at job hunting as an employed person than as an unemployed person. People who are employed have the economic resources to search for what they want and do not feel pressured to take the first opening that is offered. And they can appear positive about wanting to make a change for the better.

THE FORCED JOB LOSS

You may lose your job without choosing to. This may occur as a result of layoffs (the status of the job changes or is eliminated) or firings (dismissal with cause—a specific, justifiable reason) during your professional career. A layoff may be temporary or permanent. If you experience a layoff, inquire about the benefits due you. Severance pay (a lump sum transition payment from the company) and/or unemployment benefits (government reimbursement of money paid in for this purpose) may be available. If you are fired, you may also explore what benefits are available. Unemployment benefits are often not available if you are fired with cause.

Any forced job loss is a blow to your feelings of self-worth. If you are forced to resign or are fired, ask for reasons, and try to understand the total situation. You may learn that the situation occurred through no fault on your part, or you may learn ways you can change to avoid losing a future job.

Of course, many people use the time after layoffs to find a new position. You might also use the time to develop new skills. The state and federal governments offer retraining for many workers who lose their jobs. Often workers learn a new trade or take courses that lead to a new career.

MANAGING YOUR PERSONAL AND PROFESSIONAL RESPONSIBILITIES

Balancing the responsibilities of a career and a home is a necessity for many couples, who have found that they cannot meet their financial responsibilities or goals on one income, or whose personal goals include the development of professional careers for both adults. A well-run, well-maintained home can provide enjoyment and comfort. However, a home like this is not achieved without effort; it is the result of organization, planning, and hard work.

When two or more adults live together, the sharing of duties and responsibilities makes their life and work easier to manage but still challenging. On the other hand, when the family has only one adult, managing a home and career is even more challenging.

MANAGING PERSONAL AND PROFESSIONAL LIVING "MAJOR CHALLENGES"

1. Child care
2. Time management
3. Fulfilling expectations for two roles
4. Career promotion
5. Money management

Research shows that these challenges exist for all people who choose to manage both family and professional life. The challenges change somewhat when people are involved in a two-career family—a family where both adults are building professional careers. For example, the couple may have differing role expectations, different views about who and how the income should be managed, and how both careers can be promoted.

REQUIREMENTS FOR MANAGING WELL

A flexible attitude toward traditional family roles and a willingness to share are critical to managing work and family responsibilities. In addition, having common goals and certain management skills are helpful.

Attitudes. If both partners are willing to share responsibilities at home, they will both benefit domestically and professionally because each will bear less of the burden. Families should set aside traditional ideas of "women's work" or "men's work" to function well together. For example, a wife may cheerfully wash the car or mow the lawn if she has more time at home than her husband; the husband can oversee the children's baths or vacuum if she is too busy. When family members accept responsibilities based on need, on ability, and available time, the family functions better.

Family Goals. It is important for families to have clear, mutually agreed-on goals; this encourages a willingness to share. For example, each wage earner in the family may contribute a portion of his or her income toward a family vacation. Or each member of the family agrees that household chores will be completed before going out or watching television.

Communication. Happy families are able to communicate their thoughts and feelings to each other. They talk together often and they listen to what the other has to say. The communication skills described earlier in this text are important for successful family life.

Organization. Organization is an important factor in a well-managed home. Organization of the physical space and equipment, organization of chores, and organization of time should be based on what the total group decides is best for the family and for each of the individual members. For example, most families have a goal of a pleasant, comfortable, and clean living space. To reach this goal, one family may work together as a group each Wednesday evening to clean the entire house; another family may prefer to divide the cleaning chores so that each individual is responsible for the condition of one room; a third family may use some of their surplus earnings to hire a person to clean on a weekly basis. The following list provides time-saving tips for families with two working members.

TIME-SAVING TIPS

- Share duties and responsibilities.
- Investigate new tools, cleaners, equipment or skills that may make tasks easier or faster.
- Learn the most efficient method of accomplishing each task; for example, keep cleaning supplies near areas that must be cleaned often.
- Take your phone off the hook or turn on your answering machine to prevent interruptions while doing chores.
- Arrange a babysitting trade-off with a friend. The friend keeps your children on your home-task day and you return the favor later.
- Do one large task a week. This is better than spending a week of your vacation performing major chores.
- Buy furnishings that require little care. Choose washable items that do not need ironing, rugs that resist stains, and wall-coverings that are washable.
- If possible, have separate laundry hampers for white and colored clothes to save time in sorting.
- Remove clothes from the dryer while they are still slightly damp. Shake and smooth clothes to remove wrinkles and avoid ironing.

Figure 14-4 Sharing responsibilities makes home life easier to manage. Sometimes dad reads to the children while mom pays the bills or works late at the office. (Photo copyright © Wayne Michael Lottinville.)

◆ Stack finished laundry into piles for each family member and have each put away his or her items.

◆ Change bed linens on laundry day so that clean sheets can be replaced on the beds instead of having to be folded and stored.

◆ Arrange floormats outside entrance ways to protect floors from unnecessary soil.

◆ Finish unpleasant tasks before beginning tasks you enjoy.

◆ Reward yourself when you finish a task. Watch a TV show, play softball, buy a new shirt, sunbathe, read a book, or do some other activity you enjoy.

◆ If possible, pay someone else to do tasks you dislike.

◆ Work with a friend to make the time spent doing unpleasant tasks a little more enjoyable.

◆ Cook large quantities of food and freeze meal-sized portions for later use.

FOCUS ON:
HOW ONE WOMAN MANAGES HER PERSONAL AND PROFESSIONAL ROLES

Joanne Edding, divorced just 3 years ago, is the mother of three children ranging in age from 4 to 15. She is among the growing number of women who, to make ends meet, must work full-time while caring for her family. At 37, Joanne is the manager of the Word Processing department at Smith and Dodd, a prestigious legal firm located in Houston, Texas. Named Woman of the Year by a local businesswomen's association, Joanne agreed to be interviewed in her office—provided it didn't take too much time.

Joanne, what are your major difficulties in managing a family and a job?

The biggest challenges are child care and finding time to get everything done. With so much to do, it is hard to set aside time for relaxation with my family and friends.

How do you manage the care of your children while you are working?

Before the divorce, my husband and I used to take turns in getting Ricky to the day care center. Thank heavens Mary and Don are older. We also used to alternate staying home if one of the children was sick. Now, I am part of a parent pool made up of working parents who share child care emergencies. I spend as much time as I can with the children during the evenings, and try to see that each of them has as much of my attention as possible. We really try to have the evening meal together. It is our time for family discussions and sharing. Each weekend we plan at least one family activity. Saturday mornings are set aside for errands, haircuts, the dentist, special shopping, etc.

Joanne, how are you able to provide nutritious meals with so little time?

By planning ahead. I cook on the weekend and prepare more than enough, so that we have leftovers for freezing and reheating. My specialty is one-dish meals. I simply don't have time to cook in the evenings. We have quick breakfasts—cereal, fruit, and milk. We each pack our own lunch. I try to see that everyone gets balanced meals instead of junk food.

Do you have time to keep your apartment neat?

Divide and conquer—that's our motto! We all have our own jobs, even Ricky. We each make our own bed when we get up. We each hang up our clothes or toss them in the laundry hamper. We all pick up after ourselves—and the boys are usually neater than Mary. I have to keep after her.

When do you do your errands?

We keep a "To Do" list on the bulletin board in the kitchen. Some things I do on the way home from work or during the noon hour. You should see us on Saturday morning! It's like Grand Central Station the way we rush around. We use the telephone a lot to cut down the number of trips by car. We don't have time for wild goose chases!

How do you manage to get everything done?

I don't! And I've stopped feeling guilty about it. I already had children when I began my career, so I realized that everything would depend on my ability to manage my time wisely. Working fewer hours wasn't really an option, but I could work more efficiently. I use the clothes dryer rather than hanging wash on the line—it's a time saver. The time I spend preparing dinner is when I usually help the children with their homework. Doing two things at once saves time. Instead of having apple pie for dessert, we have sliced apples and cookies—another time saver. I'm always looking for faster, better ways of getting things done.

Finally, do you manage to find any time for yourself?

I set aside one evening each week for myself and my friends. The kids and I have an understanding: Tuesday night is "Mom's Night Out." But during the rest of the week, I try to be available for my kids. We spend a lot of time talking while we're doing chores and running errands. Let's face it, we always manage to find the time for the things that are really important. It just takes some careful planning.

METHODS OF MANAGEMENT

As in business, successful management of the home results from trial and error. Certain techniques work for some families and not for others. By trying various methods, you can evaluate what is right for you and your family. Read the interview on page 349 to learn how one family manages their personal and professional lives.

LEADING A BALANCED LIFE

All work and no personal life makes for an unhappy person. You may wonder how a person who is committed to a career can have it all. Many people are living proof that it is possible.

First it is important to understand the importance of a balanced life. To be mentally and emotionally healthy, one needs to have a family life, social life, and work life. Many psychologists would add a spiritual life as well.

Think back to the hierarchy of needs presented in Chapter 1. We all start out just trying to meet our physical needs. Then we build our feelings of self-worth, as we work our way to the top goal: self-actualization.

In the search for happiness and a satisfying life, no one can determine what is right for another person. In the final analysis, each person must decide for himself or herself what is the most satisfying way to live. The search for satisfaction may be aided by a review of what others have found to bring fulfillment. Observe and question what you see and who you are. Evaluate your own experiences. Then make your decisions for the direction you will take to achieve your personal and professional well-being. And remember the words of wise people through the ages who have cautioned that happiness and satisfaction are *current* conditions as well as goals for the future. Abraham Lincoln spoke to this idea when he said, "Life is in the living."

REVIEW QUESTIONS

1. Write a comprehensive definition of a professional, listing at least five characteristics.
2. Describe three ways in which a person may grow professionally.
3. Explain how to build a work record.
4. Write a sample letter of resignation after 5 years as a receptionist for P&G Poultry Company. You have been happy in your job, but your family is moving to another city.
5. Name six things that a person should take into consideration about changing jobs.
6. Why is it better not to resign from a position until you have found another one?
7. Cite five advantages of membership in civic organizations.
8. Write ten tips for managing the dual role of homemaker/wage-earner.
9. Why do health experts recommend a life-style that balances family, social, and work life?
10. What do you need to add to your life to have a more balanced life-style?

ACTIVITIES

1. Interview two people who have advanced in their careers. Ask them to explain how they were able to advance to the levels they now have. Write a two-page report.

2. Research the goals and activities of at least two civic clubs in your town. Assess what membership in them might do for you. Report your conclusions to the class.

3. Interview the sponsor or head of a local professional organization. Ask about programs, membership requirements, and opportunities for professional growth. Report your findings to the class. (You may combine your information from this interview with your findings in Activity 2.)

4. Visualize your life a year from now. What type of growth activities do you plan for yourself? Visualize your life 5 years from now. What growth activities must you participate in now and next year to get where you want to be in 5 years?

5. Investigate and describe the child care options for working parents in your community. What kind of impact may these resources have on your professional well-being?

6. Interview both parents in two separate households about how they handle the dual roles of maintaining a household and holding down a job. What works well? What are their concerns? Write a two-page report.

7. Contribute to a class file of adult education opportunities in your community. These may include evening classes at a community college or technical school, a parent effectiveness course at a social agency—anything that qualifies as a way to grow and improve yourself.

INDEX

Note: Page numbers in bold type reference non-text material. Entries in bold type reference titles of publications.

A

AIDS (acquired immunodeficiency syndrome), 301–3
Airplanes, travel by, 192–94
Alcohol, abuse of, 300–301
Anger, communication and, 175
Appearance
    conflicting messages in, 73
    personal, success and, 32–34
Application
    job, 107–11
    letter, 105–7
Aptitude tests, 9
Attitude, success and, 30

B

Banks, 315
Belts, 67
Benefits
    employer sponsored day care, **136**
    health care, preventive, **132**
Births, 233
Blush, 43
    applying, **43**
Body language
    eye contact, 36
    handshakes, 35–36
    posture, 34–35
Budget, making a, 310–15
Buses, travel by, 194
Business writing, 180–87

C

Calories, 277–78, 282
    defined, 277
    expended, activities and, **282**
    reducing, menus for, 298

Career
    choices,
        goal of, 13–14
        importance of, 3–4
        information concerning, gathering, 10–11
        interviewing professionals and, 11
        investigating, 9
        reading and, 12–13
        self-assessment, 6–9
        stages in, **4**
        work place visits and, 11
    evolving, focus on, **22**
    objectives, resume and, 102–3
Catalog shopping, guidelines for, **87**
Checking accounts, 316–18, **319**
Cheek color, 43
    applying, **43**
Civic responsibilities, 339
Clients, relating to, 157–60
Clothing
    care of,
        cleaning, 87
        dry cleaning, 89
        laundry, 88–89
        repair, 89, 91–92
        storage, 92
    focus on, **59**
    importance of, 55, 57
    stains, removal chart, 90
    travel and, 196–97
    wardrobe. *See* Wardrobe
Color, 79–81
    mix and match matrix, **83**
Commercial banks, 315
Commitment, signs of, **19**
Communications
    conversation, 168–77

introducing others, 167–68
letter writing,
  business, 180–87
  personal, 177–79
presenting yourself, 166–67
skills, goal attainment and, 24
stereotyping and, **170**
Compliments, 174–77
Concern, for others, success and, 32
Condolence, letter of, 178, **179**
Congratulations, letter of, **170**, 178
Conventions, behavior guidelines, **205**
Conversation, 168–77
  guidelines for, 176–77
  listening guidelines, 169–70
  responding skillfully, 174–75
  speaking well, 171–74
  topics for, **173**
Cooperativeness, success and, 32
Coordinates, wardrobe and, 81–82
Credit, 318, 320–24
  abuse, avoiding, 323
  advantages of, 321
  cards, 320–21
  cost of, 323–24
  disadvantages of, 321–23
  types of, 320
Credit unions, 315

D
Dandruff, 41
Death, 235
Debit cards, 320–21
Decision making, poor, 17
Dental care, importance of, 40
Dependability, success and, 30
Desk, 143–44
Diet, health and, 296–98
Dietary guidelines, 279–80, 283–86
Directory of Occupational Titles, 10
Divorce, 233–34
Dress
  women, guidelines for, 75
  see also Wardrobe

Driver courtesy, 214
Dry cleaning, 89

E
Ebony, 12
Education
  reaching goals and, 19
  resume and, 103
Electrolysis, 52
Emotional health, wellness and,
    304–5
Employment
  agencies, 99
  commissions, 99
  see also Job market
Energy, success and, 30
Enrichment courses, personal, 24
Enthusiasm, success and, 30
Ethics
  business versus professional, 270
  codes of, 258
    example of, **260–61**, **264**
    personal, 263, 265–66
    as a resource, 266, 268
    sources of, 258–59, 263
  decision making and, 268–69
  defined, 257
  lie detection/honesty tests and, **262**
  personal,
    acting on, 271–73
    maintaining, 270–71
  purpose of, 257
  valued principles of, 258
Etiquette
  restaurant, 207–13
  shopping, **86**
Exercise
  benefits of, 286–87
  planning for, 287, 289
Expenditures
  analyzing, 314–15
  recording, 312, 314
Eye contact, importance of, 36
Eye liners, 44
  applications, 45

Eye shadow, 44
   applications, **45**
Eyebrow pencils, 44
   applying, **45**

F
Fabric, patterns in, 82, 84
Face
   care of, 39
   cosmetics for, 41–43
   shapes of, hair styles and, 48–50
   skin types, **40**
Falsehoods, 175
Finances
   budgeting, 310–15
   checking accounts and, 316–18, 319
   credit, using, 318, 320–24
   expenditures,
      analyzing, 314–15
      recording, 312, 314
   goals,
      establishing, 311
      short-term, **311**
   income, identifying, 312
   insurance,
      automobile, 325–26
      health, 326–27
      life, 324–25
      residential, 327
   paycheck stub, 312
      example of, **313**
   plan, managing, 329
   savings, 327–29
   taxes and, 329–32
Financial institutions, 315
Food
   nutrition basics, 277
   pyramid, 284
   wellness and, 276–77
Foundations, cosmetic, 41–43

G
Gift giving, 236–37
Glasses, hair styles and, 50

Goals
   activities related to, 24–25
   defined, 13–14
   failure to reach, reasons for, 17–19
   long-term, 14
   reaching, 14, 16
      preparing to, 19–21
   sample of, **15**
   short-term, 14
Gossip, 176
Grooming
   checklist, **53**
   cosmetics, face, 41–43
   hair,
      color and, 50–51
      facial, 51
      removal, 52
   hair styles, 46–50
      glasses and, 50
Groups, working in, 155–57
Guest of honor, behavior as, 219

H
Hair
   care, importance of, 41
   color, grooming and, 50–51
   facial, grooming and, 51
   removal, 52
   styles, 46–50
Handbags, 67, 69
Handshakes, importance of, 35–36
Health
   AIDS and, 301–3
   care, obtaining, 303–4
   emotional, wellness and, 304–5
   insurance, 326–27
   risks, diet, 296–98
   stress and, 289–96
   substance abuse and, 299–300
      alcohol, 300–301
   weight table, **297**
   see also Wellness
Hierarchy of needs, **20**
Honesty, success and, 30

Hosiery, 66–67
Hotel accommodations, 194–95
House guest, behavior as, 219
Hygiene
    dental care and, 40
    face care, 39
    hair care and, 41
    importance of, 37–40
    nail care, 38
    skin care, 39–40
        skin types and, **40**

I

Income, identifying, 312
Insurance
    health, 326–27
    life, 324–25
    residential, 327
Interest inventories, 9
Interpersonal relationships, 21–24
Interviewing
    after, 118, 120–21
    frequently asked questions during, **113,**
        116–17
    inappropriate questions during, 117
    preparation for, 111–12
    successfully, **119**
Invitations
    issuing, 220–22
    responding to, 217–18

J

Jewelry, 67
Job market, 114–18
    applications,
        completing, 107–11
        letter and, 105–7
    direct contact and, 99
    employment,
        agencies and, 99
        commissions and, 99
    experiences, checklist, **8**
    fastest growing segment, **97**
    interviewing,
        frequently asked questions in, **113,** 116–17

inappropriate topics during, 117
    preparation for, 111–12
    newspapers and, 98
    personal contacts and, 98
    school placement office and, 96–97
    search preparation, 99–100
        resume, 100–105
    understanding, 95
    see also Employment

K

Knowledge
    reaching goals and, 19
    success and, 30

L

Laundry, 88–89
    terms associated with, **88**
Learning experience, informal, 336
Letter writing, personal, 177–79
Life, 12
Life
    experiences, evaluating, 7
    insurance, 324–25
Line
    described, 78–79
    use of, **80**
Lip color, 44
Listening, guidelines, 169–70
Loyalty, success and, 32

M

Marriage, 230–33
Mascara, 44
    applying, **45**
Maslow, Abraham, hierarchy of needs and, **20**
Means-end goals, 13
Motel accommodations, 194–95

N

Nail care, importance of, 38
Newspapers, job market and, 98

Nutrition
    basics of, 277
    calories and, 277–78, 282
    dietary guidelines, 279–80, 283–86

O

Occupational Outlook Handbook, 10
Organizations
    ceremonies and, 129–30
    culture,
        functions of, 131–33
        importance of, 127–28
        reading, 133–39
    history and, 130
    language and, 128–29
    structure, 128–30
    success and, 30, 32

P

Packing, travel and, 197–99
People, 12
Perfume, use of, 46
Permanent insurance, 325
Personal
    appearance, success and, 32–34
    contacts, employment and, 98
    finance. *See* Finance
    health. *See* Health
Personality
    characteristics of, checklist, **10**
    inventories, 9
Planes, travel by, 192–94
Posture, importance of, 34–35
Praise, letter of, 178
Principles. *See* Ethics
Productivity
    importance of, 242
    qualities needed for, 250–53
    techniques for, 242–45
Professional
    changing jobs and, 338–39
    civic responsibilities and, 339
    defining the, 333–34
    formal education and, 335–36

informal experiences and, 336
    organizations, 340–41
    profile of a, **334**
    social activities and, 339–40
    work experience and, 336
    worth, communicating your, 341–42
Promotions
    asking for, 247–48
    guidelines, to be considered for, 246
    qualities needed for, 250–53
    reactions to, 248–49
    reasons for, 246
Public appearance, 214
Public places, behavior in, 213–14
Purses, 67, 69

R

Relationships
    clients, 157–60
    coworkers, 151, 153
    groups and, 155–57
    irritating work habits, 153
    men and women working together, 161
    new worker and, 148–49
    sexual harassment and, 161–63
    subordinates and, 154
    superiors and, 149–50
Rental cars, 192
Residential insurance, 327
Resignation
    behavior after, 345
    notice of, 343–44
    time of, 344, 345
Responsibilities, managing, 346–48, 350
Restaurant
    etiquette, 207–13
    menu items, **209,** 210–11
    special foods, 211–12
Resume, 100–105

S

Savings, 327–29
Savings and loan associations, 315
Scarves, 67

School placement office, job market and, 96–97
Self, 12
Self-assessment, 6–9
Self-control, success and, 32
Self-esteem, reaching goals and, 19–21
Sensitivity to others, importance of, 21–22
Sexual harassment, 161–63
Shoes, 66
Shopping
    catalog, guidelines for, **87**
    etiquette, **86**
    guidelines for, **86**
    satisfaction with, 84–87
Skin
    care of, importance of, 39–40
    face, **40**
    tones, 80–81
Social activities, professionalism and, 339–40
Social events
    beverages for, 226
    food,
        arranging for, 222–26
        sample menus, 224–26
    as guest at, 218–19
    as guest of honor, 219
    hosting, 227–29
    as house guest, 219
    invitations,
        issuing, 220–22
        responding, 217–18
    physical facilities for, 226
    planning, 219–27
    types of, 227
Stains, removal of, **90**
Stereotyping, **170**
Storage, clothing, 92
Stress, managing, 289–96
Substance abuse, 299–300
    alcohol, 300–301
Success
    hygiene and, 37–40
    posture and, 34–35
    qualities needed for,
        internal factors, 30, 32
        Personal, appearance, 32–34

Suit
    variations on the, 63–69
    wearing of, 60–63
Suitcases, packing, 197–99
Supervision, accepting, success and, 30
Suspenders, 67

T
Taxes, 329–32
Teamwork, focus on, **33**
Term insurance, 324
Texture, described, 79
Thanks, letter of, 178, **179**
Ties, 64–66
Time management
    avoiding time wasters, 147–48
    goal setting, 145–46
    setting deadlines, 146
    task prioritization, 146
Tipping guide, 202, **203**
Trains, travel by, 194
Transportation, business travel, 191–94
Travel
    accommodations, 194–95
    behavior while, **205**
    clothing for, 196–97
    costs, 200
    documents, 190
    eating and, 204, 206
    guidelines, 202–4
    itinerary, 200–201
    packing for, 197–99
    restaurant,
        etiquette, 207–13
        menu terms, 210–11
    safety in, 199–200
    special foods at, 211–12
    transportation, 191–94

W
Want ads, **13**
Wardrobe
    adding to,
        color, 79–81
        coordinates, 81–82

line, 78–79
    patterns in fabrics, 82, 84
    shopping with satisfaction, 84–87
    texture, 79
assessing, 73–78
basics, 57–58, 60
color mix and match matrix, **83**
starting,
    man's, 69, 71
    woman's, 70, 72–73, 74
suit, 60–63
    variations on, 63–69
    wearing, 60–63
terminology, men's, 72
see also Dress
Weight, suggested, **297**
Wellness
    dietary guidelines, 279–80, 283–86
    emotional health and, 304–5
    exercise for, 286–89
    food for, 276–77
    maintaining, 276

signs of, 276
    stress management and, 289–96
Work
    changing, 338–39
    experience, 336
        checklist, **8**
        goal attainment and, 24–25
        resume and, 104–5
    forced loss of, 345
    irritating habits at, 153
    preferences, checklist, 7
    record, building, 342–43
    resigning from, 343–45
Working Woman, 12
Workplace, essentials of, **28–29**
Workstation
    desk, 143–44
    equipment, 144
    shelves/walls, 144–45
Writing
    business, 180–87
    Personal, 177–79